Chartism after 1848

**Merlin Press Chartist Studies**
Series editor: Owen R. Ashton

**The Chartist Legacy**
Edited by Owen Ashton, Robert Fyson & Stephen Roberts

**Images of Chartism**
by Stephen Roberts & Dorothy Thompson

**The People's Charter**
*Democratic Agitation in Early Victorian Britain*
Edited by Stephen Roberts

**Friends of the People**
*'Uneasy' Radicals in the Age of the Chartists*
by Owen R. Ashton & Paul A. Pickering

**Papers for the People**
*A study of the Chartist press*
Edited by Joan Allen & Owen R. Ashton


Forthcoming

**Voices of the People**
*Work, Democracy and the Making
of Chartist Political Identities, 1830-1860*
by Robert G. Hall

# Chartism after 1848
the working class and the politics of radical education

### Keith Flett

THE MERLIN PRESS

First published 2006 by The Merlin Press Ltd.
96 Monnow Street
Monmouth
NP4 0AA
www.merlinpress.co.uk

© Keith Flett, 2006
The author asserts the right to be identified as the
author of this work

Paperback:
ISBN-13: 9780850365399
ISBN-10: 0850365392

Hardback:
ISBN-13:9780850365443
ISBN-10:0850365449


British Library Cataloguing in Publication Data
is available from the British Library


All rights reserved. No part of this publication may be
reproduced, stored in a retrieval system, or transmitted,
in any form or by any means, electronic, mechanical,
photocopying, recording or otherwise, without the
prior permission of the publisher.


Printed in Great Britain by Cromwell Press, Trowbridge, UK

For my father Graham and my late mother Ronnie

# Contents

| | |
|---|---|
| Timeline | vi |
| Introduction | 1 |
| 1. 1848: political protest and the communication of radical ideas | 29 |
| 2. The Chartist Meetings of 1848: discussing and acting on radical ideas and strategies | 54 |
| 3. The Impact of Defeat on Radical Ideas in 1848 | 80 |
| 4. The Battle of Ideas, 1848-1851: location, influences, results | 98 |
| 5. The Breaking and Making of Radical Education and Ideas in the Late 1850s | 124 |
| 6. Beyond Chartism: radical education and radical politics in the later 1850s | 146 |
| 7. The Politics of Radical Education in the 1860s: 'Really Useful Knowledge' and the 1870 Education Act | 174 |
| 8. Conclusion | 194 |
| Glossary | 201 |
| Biographies | 206 |
| Bibliography | 209 |
| Index | 219 |

## Timeline of Late Chartism

1848: 10th April, Kennington Common demonstration.

1848: Summer onwards – secular schools formed in London.

1850: *Red Republican* begins publication.

1850: July – Ernest Jones released from prison.

1851: April – The 'Charter and Something More' programmed adopted.

1852: May – *People's Paper* begins publication.

1853: Repeal of the newspaper stamp.

1854: March – The Labour Parliament, Manchester.

1855: Aug/Sept – Death of Feargus O'Connor. 40,000 attend funeral.

1858: February – Last Chartist conference.

1860: End of Chartist press and the NCA.

1870: Education Act.

# Introduction

## The approach of this study

This work looks at independent working-class radical education in England from 1848, the year of revolutions, to the passage of the 1870 Education Act. It takes as its starting point Richard Johnson's analysis of 'really useful knowledge', but differing from Johnson it argues that radical ideas and radical working-class education and schools, far from disappearing after 1848, in fact flourished. It takes as its main source the often overlooked pages of the late Chartist and radical working-class press, and focuses on the detail of radical meetings and events and the ideas that informed them.

After an introduction which firmly situates the research in its theoretical, historical and particularly chronological context, the following three chapters provide a detailed examination of Chartism in 1848 and how the discussions, ideas and strategies of Chartists and Chartism in that year influenced working-class ideas and education. The experience of radicals in the period after 1848 is then considered, when support for Chartism declined but Chartist ideas moved further to the left. Historians have rarely studied this crucial period in the development of late Chartism. Two chapters look at the later 1850s, how Chartism developed under the leadership of Ernest Jones and the little discussed educational strategy for political change put forward by G.J. Holyoake and opposed by W.E. Adams. A final two chapters examine the world of post-Chartist working-class politics, with a focus on the ideas, strategies and organisation that led first of all to the Reform League and the International Working Men's Association and then to the Land and Labour League, the Paris Commune and the 1870 Education Act.

This study seeks to address two major questions posed by the development of mid-Victorian working-class radicalism. Firstly, it looks at what happened to Chartism after 1848. Secondly, it examines what happened to the provision of radical independent working-class education in the period between 1848 and the 1870 Education Act. Crucially, it seeks to tie together changes in these two areas. The research demonstrates in particular that Chartism did continue after 1848 and that radical education, far from falling away, in fact developed and changed significantly in the 1850s and 1860s. Within these guidelines the approach taken in the chapters that follow has specific theoretical and methodological parameters which have been too little used by historians of education.

The book focuses on three areas: London, the great centre of late and post-Chartism; the north-east, particularly Newcastle; and the north-west[1] around Manchester, where the demise of the national centre of Chartism led to very different profiles for the regional working-class radicalism and the radical press, whether the *Beehive* in London or the *Newcastle Daily Chronicle* that replaced it.

For historians Chartism has become something of a historiographical touchstone. Certainly the influence of Foucault has been felt. According to Jeffrey Weeks 'Foucault is ultimately interested not in "the past" as such but in a "history of the present".[2] John Host, who has written a book on 'Victorian labour history' and is influenced by Foucault, has noted the 'extent to which the meaning of the past is formulated to the present'.[3] The approach in this book is rather different. The view that the struggles of Chartism speak to the present day is not discounted; the structures of capitalism against which the Chartists fought have not fundamentally changed in Britain since the 1840s. We still live in a market capitalist society, albeit one that is now mature or perhaps even over-ripe rather than youthful. This means that we need to understand how the struggles of the Chartists were both similar to but also very different from those faced today.

Firstly, the material basis of interest in radical ideas and really useful knowledge is insisted upon. As the nature of production and workers' experience of it changed – for example, as more and more people became factory workers after mid-century – so did the basis and demand for radical ideas and knowledge. However, the overriding concern to discover the nature of exploitation in a capitalist economic system and ways to overcome or avoid it remained.

Secondly, the chronology of events is all important. Too many works that purport to deal with what happened to Chartism after 1848, notably the influential essay by Gareth Stedman Jones, 'Rethinking Chartism',[4] show little evidence of consultation of sources from this period. The vast bulk of published research on Chartism has relied on source material for the period before 1848[5] and of this material much is from the 1830s. The working class of 1832 was not the same as that of 1852 or 1862. It is a mistake to read working-class history as a simple progression. However, those influenced by Stedman Jones often pursue such an approach where Chartism is seen as an aberration to a radical liberal tradition. The volume of essays edited by Biagini and Reid under the title *Currents of Radicalism*[6] (1991) is perhaps the key text here. Historians need to be much more attentive to changes that took place within specific timescales. With the Chartist defeats in 1848, and as it became clearer in the 1850s that while Chartism could survive it was unlikely to regain all of its former support, a period of reassessment got underway. The changes that flowed from this reassessment still had a real impact in the 1870s, though they did not wait that long to be implemented. Fundamental changes often took place very quickly. An approach which is not based on chronology and thematically quotes from the 1830s, 40s and 50s to underline research findings is flawed. It can miss altogether the specific character of the working class after 1848: the reasons why it held certain ideas and shunned others. Chronological approaches are comparatively rare in British labour history, although Eric Hobsbawm has sometimes suggested such an approach. He has, however, always qualified any simple chronologically based historical study. For example, he has argued that the British working class was formed between 1870 and 1914 and not at an earlier date as E.P. Thompson has suggested. However, he has also noted of the process that the 'formation of this or any other class is [not] a once-for-all process like the building of a house. Classes are never made in the sense of being finished or having acquired their definitive shape. They keep on changing'.[7]

An approach based on a chronological view of history **is** important for an understanding of how Chartism and its relation to education and radical ideas changed. Professor Brian Simon followed such an approach in his pioneering studies of the history of labour and education. However, it is important to grasp that within the chronological approach there are different methods. There is what might be called a simple chronological approach which, empirically driven, sees history as a straight progress from date A to date B. Unfortunately this approach can hardly begin to grasp the ebbs and flows of real historical change. The model employed here is a more complex chronological one, recognising that there is no simple linear progression in history or a series of economic and social stages which have to be gone through in a particular order. Rather history is seen as a process, a struggle where the influence and power of contending classes ebbs and flows over specific periods of time. A complex chronological model does, therefore, see key moments and dates as central to an understanding of history. However, it is essential that these are seen in context. It is impossible to understand the 'British 1848' without grasping something of the nature of the 1832 Reform Act. It is also impossible to understand it without understanding wider economic trends in the development of British capitalism and the longer term impact of the events of 1848 elsewhere and particularly in France.

For this reason the study takes as its starting point a detailed study of 1848 and then proceeds chronologically to 1870. However, the model employed – that of a complex chronology – does not indicate a straight line of development between the two dates, but rather a contested process about how what happened in 1848 continued to influence events twenty-five years later.

Hence, in 1870 there remained echoes of the events of 1848, together with ideas and strategies which were precursors of the socialist movement of the 1880s.

In his recent book *In Defence of History*[8] Richard Evans has taken on postmodernist views of history which attack notions of linearity, causality and a sense of time in history. As is often the case, the postmodernist attack is not made on existing historical practice but a caricature of it. It is certainly true that this work seeks to establish causes for developments and changes in radical education which are placed in the context of wider changes in the economy and social and political relations. Within this it also seeks to establish an overall understanding of what has happened and the major themes to be considered. In particular, for example, the role played by the radical press against the background of a changing radical working class. What it does not do is to suggest a simple and straightforward progression in history. Particularly, in the period after 1848, it is vital to understand that history can flow in two directions, backwards and forwards. Pressure from the working class could produce change and concessions from the government. On the other hand, in other periods the pressure could flow the other way, making working-class activists moderate their demands. Finally, as John Rees has noted in a recent study of the marxist dialectic, 'what unites all these [non-marxist] explanations is that they see the totality as static...Change, development, instability, on the other hand are the very conditions for which a dialectical approach is designed'.[9] As Engels argued, '[h]istory often moves in leaps and zigzags'.[10]

Thirdly, and perhaps most importantly, this work does not agree with arguments which suggest that a labour aristocracy was to blame for the rise of reformism and reformist ideas in the mid-Victorian working class.[11] While the development of a labour aristocracy has been a key element of many explanations for changes in working-class politics after 1848, for reasons of both space nd choice it does not feature centrally in this book. It is argued instead that the key layer was a labour bureaucracy of working-class organisers and leaders rather than a layer based specifically on skill and occupation.[12] If the concept of a labour bureaucracy is accepted then it also becomes apparent that there was a related educational aristocracy. Partly this was constructed, as Alistair Reid has argued, to match middle-class conceptions of who was and was not eligible to receive the vote.[13] It was also, however, an important reflection of the reality that in a period of relatively low working-class struggle, there was a premium on people who already had ideas. Those who had a worked out view of the world and some solutions to the questions posed by the material existence of workers suggested above found support in the working class. The 'educational aristocracy' was not a united group. It stretched from the supporters of George Jacob Holyoake on the right to the followers of Bronterre O'Brien on the left. It was important, however, in terms of arguing for a strategy focused on manhood suffrage and the gradual extension of the ballot as opposed to revolutionary change. The dominant ideas in the working class of the 1860s came from this layer of people. They were vital both in facilitating real progress for working people and in marginalising revolutionary challenges to the left. This study suggests that there is more than one kind of 'gentleman leader'.[14]

The research which follows is characterised by a number of specific parameters. Firstly, that radical education did continue after 1848. However its nature and form had changed somewhat by the time of the 1870 Education Act. This is distinct from Professor Brian Simon's focus on state inquiry and provision after 1848 and Phil Gardner's emphasis on non-political working class education.[15] Secondly it is demonstrated that Chartist organisation and Chartist ideas continued to be a considerable force in working-class politics after 1848. Indeed, this period of late Chartism, which still remains little studied, is vital for an understanding of how radical education developed.

The approach of this study is firmly chronological. The specific nature of post-1848 Chartism is insisted upon. From this it can be seen that Chartism as a nationally organised force suffered a final crisis between 1858 and 1860 and after this date continued, organisationally, on a regional basis only. There were noticeable differences between regions, for example London and the north-west and north-east, as to the precise impact of post-Chartist politics and ideas.[16] The impact as a result on radical education was considerable.

The emphasis that Gareth Stedman Jones placed on language as a way of understanding Chartism was an important step forward for grasping the dynamics of Chartist thought. It was, however, limited, both in terms of the understanding it did actually provide in the case of Stedman Jones's analysis and in the mechanical nature of his use of language as a theoretical tool. Language here is understood as a process whereby words, meanings and ideas change within a framework of class politics. What Chartists and other radicals said cannot simply be taken at face value. As Neville Kirk has argued it is the context in which language is used which provides the vital key to understanding.[17]

Although this study is sceptical of the value of any form of explanation for changes in the post-1848 working class that focuses on a labour aristocracy, it does emphasise that an educational aristocracy did play an important role in reinforcing changes to working-class politics and ideas after 1848. The educational aristocracy had a material base in that it seized the limited opportunity for reform from above opened up by the changes in the economy and economic relations since 1848. Co-operators can be seen, in another and sometimes related field, to have seized the same opportunity. Its emphasis on education and learning as the key to extending the suffrage appealed precisely to the radical layer of political activists who had developed during the Chartist years. This layer of what might be called working-class leaders and opinion formers provides a more substantial basis to Ray Challinor's suggestion that a labour bureaucracy was the key to understanding the rise of political reformism in the working class.[18] The labour bureaucracy as a layer was far too small to have a decisive influence. It did, as Challinor notes, give the kind of wider stability and durability to class relations that provided a framework for the rise of reformism. The educational aristocracy, by contrast, at least potentially, was much broader and more influential as the 1850s turned to the 1860s.

The trend of the educational aristocracy did not, however, find total support from all radicals. Some went against the stream of mainstream radical thought. Key figures like Ernest Jones[19] and a number of second rank leaders like W. E. Adams[20] still focused on a more political and class based knowledge. The importance, particularly of the second rank leaders, after the demise of Chartism cannot be over estimated. In many areas and industries they were able to provide a pole of attraction for those whose ideas did not fit with the progressive ethos of Gladstonian liberalism. They were essential to the continuation of radical education.

The radical press, and particularly the flagship Chartist papers the *Northern Star* and the *People's Paper* and the secularist *Reasoner* provide the major source for the research presented here. This is no accident. Radical activity, and especially radical educational activity, which was demanding of both time and money, were of necessity ephemeral activities. Official histories were not written and if mention is made in memoirs or biographies, this is invariably long after the event and frequently with a large dose of hindsight. The radical press provides the best understanding of what might be termed the ethos of post-1848 radicalism. It is in reports of meetings and protests, letters, notices and advertisements that one finds not only the details of ideas which were being discussed, but how exactly they were discussed and received. Of course, this was not an entirely free press – the government could, and did, read it as a basis for prosecution.[21] Not everything was reported. But it remains, particularly through the mechanism of checking one radical paper and its reports against another, the best source of information on radical education and the one best suited to the forms which radical education took. Gareth Stedman Jones, as noted, does focus on the radical press for his sources, but only a minority of his information comes from reports of meetings and protests. The majority is sourced from editorial statements and articles. These more considered pieces are helpful in understanding what the formal positions of radicalism were. They cannot focus on the day-to-day process of discussion and interaction of ideas with radical strategies and tactics that was the core of radical education.

There is a very noticeable lack of secondary work on the radical press of the Chartist period from 1837-1848 and the late Chartist period from 1848-1860. There are several books on what may be seen as the heroic, Unstamped,[22] period of the radical press, and several more on the post-1860 period which look at the origins of the tradition of radical-liberal papers.[23] Not only, however, do the *Northern Star* and the *People's Paper* lack an historian; so does the mass selling *Reynolds's News*, which was commercially successful and led the way for the assimilation of some radical papers into the existing press system.[24]

The key framework for radical papers in Britain is provided by the *Warwick Guide to British Labour Periodicals*,[25] which lays down criteria for different types of radical, socialist and labour papers. However, it is not just the historical categorisation of the radical press which is of concern in a study of radical education but also the sociology of the papers. Who wrote for them, who sold them, who read them and what they read are all important questions in understanding the impact of radical education.

Richard Johnson's theorisation of independent working-class ideas and education was excellent at describing how ideas were held when the working-class movement was in full flow.[26] It is also a helpful way of looking at the kind of ideas held by radicals who went against the stream of dominant ideas in quieter periods. However, really useful knowledge is much less helpful when dealing with questions of false consciousness, or how it is possible for workers to hold radical and reactionary ideas at the same time. It also finds it difficult to account for periods when class struggle is ebbing. Richard Johnson has tended to argue that really useful knowledge did not exist in such periods. In reality it was not that radical ideas were not forcibly held but that they were less forcibly expressed.

In addition to the parameters above a number of other key points about the post-1848 working class are made. Firstly that even after the demise of Chartism as a national organisation in 1858-60 working-class political independence continued both at the level of organisation and at the level of ideas. While national organisation after 1860 remained at the level of single issue campaigns on the American Civil War, the suffrage and the land question amongst others, local and regional organisation continued on a broader basis, often focused around a range of local issues. The formation of the National Secular Society in 1866 suggested a continuity of organisation of working-class radicalism, although at a much reduced level to that of the 1840s.

While the support for the Liberal Party amongst radical workers has often been taken for granted in more recent research, this support was in fact the basis for a continued battle of ideas and strategies. Where support was given or withheld depended on what view was taken of the prospects of change coming through Parliamentary action.[27] In his book *Liberty, Retrenchment and Reform* Eugenio Biagini has written that 'Gladstonian Liberalism had a remarkable "ideological" cohesion, greater than that of any continental socialism'.[28] Biagini has argued that 'working-class liberalism was not the fruit of the ideological success of bourgeois ideas during the mid-Victorian decades but rather the continuation of older and genuinely popular plebeian traditions'.[29]

Biagini, along with other historians who are very much in the wake of Gareth Stedman Jones, has developed a subtle argument about working-class liberalism. It is of course at odds with Stedman Jones, who has argued for a distinctive break in working-class political attitudes in the 1840s. Biagini rather sees the continuation of popular radicalism which is subsumed under the hegemony of Gladstonian liberalism. There are two issues here which Biagini avoids. Firstly, the subsumption was far from complete. Radical working men in the main voted Liberal, but often went further politically than the Liberal Party was prepared to go. The real issue here then is not Liberal hegemony but the absence of a national organised independent working-class political force. Secondly, while there were elements of continuity in radical politics, it is far from clear that some of the main strands of these, Fenianism and land nationalisation for example, were in fact inside Liberal politics. The basis for interest in radical education was not simply that there was radical political organisation to provide it. There was, before this, a material basis for radical education which stemmed from the desire to understand and attempts to change conditions at work and at home.

Study of the role of the state is very much neglected in relation to radical education after 1848. Essentially there are three models. John Saville sees a mellowing of the internal security state of 1848 and before, once successful repression of working-class challenges to it had taken place.[30] Brian Simon takes a more positive position in viewing the state, not without pressure, as the provider of a national elementary education system by 1870.[31] Finally Phil Gardner sees the state as fundamentally intrusive on an already existing structure of working-class elementary schools.[32] In the analysis that follows the state is viewed as a structure which, more or less successfully, includes people within the developing political system. In doing so it persuades them that reform rather than more radical strategies is the best way of making progress. This had a significant impact both on radical ideas and on how the development of working-class education was viewed by radical workers themselves.

Within the argument that working-class radical politics were significant after 1848 there is also an argument about what kind of working class actually existed at this time. Recent work by Anna Clark and Trevor Lummis has emphasised gender and age as crucial factors.[33]

Earlier drafts of this book carried far more about gender, class and education. The relationship between sex and class in radical education in the nineteenth century is an important one. In a recent essay, 'Gendering the stories of Socialism: An Essay in Historical Criticism',[34] June Hannam and Karen Hunt have asked, 'why do labour historians seem to find it so difficult to integrate gender into the historiography of British socialism'.[35] The authors argue for consideration of other narratives and perspectives than the dominant one of male labourism. It is an important argument and one that takes the historical debate on from the sex versus class discussions of previous decades. In terms of radical education, while there was clearly a generally accepted agenda of issues and interests which spanned the entire radical working class, there were also specific angles relating to the position in the labour force in which people found themselves. Depending on whether class struggle was advancing or retreating these could be a source of strength or division both at the level of ideas and of organisation.

A key question which remains implicit in much of the research here is how much of the working class can be categorised as radical and therefore the basis for radical education. Even during the peak of the Chartist period between 1837 and 1848 there were 'conservative operative' societies and trades and locations where radical ideas were not strong. The support, albeit limited in its enthusiasm, of a layer of London workers for the Government side on 10 April 1848 highlights the reality that not every worker was a radical even when radical politics were at a peak. After 1848, particularly in the northwest, there was a growth of religious division and extreme Protestant politics amongst significant sections of the workforce. Neville Kirk has argued that the politics of ethnic division arose precisely because of the defeat of Chartism.[36] It is clear that in a period of retreat and defeat for the worker's movement, while there was a demand from radical activists for an explanation as to what had gone wrong, for many others a turn away from radical ideas altogether took place.

It is a mistake, however, to see workers as either radical or not radical. Some trades, particularly the shoe makers, had a reputation for consistent radicalism. For many others radical ideas, politics and interest in radical education came and went, depending on their material circumstances and their experiences. The continuity of the layer of activists who provided the basis for radical education was the coherent centre in a situation where interest ebbed and flowed.

As for the general approach towards the development of working-class politics and organisation after 1848, it is very much along the lines of work by Neville Kirk, A.D. Taylor and Martin Hewitt.

The model of radical education which is used in the following research has two main elements. Firstly, as outlined above, there was in 1848 and afterwards, a material basis to the demand and provision of radical education. Interest in and support for radical ideas arose as a direct result of the experiences of workers. While these clearly changed, the underlying focus was on how to understand and come to terms with a system based on alienated labour and the extraction of surplus value. This model itself is based on a Marxist understanding of capitalist political economy. The key point here was that it was an understanding of these issues that was sought, rather than the propagation of a finished and accepted Marxist text. Secondly, that in the period after 1848 the context of radical education was one where there was a desire to develop a vision of an alternative to the existing market economy. It was also a period when some state provision of education was thought both desirable and possible to achieve through agitation.

In this sense Edward Thompson's concept that the working class 'warrened' capitalism from 'end to end' does explain the often uneven but combined progress that radical working-class education made in the period after 1848.[37] On the one hand an element of democratically controlled state provision was won. On the other, independent radical education did also continue in one form or another.

Models which are available from the history of education are quite limited. Brian Simon follows, certainly for the period up to 1870, a statist model which sees all working-class attention focused on winning state provision. Phil Gardner suggests a diametrically opposed model with most working-class interest beyond a layer of radical activists focused on keeping the state out of educational provision for the working class.

Finally, there are models of independent working-class education. As noted above Richard Johnson's concept of really useful knowledge is excellent at explaining how a layer of radicals fought against the stream of existing society and its ideas. It does not explain the battle which took place for the meaning of ideas and language which were held in common between the working and middle class. Other analysis of independent working-class organisation has focused not so much on ideas but precisely on the layer of autodidacts and activists who kept alive radical ideas, frequently in isolation from the mainstream of the working class.

## In Defence of Class

The parameters by which working-class radical education is viewed in this study are laid out below.

Firstly, the work is rooted in the concept of a class analysis of society. It is argued that social class and particularly the relationship to the means of production did make a key difference in how workers understood ideas and what kind of radical education they chose to pursue. It is also argued that an outlook based on class largely determined how they put ideas into practice. To situate this statement historically it is argued, in line with E.P. Thompson's seminal work, that the British working class was made in the period after the 1832 Reform Act.[38] However, if Thompson's definition of class is followed it may be seen that class is not a mechanical or fixed entity. In his mould-setting introduction to the *Making of the English Working Class* Thompson emphasises that 'class is a relationship and not a thing'.[39] He expands on this to include specifically the relationship between class and radical ideas and education. He notes that 'class happens when some men as a result of common experiences [inherited or shared] feel and articulate the identity of their interests as between themselves and as against other men whose interests are different from and usually opposed to theirs'.[40] Thompson sees class as a 'cultural as much as an economic function'.[41] In doing so he specifically includes radical education as a key determinant of the formation of class. The concept of class used here, therefore, is an historical, not a sociological one. Again, Edward Thompson has noted that 'if we remember that class is a relationship and not a thing, we cannot think in this way'. 'It' does not exist, either to have an ideal interest or consciousness, or to lie as a patient on the adjusters table'.[42] The working class of 1832 was not that of 1848 or of 1870. As the working class developed it changed, advanced and retreated and looked to different forms and kinds of radical education.

While this research is grounded firmly within a materialist class-based approach to history this does not mean accepting the kind of mechanical and rigid caricatures postmodern historians often seem to set up about class and how it should be defined. As Neville Kirk, writing from within the Marxist tradition, has noted of Robert Glen's work on Stockport, 'Glen operates with…an absolute or 'true' view of class. According to this view a 'true' class must possess total unity of experience, values and purpose. A group of people who do not measure up to this absolute standard cannot be said to constitute a class'.[43] Kirk has suggested that 'The notion of a totally unified working class in the early decades of nineteenth-century England belongs to the world of fantasy rather than to Engels or Thompson'.[44] Similarly, Dorothy Thompson has suggested of Gareth Stedman Jones's *Languages of Class* that a major concern is that 'behind the discussion lurks a definition of "class" which is never clearly stated but against which Chartist responses are measured and found wanting'.[45] As Thompson notes, there is no substitute for a 'close study of the history of the working people [which] will inevitably lead us to modify and elaborate our definitions'.[46]

Postmodernism, while raising important questions for historians, also has a habit of providing quite destructive answers to them. Most postmodernists would deny that it is possible to do what is attempted here, namely to recover and understand what is meant by the vision and language of late and post-Chartism. For them there are multiple visions, all equally valid. Neville Kirk has recently criticised Patrick Joyce for taking just such an approach to north-west Chartism. For example, Joyce suggests of Feargus O'Connor's most well-known gesture towards his working-class supporters, the wearing of a fustian jacket, that 'what is demonstrated is the employment of a particular appeal, the character of which can be open to all manner of interpretations'.[47] A glance at the more recent work of Joyce surely underlines that the adoption of a free-floating approach to historical inquiry can lead us away from serious historical work altogether. For example, Joyce has noted that 'Class is seen by some to be unequal to the task of explaining our present reality. And this view has been of great effect among historians too: if class fails to interpret the present, perhaps it has not given an adequate account of our past either'.[48]

It follows that this study defends an approach to class and class relations which emphasises flexibility. James Epstein, for example, has noted that the

> struggle over political and cultural values that transcends class...the struggle over whose voices and what forms of political language possess authority within the public sphere of discourse is essential to the reproduction of relationships of dominance or broadening and subordination in modern society. The struggle over the narrowing or broadening of this sphere is also crucial to levels and forms of resistance.[49]

The changing nature of such relations within the overall framework of the relations of production is a central part of understanding what happened to radical education and ideas after 1848. This does not however imply any support for postmodernist approaches to history. By focusing on what people said, their experiences and the signs and symbols by which they made sense of reality postmodernists have offered valuable insights into the processes of radical education. For example Raphael Samuel in *Reading the Signs* noted that this approach 'invites us to consider society as a spectacle, one in which appearances are double-coded, meanings occult and images opaque...reading the signs invests enormous symbolic significance in the small details of everyday life...in the case of Montaillou, states of dress or undress, greetings, rituals and handshakes'.[50] The idea that there are many competing narratives, as Patrick Joyce notes, 'the vocabulary of class was itself unstable, and cannot automatically be given the meanings so often imputed to it',[51] cannot explain, however, why nearly all radicals focused firstly around the suffrage and then around the 1870 Education Act. No doubt different radicals viewed the world differently and perhaps even saw different things in the suffrage and in State provision of education. Ultimately, however, they still shared enough of the same views and understandings to support political campaigns which actually changed things.

Class is the organising concept of this study because such an approach to history is best able to explain the development of radical education. The search for alternative explanations to those provided by official society about how, for example, the work relationship operated – enshrined in Master and Servant legislation – and the desire to provide a coherent alternative to such ideas in terms of the provision of radical education, was rooted in the experience of class. This was a political experience, namely that the 1832 Reform Act and the subsequent Whig/Liberal government had not delivered real change for ordinary people. It was also, as with the Poor Law of 1834, an economic experience in the factories and workshops, where the new masters were increasingly the same people as those who ran the government. The defining moments of the development of radical education can be seen in terms of class confrontations. Radical education contained many ideas and strategies that had little direct relationship to such confrontations, particularly many of the views of utopian socialists and secularists. However, key changes and advances in understanding always followed central points of confrontation. The social-democratic 1851 Chartist Programme, for example, flowed from a consideration of the lessons of the events of 1848. This consideration was not just at the level of ideas, but in terms of the impact on workplace relations as well.

There is no need to adopt a postmodernist approach to have a more nuanced and accurate picture of what class and class relations meant for radical workers. Engels wrote to Joseph Bloch in 1890 that

> The economic situation is the basis, but the various elements of the superstructure – political forms of the class struggle and its results...especially the reflections of all these real struggles in the brains of the participants, political, legal, philosophical theories, religious views and their further development into systems of dogmas – also exercise their influence upon the course of historical struggles and in many cases determine their form in particular.[52]

The key point here is that while the foundation of the search for alternative views of society and ways to change it is to be found at the point of production, in the labour process itself, the form which these views and strategies take is very much determined within the superstructure of society in precisely the kind of radical papers and radical educational forums which this study looks at. These ideas themselves then, in turn, impacted on how people reacted to their position at work. They might, for example, have seen the political demands of the Charter or the industrial struggles of the early trade unions as the best way to improve that position. Perhaps more likely was a combination of these factors depending on the precise situation.

It follows, therefore, that this study argues that approaches which focus on a direct connection between working-class respectability and support for some kind of educational activity are too simplistic. It was not just those workers who were deemed or saw themselves as respectable that were interested in radical education. This connection has been drawn by both John Foster and, more critically, Neville Kirk. Kirk warns specifically of 'the pitfalls of the claim that respectability signified capitulation to bourgeois values and patterns of behaviour'.[53] On the other hand the suggestion by Alistair Reid that there is no perceivable or meaningful connection at all between education, class and skill must be rejected. So too must his assertion that whether a worker was educated or not and what role they played if they were was purely a matter of accident.[54]

The organising method of the research and the way in which evidence is approached owes something to Peter Bailey's seminal text, *Will the Real Bill Banks Please Stand Up.*[55] Bailey's article, based on Thomas Wright's *Bill Banks' Day Out* follows a day in the life of a respectable working man and his wife. Unfortunately the equally interesting article, 'Will the Real Mrs Bill Banks Please Stand Up?' remains unwritten. Bailey underlines how Bill Banks reads books to improve himself. On deciding to take a rare half-holiday he uses this also as an attempt to better himself. However, this is not quite the whole story. Bill Banks, his wife and others set off for Hampton Court in a cart laden with food and beer for a picnic. Before they set off they stop off at a pub for some refreshment. On arrival they consume their picnic including the beer and then proceed to have an argument. In the evening they proceed to the music hall in central London and then take a cab home. Bailey's point is that respectable and unrespectable behaviour did not belong to two entirely different groups of people but could found in the same person, depending on time and circumstances. Bill Banks was an utterly respectable working man, except on the occasions when he was not.

This is not to deny the importance of temperance and its links to respectability and education. In Patrick Joyce's idiom this is another story. The reality is that temperance was a significant but minority pursuit amongst the working classes and it was not necessarily the key or dominant issue in how such people understood the world. For the working class in mid-nineteenth century Britain daily life was, above all, a question of survival, survival often based on a frugal lifestyle that allowed little space for half holidays or drinking. It follows that this study sees radical workers, the ideas they held and the radical educational forms these ideas took as being living subjects rather than one-dimensional wooden figures. There was a plasticity to the daily existence of many which meant that it was quite possible to 'think and drink'.

It is particularly important to understand the realities of the everyday lives of ordinary people and how they experienced them in terms of the range of working-class reactions and attitudes towards political ideas, culture and change. Making time for education or to discover and discuss radical ideas was a struggle. The milieu in which this could be done was often not of the workers own choosing. Some might prefer the informal atmosphere of the working mens club, others the more severe environment of an institute. In either case, while literacy and learning might mark someone out from the general ranks of the working class, as Thomas Wright argued, it is unlikely that their attitudes varied significantly. Respectability or unrespectability were the products of the lived environment, milieu and economic and social circumstances as much as a deliberate and conscious construction.

### The material basis of radical education

As noted above, for the historian of radical education postmodernism has considerable attractions.[56] Patrick Joyce, a central figure in recent attempts to revise the history of what workers actually thought in the nineteenth century, has written that,

> Class identities were, therefore, a product of arguments about meanings, arguments which were primarily political in character. Class does not seem to have been the collective cultural experience of new economic classes produced by the Industrial Revolution.[57]

Postmodernism which focuses on identities, languages and understandings of the world that can be lost in more mechanical histories may be able to help a focus on the complexity of workers thought in the nineteenth century and how this complexity could lead to different and parallel conclusions as to what should be done. This is not in any sense new. *The Making of the English Working Class* famously examines working-class experiences and is firmly based on traditional historical methods of research.[58] What postmodernism cannot do is provide an understanding or analysis of why workers developed particular understandings of the world in certain times and circumstances and, crucially, what made them change that understanding.[59] These are surely the key questions for any historian of radical education.

Marx noted that the nature and development of economic relations of production gave rise to new classes, the bourgeoisie and the proletariat, and to struggles between them.[60] These developments and struggles also gave rise to a quest to understand the changes in society that were going on. For the middle class the quest was mainly based in the natural and physical sciences, and it was underwritten by a desire to prove the permanency of capitalist relations of production.[61] For the working class the quest was about understanding how a system which proclaimed the freedom of all, including the labourer, was fundamentally exploitative. This went hand in hand with the attempt to discover effective strategies and tactics to change this system. It is important, too, to grasp that this attempt to understand a new system took place not just at the workplace but as part of the social relations in society as a whole, in meetings, at the pub and in the home.[61]

The content of the really useful knowledge which working-class radicals developed as a result was a complex and changing set of ideas and analyses. Crucially it was determined first of all and above all else by the experiences of working-class radicals as capitalist society developed.[63] The attack on a peaceful demonstration at Peterloo in August 1819 and the repressive laws relating to political meetings and combinations told radicals the reality of the nature of the British state. If 1832 suggested that some change was possible within existing structures, the 1834 Poor Law underlined that the resulting Whig administration was no friend of the working classes. The day to day experience of work, or the lack of it on many occasions, undermined any grand notions that all would benefit from the development of a factory system of production. It became then a question for workers of understanding precisely what function they fulfilled in the new set up, of attempting to control their exploitation within the new relations of production and of working out how things might be changed.[64]

Richard Johnson has termed this quest for understanding 'really useful knowledge', a term derived in part from William Cobbett. It may be noted however that the material basis for such knowledge arose from the new relations of production which developed in the first half of the nineteenth century and which are shown at their most acute in Engels's survey of Manchester in 1844.[65] Such knowledge was not static, as can be seen from the development in ideas from the original Charter of six points in 1837 to the Charter and Something More, agreed in 1851. At its core was a grasp of the labour theory of value, which at its most basic was a sense that workers put more into their work than they got out if it, and an attempt to understand and change this situation.[66]

This was not done on an individual basis, although the consciousness of really useful knowledge did have to come to each person individually; rather the material basis for radical ideas and education expressed itself primarily in collective terms. The radical press, from the unstamped and factory papers to the *Northern Star*, provided the crucial framework in which ideas and strategies could be raised, discussed and changed.[67] Radical organisation, particularly, from 1841, the National Charter Association, provided the focus whereby ideas could be tested in the practice and experience of political agitation.

In terms of radical education and ideas the key issue in material terms was what was seen as possible and what was not. The more recent work of Patrick Joyce has suggested that it was up to people to choose their vision of what was possible and what was not in the sense that they could construct their own vision of class. Clearly self definition is one meaning and understanding of class and it is important to understand historically how people saw their position subjectively. This cannot however release the historian from the task of making a more objective assessment. As Engels noted,

> We make our history ourselves but, in the first place under very definite antecedents and conditions. Among these the economic ones are ultimately decisive. But the political ones, and indeed even the traditions which haunt human minds also play a part, although not the decisive one.[68]

People were free to construct their own visions but only within the material constraints of their own experience, memory and consciousness. For a politically active worker in the 1850s, therefore, any available vision would have focused particularly on the experience of French, and perhaps American, politics from the 1790s onwards and on the experience of defeat represented by Chartism. As material conditions changed, and there was a little more space in the political and economic system to accommodate the demands of labour after 1848, so the nature of really useful knowledge, the demand for it, and the space in which it could be discussed and developed also changed. Such changes, however, took place in complex ways. For example, while the worker of 1860 might have abandoned any specific hope of the demands of the People's Charter being enacted and may have been looking at other ways of changing their position in society such as trade unionism, this did not necessarily mean that they had abandoned the frames of thought and reference points of Chartism. The development of the economy, of the workforce and, at several removes, the ways in which workers understood and sought to change this was an uneven process. Eric Hobsbawm, for example, has placed the formation of the working class in the 1870s and 1880s without seeing how the lessons of an earlier model of working-class development influence the later period.[69] The level of change in radical ideas was dictated at root by the everyday experiences of workers. Neville Kirk has noted that:

> It was within this determining context of experience, as opposed to abstract theory, that the Chartists formulated their profoundly class-based ideas, tactics and strategies....The Chartists welcomed genuine offers of friendship and support from the middle class, but experience demonstrated the rarity of such occurrences.[70]

For example by the mid-1860s radical workers may have found the political ideas of the Liberal Party appealing. They may also have found the activities of their Liberal employer in terms of trade union recognition and wage rises much less appealing. When workers came together to press for a change in the system, for example the fight over the suffrage in 1866 and 1867, ideas could change quickly and easily outstrip anything on offer from either middle-class or working-class radical leaders. When things were quieter the fact that these very same leaders did have coherent views and ideas meant that they had a much greater weight in the working class than could be justified simply by their position. The trajectory in the 1860s of the two key radical leaders of the post-1848 era, G.J. Holyoake and Ernest Jones, underlines the point. Holyoake found greatest interest for his ideas of accommodation when political activity was at a lower ebb. Jones, on the other hand, despite real and significant concessions to the ideas of liberalism, remained the focus for those with more advanced ideas when these came to the fore.

What kind of radical ideas workers picked up was determined by a complex mixture of workplace and political experience, age, gender and location. What is not in doubt is that it was the material impact of a developing system of market economics which led to the search for radical ideas. It also provoked the demand for radical education so that these ideas could be transmitted and discussed with wider layers of workers.

### Arguments on radical education after 1848

While the intervention of the state into working-class education with the 1870 Act represented a decisive moment in both working-class and educational history, this change has been little discussed historiographically. Indeed, the history of working-class education has been considered mainly through the prism of a wider labour history which focuses either on a forward march of labour or emphasises the problems involved with any state involvement in working-class affairs.

Within this framework there have been two dominant ideas about what happened to radical education after 1848. The first and certainly the most authoritative is that suggested by Professor Brian Simon.[71] Here radical workers increasingly looked towards the state to provide at least a basic education for their children. There is no doubt that there is an important truth in this position.

The second is that where radical education outside state control did continue after 1848 it increasingly became the preserve of skilled workers who used it as a means of 'getting on' within the existing system rather than as a means of opposing or overthrowing it. The origins of this view can be traced to John Foster[72] but it also finds more qualified and tentative echoes in work by Neville Kirk on the origins of working-class reformism in the mid nineteenth century.[73]

An important question is raised by the second position. Was working-class education important in helping to secure the comparative stability of class relations and the progress of a small minority of workers through the system after 1848? If it was, this was not the whole picture. Education could be used for a number of ends ranging from promotion within the system, through organising limited alternatives to it such as trade unions and co-operatives, to outright opposition. Which particular end was chosen often depended on circumstances, conjuncture and perceived possibilities. For example, Thomas Martin Wheeler, who was jailed in 1858 as a surety for debt on Ernest Jones's *People's Paper*, was at the same time the head of a significant and successful life assurance company.

There seems little doubt that the skilled did use education to advance their position in society. Such education was unlikely in any real sense to have been radical. Radical education, for different ends than making one's way through the system, did continue after 1848 and it is this which existing commentators miss out on almost entirely.

There are also two traditions in the historiography of working-class education after 1848 which are sharply opposed to one another and which rest, arguably, on very different conceptions of the working class in this period. For Professor Simon the period after 1848 is one of working-class pressure and government enquiries that led to the 1870 Education Act. This put in place the framework of state provision of education which was to form the basis for the progressive measures of the twentieth century.

For Phil Gardner,[74] on the other hand, the 1870 Act was a conscious attempt by the state to eliminate private elementary working-class education, primarily by inspecting it and labelling it 'inefficient'. Gardner cautions against examining the pre-1870 period through the later experience of state education. He notes that 'we have been content to extol the expansion of publicly provided schooling after 1870 while we have remained ignorant of the catastrophic decline in private elementary schooling in the same period'.[75] For Gardner it is a matter of recovering and understanding a tradition of private working-class elementary schooling that existed outside the control of authority. Unfortunately he does not situate schools fully in the context of the working-class cultures and politics from which they sprang.

A number of general positions on radical education after 1848 may be developed. Both Professor Brian Simon and Dr Phil Gardner are products of their respective historiographical periods. Brian Simon wrote in a time of optimism about the involvement of the state in education, and played a central role in the development of comprehensive state education. From this perspective the 1870 Education Act could be seen as the beginning of a positive tradition of state involvement. Phil Gardner's research, by contrast, reflects a more critical view of what the state could achieve in education, following some years of experience of the comprehensive model, and a much greater interest in specifically working-class alternatives to state education.

State concessions were the result of earlier pressure. Whichever position is taken, and this study sees merit in both, there seems little doubt that the reason for the 1870 Act was less to do with the national enquiries into education which characterised the years before its passage and more to do with the pressure for change that had built up during the Chartist years. The debate in the 1860s was not really about whether the state should intervene in education, but how this intervention should occur.

Organised labour warrened capitalist society. Working-class attitudes towards state intervention in education were more complex than either Simon's or Gardner's theses permit. While the statist road was the one eventually taken by the labour movement this was not pre-determined in the 1860s. During the post-Chartist period it was a question of seeing what could work in terms of achieving change. A demand for state education had been an advanced radical demand since the 1851 Chartist Programme. This did not mean, however, that state provision was the desired end for radical working-class politics in itself. There were also questions of how state provision should be controlled and how much space there would be for independent working-class education outside the state sphere.

State intervention in education resulted in some losses and some gains for working-class education. The move towards state provision which required considerable pressure from working-class and radical middle-class organisations was not simply a matter of gain or loss for working-class education. Gains were made in the extent of provision of some form of basic education, which now stretched far wider than independent working-class initiative could ever hope to achieve. Losses were made in the amount of direct control that the working-class now had over educational provision. The judgement to be made was how far gains and losses could be balanced.

Phil Gardner's work has raised important correctives to any uncomplicated theory that state education was simply welcomed by working-class adults and children. He highlights how the form in which state education was provided was precisely not the form which suited existing working-class social relations and family structures. This, of course, was no accident.

There was a combined and uneven development of working-class attitudes on education. On the one hand there was pressure for State provision, on the other there was concern about what the content of that provision would be and, crucially, whether workers representatives would be able to exercise any control over it. With this perspective it is possible to move beyond the work of both Brian Simon and Phil Gardner and grasp that working-class attitudes towards State education in the 1860s were ambivalent. Most radical working-class activists supported it and had to press for it to come about in a way which provided for some local and democratic control. However much control was given the education was still provided from above and this cut across much existing working-class practice. The 1870 Act may be seen as an early lesson of what reforms within the existing structure of society were to mean.

The question of gender is a key issue which remains under-researched. It is almost certainly the case that the 1870 Act meant that more girls got some kind of basic education than previously.[76] It may be seen therefore as a significant advance for working-class women. The division between child and adult is also an important but neglected factor in the development of radical education. The 1870 Act reinforced the division between child and adult in working-class life, and as school inspectors began to make their presence felt drew an increasingly sharp line between the worlds of work and school. This clearly had a major impact on the shape and form of radical educational provision outside the new state system.

Finally there is the issue of the making and breaking of systems of education. After the 1870 Act, at least partly because of the considerable support shown by organised labour for the Act, the state invested considerable energy in removing informal and private schools. Phil Gardner has detailed this process and emphasised that it was a lengthy one. At the same time as the old system of working-class education was broken, however, the inadequacies in the new state system began to throw up a fresh demand for independent working-class education. This found expression, for example, in the continuation of secular and then socialist Sunday schools. The development of working-class education was never a straightforward and linear process but one which was argued over all the way.

## Really Useful Knowledge: A Critique

One of the most interesting concepts to arise from the explosion of socialist and social history after 1968 was Richard Johnson's 'Really Useful Knowledge'.[77] Johnson did not, of course, pluck the concept from thin air. As a term and an idea it was in use by radical workers in the first half of the nineteenth century. Yet Johnson's rediscovery of the term, which was first published in the journal *Radical Education*, had a definite political context that belonged to the 1970s rather than the 1840s.

*Radical Education* was a magazine of left-wing teachers and educational theorists and the publication of 'Really Useful Knowledge' as a two part article in 1976 can be seen as an attempt to give radical educational practice an historical and theoretical grounding. The themes of oppositional knowledge, of ideas which were not available officially, and of real as opposed to superficial understandings of capitalism were strong themes amongst post-1968 radicals.[78] Following his 1976 article Johnson went on, in a series of essays published over the next fifteen years, to further refine the historical context of really useful knowledge and to suggest political implications as the right seized the educational initiative.[79]

Historically, really useful knowledge had a clear meaning. It was used to differentiate the ideas of working-class political radicalism from middle-class notions of useful knowledge or what were alternatively known as really useless knowledge or merely useful knowledge. The break had come not just at the level of ideas but in practice too. The Six Acts after Peterloo in 1819 suppressed the expression of working-class opinion. The war of the unstamped had seen a liberal government, elected after the 1832 Reform Act, imprison sellers of the working-class press. The era of Chartism after 1838 had seen numerous collisions with authority over the right not only to hold ideas but also to express them in public meetings and public places.

The concept of really useful knowledge, although immensely useful at the time, had problems from the outset. Johnson dealt with the period up to 1848 and could only sketch out what happened after this. His view is clearly that the rise of state intervention in the educational and cultural fields undercut the basis for the existence of really useful knowledge. He does not, therefore, address the issue of really useful knowledge as a theory which can explain oppositional ideas in a capitalist society at any given time.

To this extent it is a flawed concept. It focuses on the moment of the formation radical ideas and education in the immediate pre-Chartist period. However, in Johnson's analysis this 'moment' remains largely static. There is no more than an outline sketch of how the really useful knowledge forged in the battles around Peterloo and for the unstamped press, changed with the experience of the Chartist years. There were, of course, many 'really useful knowledges', the genius of the Chartist leadership being to focus this on to one political programme – the Six Points of the Charter. However, the unified vision of really useful knowledge which existed in 1848 was very different to that which had developed in the 1837-8 period. The 1851 programme of the Charter and Something More represented a major advance in Chartist thinking. By the late 1850s these ideas had been largely, although not entirely, forgotten. Really Useful Knowledge was remade in the 1860s on a different basis, very much on a trade union/International Working Men's Association axis, but with the memory of Chartist ideas still very much in mind.

At the same time, by focusing entirely on oppositional or 'spearhead' knowledge Johnson misses much of the complexity of the battle for ideas, knowledge and radical education which was a central feature of working-class politics and battles between the working- and middle-class during our period. Many ideas and understandings, for example those around the suffrage, independence and respectability, had common currency amongst both the middle and working classes.[80] Their precise meaning was fiercely fought over, and often the same term was differently understood by different people, depending on their economic and political position. This was arguably all the more so when radicals came together, for example in the Reform League, to campaign around a key idea and demand such as the extension of the suffrage.

Johnson focuses on two main sources for his analysis of really useful knowledge: the radical press and working-class autobiographies. In reality, however, it is only the radical press which provided a contemporaneous source. The radical press reported many of the radical protests, meetings and events which went to form the core of really useful knowledge in the first place. It also, by reporting and commentating on the radical movement, played a central role in taking the analysis of really useful knowledge further than direct experience. The *Poor Mans Guardian*, the *Northern Star* and the *People's Paper* were the most widely and collectively read, but *Reynolds's* whose circulation far outstripped these papers, played an even more central role in shaping post-Chartist 'really useful knowledge'.[81]

The dynamic nature of 'really useful knowledge' can be demonstrated by a brief examination of the trend of ideas in working-class radicalism after 1848. In the period from the Autumn of 1848 to the end of 1850 a major reassessment of the ideas of Chartism was undertaken. The repression of 1848 probably convinced significant numbers that Chartism was no longer the way that change could be achieved. The remainder of Chartism moved sharply to the left with the adoption of the Spring 1851 programme which came to be known as the Charter and Something More.[82] By the Chartist Conference of 1858 this move to the left in ideas had been formally abandoned as a strategy in favour of a focus specifically on the suffrage and middle-class cooperation to help achieve it. By the 1860s, however, the core demand of the suffrage was to be found in two new sets of radical ideas and understandings – those of the newly powerful trade unions and those of secularism, moving as it was at this time towards a political party type organisation in the National Secular Society. The change in knowledge over fifteen years from a broad left-wing programme to a much narrower practical focus and then a broader but sectional platform with the common basis of the suffrage was considerable.[83]

The twists and turns in really useful knowledge after 1848, dictated by ebbs and flows in class struggle and by changes in the material factors which motivated workers to look towards radical ideas and education, were considerably more complex than the schematic approach of Richard Johnson allows for. Some of this complexity and detail is shown below.

The research takes as its starting point the turmoil of events and ideas that was the British 1848 and ends just over twenty years later with the 1870 Education Act and the Paris Commune. What happened in 1848 set much of the tone for the subsequent two decades. For that reason three chapters are devoted to that year. A further chapter traces the sharp move to the left in Chartist thinking between 1849 and 1851. The late 1850s are considered in some detail as a key turning point for radical ideas and organisation, with the rise of what is termed as an educational aristocracy that linked the extension of the suffrage firmly with educational provision. A final chapter looks at the 1860s, and examines the state of radical education up to 1870 as the government intervened in education in a significant way for the first time. Finally, the conclusion draws together the arguments and key issues of the study and looks forward to the impact of radical education on the final quarter of the nineteenth century.

The debates on Chartism go wider than just the academic community. They are also to be found in the anti-capitalist movement. For example, John Charlton, himself an historian of Chartism, has written of a link between the mood of the peaks of Chartist struggle in 1839, 1842 and 1848, and the birth of the modern anti-capitalist movement in Seattle in 1999.[84] Beyond this, however, lies a new challenge. Implicit in Miles Taylor's biography of Ernest Jones, and explicit in some of his more recent work on the ballot and colonialism,[85] is the need for a total history that understands the development of both the working classes and the ruling and governmental classes, and the interplay between them. Geoff Eley's recent book on the history of the left[86] makes a similar point about what he sees as the turning point of the 1860s. Changes in working-class politics and organisation can only be fully appreciated against the wider backdrop of changes at the top of society and in the economy.

## Notes

1. However, for Carlisle see J.C.F. Barnes, 'Popular Protest and Radical Politics: Carlisle 1780-1850'; Ph.D. thesis, University of Lancaster, 1981.
2. Jeffrey Weeks, *The uses and abuses of Michel Foucault in Against Nature*, London, 1991.
3. John Host, *Victorian Labour History, experience, identity and the politics of representation*, London, 1998, p. 59.
4. Gareth Stedman Jones, *Rethinking Chartism* in *The Languages of Class*, Cambridge, 1982.
5. There remains very little about Chartism after 1848. See Kate Tiller, 'Halifax 1847-1858' in *The Chartist Experience*, eds James Epstein and Dorothy Thompson, London, 1982.
6. E Biagini and A Reid, *Currents of Radicalism*, Cambridge, 1992.
7. Eric Hobsbawm, *The Making of the English Working-Class 1890-1914*, Worlds of Labour, London, 1984, p. 195.
8. Richard Evans, *In Defence of History*, London, 1997.
9. John Rees, *The Algebra of Revolution*, London, 1998.
10. Frederick Engels, *A Contribution to the Critique of Political Economy* in Karl Marx, *Preface and Introduction to A Contribution to the Critique of Political Economy*, Peking, 1976, p. 55.
11. Eric Hobsbawm, *Labouring Men*, London, 1954.
12. Ray Challinor, *A radical lawyer in Victorian England, W.P. Roberts and the struggle for workers' rights*, London, 1990.
13. A.J. Reid, *Social Classes and Social Relations in Britain, 1850-1914*, London, 1992, p. 6.
14. A.D. Taylor, 'The Best Way to Get What He Wanted': Ernest Jones and the Boundaries of Liberalism in the Manchester Election of 1868. *Parliamentary History Vol 16, 1997; Modes of Political Expression and Working-Class Radicalism 1848-1874*. University of Manchester, 1992. Owen Ashton and Paul Pickering, *Friends of the People. Uneasy radicals in the age of the Chartists*, London, 2002. Owen Ashton, Robert Fyson and Stephen Roberts (Eds.), *The Chartist Legacy*, Woodbridge, 1999. Miles Taylor, *Ernest Jones. Chartism and the Romance of Politics, 1819-1869*, Oxford, 2003.
15. Professor Brian Simon, *Studies in the History of Education*, London, 1960; Phil Gardner, *The Lost Elementary Schools of Victorian England*, London, 1984.
16. John Breuilly, *Labour and Liberalism in Nineteenth Century Europe, Essays in Comparative History*, Manchester, 1992.
17. For an example of this argument see Neville Kirk's comments in *Labour History Review*, 60/2, 1995.
18. Ray Challinor op. cit.
19. John Saville, *Ernest Jones*, London, 1952 was the only modern biography, until Miles Taylor's *Ernest Jones*, Cambridge, 2003.
20. Owen Ashton, *W.E. Adams: Chartist, Radical and Journalist, 1832-1906* Whitley Bay, 1991.
21. James Epstein, *Radical Expression, political language, ritual and symbol in England, 1790-1850*, Oxford, 1994.

22  Patricia Hollis, *The Pauper Press: a study in working class radicalism of the 1830s*, London, 1970; Joel Weiner, *The War of the Unstamped: the movement to repeal the British newspaper tax 1830-1860*, London, 1969.
23  Nigel Todd, *The Militant Democracy. Joseph Cowen and Victorian Radicalism*, Whitley Bay, 1991; A.J. Lee, *The Origins of the Popular Press in England 1855-1914*, London, 1976.
24  But see Rohan McWilliam, *Popular Politics in Nineteenth Century England*, London, 1998.
25  *Warwick Guide to British Labour Periodicals*, Brighton, 1970.
26  Richard Johnson, *Really Useful Knowledge* in *Radical Education*, No. 2, 7 & 8, 1976.
27  Miles Taylor, *The Decline of British Radicalism, 1847-1860*, Oxford, 1995.
28  Eugenio Biagini, *Liberty, Retrenchment and Reform*, Cambridge, 1992, p. 7.
29  Ibid., p. 6.
30  John Saville, *1848, The British State and the Chartist Movement*, Cambridge, 1987.
31  Brian Simon, *The two nations and the educational structure, 1780-1870*, Studies in the History of Education, London, 1960, Chapter V11.
32  Phil Gardner, *The Lost Elementary Schools of Victorian England*, London, 1984.
33  Anna Clarke, *The Struggle for the Breeches. Gender and the Making of the English Working Class*, London, 1995; Trevor Lummis, *The Labour Aristocracy, 1851-1914*, Aldershot, 1994.
34  June Hannam and Karen Hunt, 'Gendering the stories of Socialism: An Essay in Historical Criticism', in Margaret Walsh (Ed.), *Working Out gender: perspectives from labour history*, Aldershot 1999.
35  Ibid., p. 102.
36  Neville Kirk, *The Growth of Working Class Reformism in Mid-Victorian England*, London, 1985.
37  E.P. Thompson, *The Pecularities of the English* in *The Poverty of Theory*, London, 1978.
38  E.P.Thompson, *The Making of the English Working Class*, Harmondsworth, 1968.
39  Ibid., p. 11.
40  Ibid., pp. 9-10.
41  Ibid., pp. 13-14.
42  Ibid., p. 11.
43  Neville Kirk, review of R. Glen, *Urban Workers in the Early Industrial Revolution*, London, 1984, in *Labour History Review* 52.1, 1997.
44  Ibid.
45  Dorothy Thompson, review of Gareth Stedman Jones, *Languages of Class*, Cambridge, 1982 in *Labour History Review*, 52.1, 1997.
46  Ibid.
47  Patrick Joyce, *Visions of the People*, Cambridge, 1994.
48  Patrick Joyce, Introduction to Patrick Joyce [edited] *Class*, Oxford, 1995
49  James Epstein, op. cit. , pp. 27-8.

50 Raphael Samuel, *'Reading the Signs' History Workshop Journal* 32, Autumn, 1991
51 Patrick Joyce, op. cit. p. 327.
52 Frederick Engels, letter to Joseph Bloch, September 21st 1890, *Letters on Historical Materialism*, Moscow, 1980.
53 Neville Kirk, *The Growth of Working Class Reformism in Mid-Victorian England*, London, 1985, p. 213.
54 Alistair Reid, op. cit., p. 6.
55 Peter Bailey, *'Will the real Bill Banks please stand up?' A role analysis of mid-Victorian working class respectability. Journal of Social History* 12, 1979, pp. 336-53.
56 William H Sewell Jnr, *'Towards a Post-Materialist Rhetoric for Labour History'* L.R. Barlanstein ed. *Rethinking Labour History: Essays on Class and Discourse Analysis*, US, 1993.
57 Patrick Joyce, op. cit., p. 322.
58 Alex Callinicos, *Against Postmodernism, a Marxist critique*, Cambridge, 1989.
59 Alex Callinicos, *Theories and Narratives, reflections on the philosophy of history*, Cambridge, 1995.
60 Karl Marx and Fredriech Engels, *The Communist Manifesto*, Part 1, Socialist Register, Suffolk, 1998.
61 Alan J Kidd, K.W. Roberts eds. *City, class and culture. Studies of social policy and cultural production in Victorian Manchester*, Manchester, 1985.
62 Richard Johnson, *Really Useful Knowledge* in *Radical Education* Nos 7 & 8, 1976; Herbert Gutman, *Power and Culture, Essays on the American Working Class*, edited by Ira Berlin, New York, 1987.
63 On the question of the use of the category of experience, see Neville Kirk, op. cit., 1985, p. 30.
64 Neville Kirk, *Labour History Review*, Volume 60/2, 1995, p. 9.
65 *Exploring the urban past, Essays in Urban History* by H.J. Dyos, edited by David Cannadine and David Reeder, Cambridge, 1982; Steven Marcus, *Engels, Manchester and the Working Class*, London, 1974.
66 Gregory Claeys, *Machinery, Money and the Millennium, from moral economy to socialism 1815-1860*, Cambridge, 1987.
67 P. Hollis; J.Weiner op. cit.
68 Frederich Engels, op. cit., Moscow, 1980.
69 Eric Hobsbawm, *Worlds of Labour*, London, 1984.
70 Neville Kirk, op cit., 1985.
71 Brian Simon, op cit., Chapter V11, Part 2.
72 John Foster, *Class Struggle and the Industrial Revolution*, London, 1974.
73 Neville Kirk, op. cit., 1985.
74 Phil Gardner, op. cit.
75 Ibid., p. 189.
76 Anna Davin, *Growing up Poor, Home, School and Street in London, 1970-1914*, London, 1996.
77 Radical Education, op. cit.

78  Chris Harman, *The Fire Last Time*, Chapter 3. *The Student Revolt*, London, 1998.
79  See for example, *Working Class Culture, Studies in history and theory*, edited John Clarke, Chas Critcher and Richard Johnson, London, 1979 and *Making Histories, Studies in History Writing and Politics*, edited by Richard Johnson, London, 1982.
80  James Epstein op. cit.
81  Rohan McWilliam op. cit.
82  'The Charter and Something More' in John Saville, *Ernest Jones*, London, 1952.
83  Margot Finn, *After Chartism*, Cambridge 1993; Edward Royle, *Owenism and the Secularist Tradition: the Huddersfield Secular Society and Sunday School* in *Living and Learning, Essays in Honour of J.F.C. Harrison*, eds. Malcolm Chase and Ian Dyck, Aldershot, 1996.
84  Keith Flett and David Renton (Eds.) *New Approaches to Socialist History*, Cheltenham, 2003. John Charlton, *The pre-history of social movements*, p. 101.
85  Miles Taylor, 'Queen Victoria and India, 1837-61' in *Victorian Studies*, Winter 2004.
86  Geoff Eley, *Forging Democracy: The History of the Left in Europe, 1850-2000*, Oxford, 2002, p. 109.

## Chapter 1
# 1848: political protest and the communication of radical ideas

### The importance of 1848

1848 was a key moment for working-class radicalism in Britain as elsewhere in Europe. Revolution swept Europe and while it found an echo in Ireland and the British mainland, there was no transfer of power to a more plebeian government as happened, however temporarily, in some other countries. Historians have discussed the question of whether the development of the British political system was exceptional in 1848 and afterwards. The most famous representation of this was the debate between Perry Anderson and Tom Nairn on British labourism. In more recent years the historiography of this period has focused on what has become a rather sterile debate about whether the events of 1848 could be seen to represent a watershed or not. In reality trends of both continuity and discontinuity can be established for 1848. It is more important historically to understand these trends, their interplay and their impact after 1848 than it is to try and fit the process into a category.

There is no question that 1848 represented a crisis year for the government. The winter of 1847 had been a harsh one with serious economic problems. The move to free trade had posed sharply for the government the question of where it would get tax revenue. Its answer, to double income tax, which Russell proposed in February 1848, was problematic. Firstly, income tax was not a popular tax, and secondly the Liberals in particular had opposed it. As Parry has noted 'Parliament's consent to the tax had to be renewed in 1848. This was bad timing....'[1] Further, while the Chartist petition of April 1848 has received most historical attention, as Miles Taylor has pointed out,[2] in the wake of European events parliament received a huge number of petitions for suffrage reform in 1848, often from middle-class radicals.

The reaction of the authorities to the Chartist protest of 10 April 1848 may be seen, therefore, not so much as stage managed affair to prove that the government was firmly in control, but rather a reaction to a backdrop of a crisis. Certainly Wellington did see the use of force on 10th April as a way of reinforcing government authority. However, as Miles Taylor points out, the impact was to arouse the sympathies of middle-class radicals for the Chartists, not to subdue the movement for change.[3]

Contemporary accounts of 10th April suggest a far greater uncertainty on both sides about how events might have turned out than the historical record has so far allowed. For example, a government minister, Lord Campbell, wrote to his brother that 'many people believe that by Monday evening we shall be under a Provisional Government'.[4] On the other side a Chartist participant Thomas Frost noted 'It was impossible not to feel some degree of anxiety as to the end – the feeling increased momentarily in intensity as I proceeded towards Kennington Common ... who could say whether it would be the Government or the directors of the movement whose resolution would falter at the last moment?'[5]

Yet London was not taken over by a provisional government on April 10 or in the more troubled months that followed, while other European capitals were. David Large offers one convincing explanation as to why this was when he suggests that the government had done enough since 1832 to bring different sections of the middle-class within the political system to avoid a revolt.[6] On the other hand if there was no successful revolt, neither did reaction triumph in defeating the revolt in quite the same way that it did in Continental Europe. It was this precise conjuncture that dominated the ideas and events of the years after 1848.

This chapter and the one that follows attempt to discover the reality behind the myths of 1848. In looking at the activities of rank-and-file Chartists, as reported in the *Northern Star* and the *TheTimes*, the debates, discussions and ideas of that year are recovered. The task is an important one because it was this intense period of radical educational activity that set the framework for the years that followed up to 1860. Even then, in the subsequent ten years to the passage of the 1870 Education Act, while Chartist organisation no longer existed on a national scale, the events of 1848 were a frequent point of reference for radicals.

## What kind of picture of 1848?

While 1848 continues to be the focus of considerable historiographical attention,[7] very little has been done to dig beneath the surface of the events of that year. There is no work at all on the iconography, symbolism and language of rank and file Chartists specifically in 1848,[8] despite the fact that there is evidence in abundance in the *Northern Star*.

John Saville's analysis of how the events of 1848 were deliberately erased from parts of the popular consciousness in the 1850s reflects the fact that 1848 was not the last fling of old radicalism.[9] A recent commentator, Peter

Taylor, has suggested that, '... an examination of Chartist ideology in 1848 indicates that the themes of factory reform, trade unionism and exploitation in the productive process were not prominent features of a radical platform now anachronistic as a vehicle for addressing the relations between capital and labour.[10] In reality new ideas and alliances did develop in 1848 which the state was concerned to ensure did not find continued popular support.

An examination of what actually happened at radical gatherings in 1848 and the language used in them provides a very different picture to that suggested by Gareth Stedman Jones in his 1982 essay *Rethinking Chartism*.[11] For him language is simply what is said or written and this is taken at face value as providing meaning. He noted, of Chartism, that it was 'again to revive in 1847-8 but the staleness and anachronistic flavour of its rhetoric became apparent even to its strongest supporters'.[12] More recently Stedman Jones has noted that definitions of words and language were fought over rather than taken as a given. He has suggested that 'In the case of Chartism and its extensive employment of the language of constitutionalism, it is possible to explore the process by which new claims emerged through a process of disputation over the meaning of terms within shared political language'.[13]

For example, a meeting was held at the South London Hall in Blackfriars Road at eleven o'clock on a late August Sunday in 1848 and reported in the *Northern Star*. The aim of the meeting was to consider the 'propriety of establishing schools for the teaching of children and adults Chartist principles'. The report noted that the chair was taken by a 'young man whose name was not announced' and it complained, 'nor were any of the others who spoke'.[14] A second speaker who urged that not only should children be taught 'reading, writing and arithmetic but they should also be instructed in the glorious principles of the Charter'[15] was again reported as having been cheered. The whole report gives a powerful sense of living language in the context of a working-class meeting, quite different from the dry textual analysis which was Stedman Jones basic tool in his 1982 essay. It suggests that meaning in language was as much in the ear and mind of the listener or reader as the speaker or author and that the two could and did interact with each other in the cause of political education and political activity.

An examination of the iconography of London Chartism in 1848, not attempted even in the otherwise comprehensive work of David Goodway,[16] also provides some interesting evidence as to the real nature of rank and file Chartism and its ideas in this year. David Goodway's and John Saville's focus is on the challenge of the Chartist demonstrations of 1848 and how the State mobilised to deal with these. The report in the *Northern Star* of April 15 of the events of April 10 provided a very different picture of what took place. The impression is of a great popular festival where music and colourful banners mixed with political slogans. At Stepney Green a 'band of musicians preceeded by the flag of the Stepney Society of Cordwainers'[17] led the procession, which also contained a 'number of women, wearing the tricolour'. At Finsbury Square 'sounds of music were found to proceed from a small band';[18] the demonstration consisted mainly of 'journeymen and shoemakers' and there were 'caps of liberty fastened to the ends of bundles of twigs'.[19] At Russell Square the cordwainers were again central with their 'blue silk banner' which was inscribed with the words 'Liberty, Equality, Fraternity. The Charter and No Surrender'.[20] The Irish Confederates were also at Russell Square and one group, the Emmett Brigade, 'displayed a silk banner of crimson, white and green with the inscription 'What is life without liberty?'[21] Amongst many other banners present was a square shaped one with black writing on a white round which noted 'Every man is born free and God has given men equal rights and liberties. May it please God to give man knowledge to assert those rights'.[22]

The overall impression of the demonstration as it formed up is of one which was led by organised workers in the form of the related trades of cordwainers and shoemakers. It is also one of a group of Chartists and allied radicals, *women and men*, who were highly conscious of radical ideas and slogans. It may, of course, be argued that the slogans are those which demand political rather than economic or social democracy and that, therefore, there is substance to the point that the Chartism of 1848 was looking back to the late eighteenth century rather than forward to the twentieth. This may well have been the case for some. However, the demands of political democracy remained central to the British labour movement as it developed after 1848. Furthermore, since the core of the demonstration was to be found amongst organised workers, it is hardly appropriate to suggest that Chartist ideas were anachronistic to a developing working class. In fact organised London shoemakers were at the forefront of socialist politics in the capital in the 1860s and 1870s.

The *Northern Star's* account of the procession of the delegates to the Chartist Convention and the organisational arrangements made on Kennington Common throws further new light on the events of April 10. The banners around the procession which actually carried the National Petition included, 'We are Millions and Demand Our Rights' and 'Speak with the Voice – Not with the Musket'.[23] They can be seen to have emphasised therefore the huge, popular but peaceful intentions of those participating. This does not mean that the issue of violence was totally ignored. Indeed, the *Northern Star* reported that the on the Common 'procession was divided into 30 sections each directed and controlled by leaders who ringed them – six men deep around the greater part of the Common – thus protecting the inside from any sudden invasion on the part of the police'.[24] In terms of the actual speeches it was reported that Chartist leaders 'addressed audiences from the parts of the Common amidst great applause'.[25] Again, the overall impression is of a great political and cultural event and one in which ideas, slogans and speeches made sure that there was a fluidity of political ideas and education on the day.

An interrogation of titles in the British Library computer catalogue for 1848 provides an interesting focus on what people felt was important in that year. 179 titles mention the word 'revolution', and more precisely the threat of it. The next highest is 51 for 'land' with 26 for 'emigration' and 22 for 'labour'. These suggest quite strongly that the perception of those who did commit themselves to print in 1848 was one of the possibility of revolution from below by a labouring class which could not be controlled. This is an important indicator as to why so much effort was put in afterwards to erasing the memory of the British 1848.

## The recent historiography of 1848

A focus on the year 1848 is important to emphasise the importance of time specificity in this study and because it was, in some ways, a key turning point for working-class radical activity and most particularly for working-class radical ideas.

In terms of radical education, 1848 was the year when the ideas which had been discussed and formulated in radical meetings and educational ventures for the previous ten years came to fruition, and were lived out in practice as ideas were translated into practical strategies for action. The results of this, and the lessons learnt from it formed the basis of the ideas of radical workers for the next twenty years, until the 1867 Reform Act. As John Saville has noted, 'Chartism was the word made flesh: the Radical words of the half century following Tom Paine were gradually moulded into an organised political movement on a national scale'.[26]

Recent Chartist historiography has provided a very mixed view of 1848. Miles Taylor in his 1995 work[27] made three basic points. Firstly, that it was a return to the radical politics of 1831-2 when the working class was firmly divided from middle-class radicalism. Secondly, that it was therefore a class movement; an interesting point in the light of Gareth Stedman Jones's argument in 'Rethinking Chartism' that Chartism failed in 1848 precisely because it was still stuck in the cross-class radicalism of the late eighteenth century. Finally, Taylor suggests that the lesson learnt by those involved in 1848 was that a focus on Parliamentary radicalism was the only way forward. As Dorothy Thompson has noted in her review in *The Times Higher*,[28] this analysis does not agree with the reality of what is known about what ex-Chartist activists actually did.

Margot Finn's analysis is amongst the most nuanced in recent research.[29] She describes 1848 as a 'complex historical moment in which working and middle-class reformers were alternately swept together and driven apart by patriotic radical convictions.'[30] She also underlines that while historians may have seen Chartism as being near the end of its existence in 1848, 'contemporaries were united in the belief that the English and continental radical movements were of a revolutionary piece in 1848'.[31] Indeed, the British Library's computer database contains 179 entries for the word 'revolution' compared with handfuls for most other categories, such as 'land' and 'working classes'. There is no doubt that Finn is correct to argue that, while at least some of the middle class initially welcomed the French events, the feeling moved later towards a concern that they could be repeated in Britain. This provided powerful currents and cross-currents of ideas about how society could be changed and how quickly. In this context it is clear that many of the special constables mobilised against the Chartists were far from holding the kind of reactionary views that have been attributed to them.

John Saville has provided by far the most coherent analysis of 1848 and the balance of forces between the state and Chartism at the time. In both his book on 1848 and his later work on the consolidation of the capitalist state in Britain,[32] he has argued that Chartism did not have a coherent political strategy to take state power. He has suggested that 'while it is necessary to insist upon the presence among the committed Chartists of a general and generalised anti-capitalist ideology and of a more diffused "them against us" sentiment amongst wider sections of the working people…in the longer run there is certainly no doubt that the absence of anything approaching a theory of capitalist exploitation…seriously limited the scope of working class radicalism after the 1850s'.[33] In arguing this Saville underplays the impact of radical education and ideas in 1848 and misses the point that it was not that there was no theory of exploitation – the O'Brienites for instance had one – but that it was not sufficiently widely held. Moreover, his view of the possibilities and potential of the Chartist challenge is too one-dimensional. He argues that the state was careful not to send in the army or make mass arrests in the first months of 1848. Hence the crucial role of the special constables in maintaining order, and that it only felt able to do so once it was clear that the bulk of middle-class opinion had swung behind the established order and rejected the mood of change arising from events in France. This may of course have been a deliberate strategy on behalf of a supremely confident ruling class. It may however have been a more limited strategy that simply judged correctly when coercion could be used to break the Chartist challenge in July and August. If the state did have the forces and, in terms of some sections of the working class and the middle class, the ideas to win the battle in 1848, it had to spend the next twenty years working out ways of avoiding a re-run of the events of that year and looking at ways of bringing at least some groups of radical workers within the framework of the economic and social system. It may finally be noted that Saville very much underplays the importance of the battle of ideas between working-class and middle-class radicalism in 1848.

Middle-class opinion in 1848 was in a state of flux, ebbing and flowing between support for change and reaction. In the early months much of this opinion, which also wanted changes to the post-1832 suffrage, although not as far reaching as that demanded by the Chartists, was in support of the French Revolution. Once it became clear that revolution in France could threaten middle-class interests at home, the mood began to shift. Initially there was middle-class support for the mass appointment of special constables, and, in the summer, as reaction deepened, middle-class acquiescence in the political trials of Chartist leaders.

This did not mean that special constables themselves were uniformly reactionary. On the contrary, some expressed concern about bringing the Chartists within the existing political system. Sir Arthur Helps wrote, 'Everybody who has thought at all upon the subject must see the immense difficulty of getting at the Chartists, I mean of putting reasonable views, or at least putting the other side of the question'.[34] On the other hand, Colonel George Gawler, also a special constable, felt that revolution might be imminent. He wrote: 'My own conviction is that the next twenty years, with perhaps intervals of comparative tranquillity, will, as a period be soaked in blood and scathed in fire'.[35] It was this latter view that won out in the summer of 1848, as middle-class radicals distanced themselves from Chartism. But a few months later, no reforms having been achieved, radical sections of the middle class were again thinking of how to relate to elements of Chartism.

Finally, the European context of the British 1848 is too easily forgotten. Many radical workers were inspired by the example of French events and ideas, while the impact of Irish republicanism was central to the Chartist challenge. It is perhaps not without significance that it was on the question of Ireland and the Irish that the state, employers and the middle class focused significant attention after 1848 to avoid any repetition of the unity between Irish and English of that year.

## Chronology of 1848

*The context of the British experience*
The historical picture of the 'British 1848' has been a snapshot of the events surrounding the Chartist demonstration of April 10. In fact, what happened

before and after this is vital for an understanding of the development of and changes in radical ideas in that year. Three reasons underline the importance of understanding as precisely as possible the chronology of events in 1848. Firstly, this is the only way in which the development of and interaction between protest and ideas can be accurately plotted. Secondly, it is necessary to underline, against postmodernist histories which use evidence from different periods interchangeably, that the precise sequence of events is important. Thirdly, it is important to examine the underlying trend in protest and the ideas that it throws up, what certain historical sociologists have called 'the cycle of protest'.

Colin Barker, in his essay 'The Mass Strike and Cycles of Protest', has examined the dynamics of protest movements. He has looked at Rosa Luxembourg's classic text *The Mass Strike*, which focused on the Russian revolt of 1905 and the conditions for the outbreak of a generalised challenge to existing social relations. There were no significant strikes in Britain in 1848, but Luxembourg's method is important for a study of the British 1848. Revolts and protests do not arise in a vacuum or disappear into nothing at their demise. Barker goes on to examine theories of the dynamics of protest developed by historical sociologists in the wake of 1968. Barker rejects Sidney Tarrow's 'cycle of protest' theory[36] because it has a mechanical view of social change. Instead he prefers Victor Turner's idea that outbreaks of protest be viewed as 'social dramas'.[37] Such an analysis can help to explain some of the events of 1848. Finally Barker argues that in examining any such period of revolt 'God is in the details'.[38] This underlines the importance of the precise sequence of events and what was actually happening within them for an understanding both of the dynamics of change and of the ideas that drove the dynamic.

*The preamble to April 10 1848*
There was a pattern to the cycle of protest in 1848. The origins were firmly material, beginning with a bad winter in 1847-8 and leading to poverty and unemployment. A limited Chartist revival had already been underway in 1847. The General Election of that year was the highpoint of Chartist electoral fortunes, with considerable support from the middle class. Feargus O'Connor won a Parliamentary seat at Nottingham and, as Dorothy Thompson has noted,[39] the election also marked a revival of Chartist activity in the provincial centres. This revival, combined with worsening conditions for workers, meant that news of the revolution in France in February 1848 sparked the beginning of a new wave of protest and revolt, at first focused on poverty and jobs, but quickly broadening out to wider political demands.

Militant activity was already underway in both London and Glasgow in late February 1848, after the French Revolution but before the National Charter

Association (NCA) had begun to press home its lessons. Consequently, although protests certainly involved rank and file Chartists, it was not directed by the NCA leadership. It had a semi-spontaneous character, driven by the twin motors of economic crisis at home and revolution abroad. The nature of the protests, particularly in London, was superficially similar to the demonstrations in the summer of 1848, but the context was very different. David Goodway has suggested that the participants in both London and Glasgow were overwhelmingly working class.[40] However, the end result of the activity was not an assault on authority but rioting, looting and clashes with the police. The route taken by the London demonstrators underlines why the authorities were concerned. They started in Pall Mall on Monday March 6 1848 and went to St James Palace, St James Park, Buckingham Palace, Strutton Ground, Westminster Abbey, Parliament Street and Charing Cross. The disturbances were not in the working-class districts of the capital but in its centre.

Chartists showed sympathy for the motives of the rioters but disavowed the consequences. The *Northern Star* reported on the Glasgow disturbances:

> The crowd...broke open bakers shops, victuallers shops, gunsmiths shops and all the prominent warehouses where they could find either food, guns or pistols. We may mention that the violence was not partaken in by the unemployed directly, except in so far as the bread shops were concerned; but the thieves and blackguards of the town were the real depredators.[41]

There may well have been truth in this report. However, an alternative interpretation would have been that the NCA and in particular the *Northern Star* did not wish to publicise a growing and active physical force tendency in the Chartist ranks. This trend was alluded to by a letter which appeared in the *Northern Star* in late March:

> Whilst moral force demonstrations seem to be your only mode of action your enemies are assuming a physical force attitude; whilst you are loudly proclaiming the might of moral force and fondly felicitating yourselves upon its ultimate efficacy your foes are smiling at your folly...Democrats the necessity of this step...must be so glaringly obvious that I deem it superfluous to urge its immediate adoption. It is both lawful and constitutional to purchase fire arms and keep them in your houses...Delay not a moment...Yours fraternally John H Mackay Edinburgh.[42]

Those who wrote about such things did not always participate in them, but it was an indication that Chartist activists were learning lessons from France and were alive to the possibility of government repression. Even at this stage the debate was centrally about the merits of moral or physical force and how strategies based on them were to be understood.

## The debate after April 10 1848

April and May 1848 were taken up with the Chartist National Convention and National Assembly where organisation and policy were discussed at length. David Goodway has provided a significant reinterpretation of the events of these months.[43] At the core were arguments over strategy, particularly the question of legality, and organisation. The National Assembly in May, which O'Connor refused to support because it allowed more than the legal limit of 49 delegates, agreed a new Chartist plan of organisation designed by the Chartist left. It aimed to develop an NCA more suited to direct confrontation with the state. On the other hand, an attempt by the Assembly to criticise O'Connor failed, and even within the Chartist left there was argument about whether there should be a memorial to the Queen rather than the pursuit of 'ulterior measures'. The left was not able to successfully win an argument with the supporters of Feargus O'Connor that matters needed to be taken further than they had on April 10 and the government directly confronted. They won, temporarily, the battle of organisation but not the battle of ideas.

While the O'Connorites had not been well represented at the National Assembly, they did retain considerable support in the country. John Saville has written that

> no one matched O'Connor in the qualities demanded of a national leader, for above all others he succeeded in articulating the politics of confrontation in terms that won a response from the many different groups who came together behind his leadership. He was a superb platform speaker with a splendid presence, wonderfully racy and vivid in his language and he could be wildly funny, both on the platform and in his writings in the *Northern Star*. His extravagant language was a necessary part of the rapport between himself and the Chartist masses. O'Connor possessed, in full measures for most his career, the quality of unbounded self-confidence that has been so strikingly absent in most leaders of the British working class in the past century and a half.[44]

Feargus O'Connor did not possess an organised group of supporters in the way that the Chartist left around Julian Harney and Ernest Jones, or the Chartist right, focused on William Lovett, William Cooper and G.J. Holyoake. He had a number of very talented organisers who worked under his remit on the *Northern Star* and the National Land Company. The *Northern Star* was O'Connor's mouthpiece, although it was edited by Harney. The nature of his popular support can be better explained by his role as the 'Gentleman Leader' of Chartism. As John Saville's analysis of this leadership has suggested, it was not the ideas that O'Connor expressed but the style and form in which he expressed them that gave him the support and loyalty of thousands of new working-class followers of Chartism. It was here that the populism of O'Connor won out over the more complex arguments and ideas of the Chartist left and right.

When it came to the debate about what political strategy should be adopted after April 1848, O'Connor's deep roots within Chartist organisation and supporters gave him the upper hand. He argued that after April 10 1848 the Chartists had marginalised wider support in society and that the National Assembly should be postponed until the attitude of the middle class could be tested. O'Connor noted, with some foresight, that it was the middle class who constituted the 'jury class' who, in a few months, would sit in judgement on Chartist activists.[45] He proposed instead a Convention of forty-nine 'purely working men'. It was not dilution of Chartists demands but an alliance with radical middle-class forces which his strategy sought. While such a policy had a very limited appeal to Chartist militants in London it did find support where relations between the working class and radical middle class had remained comparatively harmonious.

Nevertheless, the organisational model which was adopted by the National Assembly was a good guide to the ideas which were to the fore in the NCA after April 1848. It was based largely on lessons and examples from France, but it also owed a considerable amount to Methodist class organisation. David Goodway has written of the new plan that 'the basic units were…the class of ten men and ward of ten classes, each locality being divided into the appropriate number of wards. Organisation in classes and wards was ideally suited to secret communication and conspiratorial preparation'.[46] In fact the new model allowed for tighter and more disciplined organisation which did not necessarily lead to conspiratorial conclusions. What was missing was effective central control which allowed local activity to flourish within the context of democracy and accountability. However, by encouraging a series of small groups the model did facilitate discussion and the transmission of ideas. The period when the new organisation swept through the NCA was the peak of the left's influence. In the early summer 1848 O'Connor's influence over Chartist activists was minimal.[47]

## April-August 1848: Militant Ideas in action

The reason for the attempted revolutionary outbreaks of late spring and summer 1848 lay both with the impact of the French Revolution on Chartist ideas and the backdrop of a developing revolution in Ireland. The apparent disappointment of Chartist plans on April 10 and the lack of public activity immediately afterwards as the Assembly met, meant that the authorities were lulled into believing that Chartism was dead. An editorial in *The Times* on May 3 stated: 'The Chartists ought for the credit of England to have done something to justify the preparations against them. After stirring us with bombast they beat us with cowardice'.[48]

A month later, at the beginning of June, the *The Times*' editorial had changed its tune. It proclaimed:

> The events of the last few days will not be lost upon the observation and reflection of Englishmen. Chartism is neither dead nor sleeping. The snake was scotched not killed on the 10 April. The advancing Spring has brought with it warmth, vigour and renovation...There is no disguise about its wishes, its intentions or its power.[49]

This was the language of a moral panic and a recognition that Chartism had retained its strength after April 10. Since some of the Chartist left had espoused the conspiratorial model of sections of the French revolutionaries, the *The Times* was able to claim that the Chartist policy was now 'secret murder' rather than 'open violence', although it would '...take some schooling...to eradicate this ancient and deeply rooted prejudice and substitute the new doctrine in its place'.[50] The paper then used this to justify the repressive measures contained in the new government Security Bill. It claimed that 'it was not opinion that was to be put down. It was action and action of the most violent, the most lawless and the most sanguinary kind'.[51] Allowing for exaggeration, the problem with conspiratorial tactics can begin to be seen. They were of little use unless they had mass support, but their very secret nature precluded such support and legitimised the use of government repression, precisely because it was seen that mass support was lacking. Naturally *The Times* was anxious to characterise all Chartist activity in this way. This ignored two points. Firstly, that a degree of secrecy was clearly desirable, and secondly, that by admitting the near success of Chartist action in a town like Bradford, it underlined what might be possible with mass support. Again *The Times* noted that 'Bradford and its neighbourhood have been with an ace of falling into the hands of a revolutionary crew. Let us do the Chartists justice. If fighting with pluck against special constables and police could make a revolution, those who fought at Bradford ought to have succeeded'.[52] What occurred in Bradford was a kind of localised dual power, where both the authorities and the Chartists had claim to be the legitimate and controlling authority. However such a challenge to authority had either to spread and consolidate or find itself isolated as the government deployed extra forces to regain control. *The Times* argued that, unlike in France, the sympathy of the soldiers and middle classes for the revolutionary attempt was absent. Even so, it went on to recognise that:

> It has been a failure. But who had guessed at the attempt? It was a failure, but of such an effort as would in some countries in Europe have made a revolution… What is to be done? Clearly separate the constituent parts of Chartism…To effect this, Government must show itself in earnest in doing all it can to promote the social welfare of the sufferers..can foster and promote those two great resources of civil wealth and power. Education and emigration…Education will give knowledge, knowledge prudence and economy.[53]

*The Times* had begun the exposition of a social programme to counter the 'Charter and Something More' of left Chartism. While this was not pursued in the context of 1848, it became of increasing significance in the years to follow.

A comparison of the news coverage of *The Times* and the *Northern Star* for the first months of 1848 is of value both in understanding how events themselves unfolded and how they were seen to unfold by participants. For example, the *The Times* gave at least as much space proportionately as the *Northern Star* to events in France. While O'Connor complained of this in respect of the *Northern Star*, there was no apparent challenge to the extent of the *The Times'* coverage. There was certainly a clear awareness by the *The Times* and the *Northern Star* that the outcome of the French 'experiment' would have considerable influence on the development of the Chartist challenge in Britain.

*The Times* stated with complete clarity that the reason a social programme was required was to head off the Chartists and nullify the impact of the 'Charter and Something More'. In its view this threatened to provide a social vision to the ideas of British radicals which would augment that provided by the French events. On July 12 1848 it noted: 'That is the choice therefore we are called upon to make – Colonisation or Revolution – a peaceful increase of the empire into its colonies or an overthrow of authority and order at home'. The paper argued in an Editorial on the same day that:

> Everybody who has given the least fraction of his time and his heart to the condition of our working population knows that the best thing an honest and hearty British labourer can do is to get a little elbow room in some less crowded part of HER MAJESTY's possessions.[54]

*The Times* went on to agree with the Chartist estimate that of 200,000 labourers and artisans in London, only a third were in full-time employment, with another third on half-time and the last third without work altogether. It concluded that 'events show that a city is on the eve of revolution when half of its inhabitants are out of work'.[55] London may not have been far off if this was correct.

Precisely because *The Times* was, on occasion, ready to take seriously the Chartist threat, it also realised the importance of arguing for alternative strategies to the Charter and strategies which took up the social dimension of the argument as well. An editorial on July 17 noted that '…we hear already of emigration clubs in the Potteries and elsewhere. These are the only land companies that will do their members any good.…'[56] *The Times* here proposed a direct alternative strategy to that of the Chartists. It was aimed not at the Chartists themselves but at middle-class radicals. The idea was to present the 'Charter and Something More' as a subject which was open to legitimate question, particularly in respect of what the 'more' might be, and then to focus on how the Chartist challenge could be headed off by pursuing alternative ideas to it.

While *The Times* articulated some of the more advanced elements of ruling-class thought, even it had to admit a large degree of surprise about developments in Chartism. Certain sections of the ruling class were now at a complete loss to understand the thinking and ideas of leading Chartists. Lord Brougham, a key figure in 1832, was reported as saying that

> he could not understand the rational soberminded people of London entering into a system of processions where there was no possibility of discussion. These peripatetic politicians did not pretend to discussion, but, they placarded the town with the words 29 May without stating wherefore those words were so placarded and then in part of the town 20,000 persons assembled.[57]

The failure to grasp what was happening and what was meant by it represented an uncontrolled fear, although Brougham probably represented a minority view, with other sections of the ruling class taking a more sober and realistic view of possibilities. Brougham's comments also underlined the degree to which the Chartist crowd was a coherent force, disciplined with a clear object. The difficulty for the historian lies with grasping what this object was felt to be and how far it accorded with official Chartist thought as expressed in the *Northern Star*.

Compared with the details of Chartist meetings, themselves often far from clear, finding an indication of what was in the mind of the Chartist crowd, or even what activity it participated in, is problematic. The *Northern Star* focused on reporting official speakers and relied largely on *The Times* and similar papers for reports of street demonstrations. There were several reasons for this. Firstly, the *Northern Star* was a weekly and did not have the space for such detail. Secondly, such events were 'immediate' and not given to accurate reporting. Thirdly, the *Northern Star* was probably less than anxious to reveal what knowledge it had of the participants and their aims. Therefore *The Times* was the most consistent source available. This must be seen in the context of its general bias against Chartism and the unreliability of its reporters, who tended to exaggerate for police benefit the unruly nature of protests. An example is the following report of events in Nottingham:

> At the close of the speeches a collection having been made to pay Blind Peter [Chartist bellman] and to purchase more newspapers, a procession was formed and several pistols were discharged into the air. While walking in military array through a great number of streets one man carried a musket over his shoulder; and cries were uttered, some for a "Revolution" and a "Republic" and others that "Mitchell should be free", "The reign of terror has begun", "death or victory". None of the leaders of the Chartists took part in these proceedings.[58]

There was a ring of truth to this report. The collection for the bellman and the newspapers and the shouts, for example, appear authentic. It is clear, however, that the procession in military array was very much a matter of judgement and might well be an exaggeration. At the same time the statement that no Chartist leaders took part does not convey whether this was because they disagreed with the proceedings or, as likely, because they feared arrest. As *The Times* report of a meeting of Chartists and Repealers at Bethnal Green made clear, demonstrations could turn into violent confrontations. The paper noted that 'the police having managed to clear one street, the fellows who had escaped retreated...there they shouted down with the police...the principal ringleaders escaped'.[59] *The Times* reports in contrast to those of the *Northern Star*, fully concentrated on events like this. There was no doubt that such events did occur and that *The Times* emphasised them in order to create a specific image of Chartism. Only rarely did it report the speeches of Chartist leaders and, as with Ernest Jones, it usually did so with the intention of providing material for prosecution. Nevertheless, the report of Jones's speech on Bishop Bonner's Fields on 5 June 1848 did contain some interesting detail. *The Times* report quoted Jones as having argued that '...Your business now is to organise. Support your class leaders, make your classes; divide yourselves into wardmotes'.[60] There is not sufficient evidence to come to a complete conclusion, but it seems that in this period the Chartist demonstrations and those who attended them were aware in a general way of the new Chartist organisation and policy. The question was whether the NCA was fully aware of and able to react to the feelings of those who attended the demonstrations, or whether it pursued separate if related policies.

By early June, and perhaps in conjunction with its editorial comments of 2 June, *The Times* urged and the government carried out a policy of repression. While it was a battle of ideas about and solutions to the crisis of 1848, the state could offer a powerful incentive for workers to come down on its side: the threat of arrest and prison. Terry Eagleton has noted

> If people do not actively combat a political regime which oppresses them it may not be because they have meekly imbibed its governing values. It may be because they are too exhausted after a hard day's work to have much energy left to engage in political activity...They may be frightened of the consequences of opposing the regime...Ruling classes have at their disposal a great many such techniques of 'negative' social control.[61]

A *Times* Editorial on 6 June 1848 argued for the arrest of Jones. It stated:

> ...for the present...we should be glad to see the experiment tried of the arrest and prosecution of the leading offenders. It is not easy to imagine that there could be any difficulty in effecting this, still less in obtaining a verdict, according to the justice of the case, from a jury of London merchants and tradesmen.[62]

It is important to note, however, that the strategy was described as an experiment. The following day after Jones and William Fussell had been arrested, the paper returned to the theme:

> The trials will be open and in the face of the country. The prisoners will be dealt with as culprits and their cases will be disposed of with as much indifference as though they had been arrested for filching pocket handkerchiefs...The energy displayed by the Government in this matter will merit general approval.[63]

It may be argued that the *The Times* had succeeded in its attempt to criminalise Chartism in the eyes of the middle classes. However, its reports for July and August 1848 indicated that Chartist organisation was maintained and that it was sufficiently tight to withstand the power of the state and the arrest of many key activists. In short, it was not coercion itself which stopped the Chartists in 1848, but, after the arrest of Jones and others, a lack of clear leadership. Additionally, the failure of the Irish revolution provided a sharp brake to revolutionary hopes and tactics. It is impossible to deny that the ruthlessness of the repression applied by the government made Chartist organisation much harder to sustain and forced a change from an offensive to a defensive strategy. As John Saville has noted, 'the Government had overwhelmed the radicals by physical force and they had triumphed in ideas'.[64]

The Times reports for high summer 1848 were the most sustained and extensive of the year and indicated the depth of concern about the Chartist challenge. There were two types of report. Firstly, there were correspondents in London, the north west and Bradford who reported on the activities of Chartists and Irish Repealers and the attempts of local authorities to suppress them. The emphasis was heavily on the latter. Secondly, there were reports of arrests and trials, which were also extensive. The paper went into a great deal of detail about Chartist organisation, although the sources, such as the police spy Powell, were often questionable. By and large, however, Chartist prisoners did not challenge the evidence of their activities. Instead they asserted that their intentions were not as alleged by the state, and, in any case, were not illegal. There was also extensive reporting of Chartist speeches. Here, the reporting was much more selective. The purpose was to provide evidence for indictment. Details of speeches were frequently challenged by Chartist prisoners. Also reported were the not infrequent cases where prisoners were discharged for lack of evidence or cases where the authorities were rebuked by judges for transgression of prisoners' rights. These, not surprisingly, were much less frequent.

What can been seen from these reports is the extent to which new Chartist organisation was adopted, while ideas about what to do remained in a state of flux. On July 26 1848 The Times reported from Liverpool that: 'Clubs to the number of 50 have been established here; that they number 160 men each – the subscription of each member is 1s a week. The money is spent in the purchase of firearms, the general price being about 12s 6d a piece'.[65] Such details were probably exaggerated, but the existence of the clubs in themselves cannot be denied. On July 29 1848 The Times reported from Manchester that 'it is notorious that organised and confederated clubs and associations have been formed in this city and elsewhere for the attainment of illegal and treasonable objects'.[66] By 17 August the fears of the Manchester bourgeoisie had reached fever point, perhaps with a degree of justification. On that day The Times reported that: 'The proceedings of the Repeal and the Chartist bodies have long been such as to excite the strongest suspicions that some secret and extensive arrangements between the various sections of the Chartists and Repealers...for a length of time past all their meetings have been with closed doors and the press have been excluded'.[67]

This kind of close knit organisation was also used extensively to promote political education. On August 4 1848 the committal proceedings against James Bryson for a speech at Webber Street in central London on 28 July were reported in The Times. Part of his speech was alleged to have been:

Men have sprung up who have declared to the people and told them and taught them what they are as men, who they should be as men and how they may obtain that which they seek...Remember I am only a working man and have not much time to study to make use of fine grammatical expressions. I sincerely and honestly cooperate with the friends of liberty as much as those who have more time to spare and devote to the cause.[68]

At another meeting of Chartists and Repealers which *The Times* reported on 19 August 1848, the anonymous speaker 'recommended that Sunday classes should be formed. Persons constituting them meet at each other's houses on Sunday evenings and might hear read to them those newspapers which espoused their cause. Thus they would obtain a vast amount of sound political information and be able in a very short time to obtain the victory.'[69]

It was clear that the new organisation was not only taken up but carried further than the NCA plan. The dentist Bryson was also secretary of the South London Life and Property Protection Society. The basic organisation was similar to the NCA model until Rule No. 3 which read: 'That every member...and convenient size to be approved by the committee and subscribed for accordingly in weekly installments'.[70] For Bryson it was clear that the key to Chartist advance was organisation. At his trial a further section of his speech on 28 July was quoted. This section read

> One question is whether we are organised or not? You all know...we are organised and that all the acknowledged Chartists belonging to this hall are organised and under the proper offices; but every individual whom comes into this hall is not under organisation, therefore we have no control over them.[71]

The new NCA model organisation designed to be inclusive was in practice both conspiratorial and exclusive. For Bryson it was not a question of organising the unorganised but of disowning them.

The relationship of the new model of organisation with Chartist ideas remained complex and raised the question for what purpose the organisation was actually organised. George Snell, a 32-year-old shoemaker, was reported as having argued that '[t]he working classes are now beginning to understand their rights and were aware that they were the producers of all wealth and they were determined to meet and discuss their grievances and endeavour to obtain those rights'.[72] This proletarian ideology must be balanced against the ideas of the old radical democracy of Bezer, later a Christian Socialist, who suggested that:

> It is not the fashion of Chartists to prevent free and fair discussion. It is the fashion of the enemies of the Chartists to prevent discussion. I love discussion...I

glory in being in a discussion and simply because I think that discussion based upon fair and equitable grounds is the best way of arriving at the truth.[73]

Bezer had at least some sense of revolutionary possibility. One resolution at a Cripplegate meeting argued that, '...Political crimes of one age are deemed virtuous in succeeding ages'.[74] His radical democracy was, however, to the left of the Chair of that meeting, Duane, when he said, 'We Chartists are not anarchists. We do not want to overthrow property in any institution that is useful to mankind but every institution that interferes with the rights of the people'.[75]

The picture of these events and the trajectory of radical ideas charted was one where activity speeded up considerably after April 10 1848. Language became more extreme as revolutionary hopes rose with the influx of Irish Repealers entering into alliance with the Chartists. The Irish had a more revolutionary temper and were not, in general, perturbed by government repression since this was their normal experience. The impact of state action from July 1848 brought a considerable degree of caution into how ideas were expressed and led, as trials started, to an increased lack of confidence if not in ideas then certainly in the relationship between ideas and political action.

It may have been at this time, in the summer of 1848, that sections of working-class radicals drew the lesson that while the ideas of the Charter were desirable they were not practically achievable at that time. It was this conclusion that led people to search out other ideas about how society might be changed in the short term, whether they were focused on the land, co-operation or trade unionism. There was, therefore, a deepening of inquiry about, and action on, specific ideas about how to survive and improve one's condition in the existing social and economic circumstances.

State repression was able to arrest the passage of advanced ideas into political practice. It was not able to obtain the consent of any but a small minority of radical workers, mainly around the Christian Socialists, for the idea that it was now possible to work within the framework of the existing, unreformed, social and political system. Change had been postponed rather than averted. In fact workers acquiesced to the existing political system. Unable to find a way of changing it, they remained unhappy about its impact on their daily lives. As the 1851 Chartist Programme underlined, the currency of radical and now social-democratic ideas continued. However, when ideas were translated into political practice after 1848, risings and general strikes were not on the immediate agenda.

## Autumn 1848: Defeat and Retreat and the rebirth of radical ideas

The months after August 1848 have been little studied by historians. Existing histories focus on the period after February through to August and then, if they are not focused only on that year, move on to the 1850s.[76] This is true of David Goodway's work on London Chartism,[77] of more general works by Dorothy Thompson[78] and John Belchem,[79] and of Henry Weisser's work on 1848 itself.[80] John Saville does, however, devote several pages to the months after August.[81] Finally, Marx and Engels, both in their published work and in correspondence, make no reference to Chartism in this period beyond that which notes its defeat and the fact of state repression and imprisonment of Chartist leaders, itself in terms of the insurgents of 1848, a Europe-wide phenomenon.[82]

In large part the neglect of the autumn and winter months is a reflection of the historiography itself. Historians have been more interested in the periods of high protest and struggle than in other periods. A focus on the times when government authority has been open to challenge is entirely justified. However, such a focus misses the point that such moments arise precisely out of the rethinking and questioning process that goes on in a period of defeat like that of Autumn 1848.

It was particularly significant that the day school at the John Street Institution, the venue from which the lead Chartist procession on 10 April started, opened on 25 September 1848. Weekly advertisements for the school appeared in *The Reasoner* during the autumn. While evidence of a direct link between the decision to open the school and the defeats of the summer of 1848 is thin, it does underline the emphasis on education, and particularly on the education of future generations, that began to develop at this time. It was not simply a displacement activity for radical protests on the streets, since most of those centrally involved, such as Thomas Cooper, had not been leading players in these protests. It suggested, rather, an alternative and much more gradual perspective about how change in society might arrive. By autumn 1849 radical education generally was beginning to thrive. On this subject G.J. Holyoake wrote in *The Reasoner* in September 1848 that:

> Recent experience, as I have elsewhere said, both at home and abroad, has absolutely manifested that educative progress is the only progress by which people advance. To multiply, therefore, the means of education, is not only a condition of private improvement, but also of public security. Activated by this conviction, the directors of the John Street Institution have afforded facilities for the establishment of A.D. Brook's Day School – noticed last week. It has been a reproach that Institutions like John Street, where so much is urged of the importance of moulding youthful character on correct principles, less has been

done throughout the land than amid sectaries. This reproach is being obviated. There is Mr Ellis's School, George Street, New Road, the National Hall School and John Street, all on secular principles. Differing in position, in sentiment and in politics as these establishments do, they are one in the great object of education.[83]

Such a perspective was not accepted by all radicals. However, it was a significant part of the reaction to the events of 1848 by people who, while on the moderate wing of Chartism in some senses, still saw themselves as Chartists. While the support amongst the working class and, perhaps, organised workers, may have been limited, there could have been no question that the issue of education was on the radical agenda in the autumn of 1848. John Saville has noted that 'Large-scale arrests are not helpful in encouraging the confidence of those left free'.[84] and by the early autumn there was widespread demoralisation among all levels of the Chartist movement. Saville has quoted the testimony of the Chartist activist George White, who toured a number of Chartist strongholds shortly before his own imprisonment in November, to the effect that while support for Chartism remained, the second rank leaders were divided amongst themselves, and, where not in jail, demoralised as to the possibility of future action. Undeniable as an analysis in itself this also poses the questions of what ideas now lay behind the divisions in Chartism, what allowed Chartist organisation to keep going as it did, and what determined its refocusing in several new directions.

During the autumn of 1848 the *The Reasoner* suggested several answers. Firstly, it was clear that there was great concern amongst secularists and radicals about the attitude of the state towards Chartism. Holyoake himself advocated that to avoid government provocation nobody but previously agreed speakers should speak at meetings and that they should say only what they had written in a previously prepared and agreed text. Other secularists wrote to the paper to disassociate themselves from the activities of Chartists. However, there remained a recognition that many secularists and radicals did support Chartism, albeit the moderate variant around the People's Charter Union. Whatever they thought about Chartism in the autumn of 1848, the government still viewed them as Chartist supporters. *The Reasoner*, while counselling the utmost caution in political activity, did not flinch from either support of Chartism or urging its readers to continue to declare themselves publicly for the Charter. At the same time, the emphasis of the paper shifted to debates and disagreements with Christian evangelisers on the one hand and discussion about the ideas of French utopian thinkers on the other. The mental horizon of *The Reasoner* reader was lifted from the hard and unpleasant reality of political activity and thought in Britain in the autumn of 1848 to other agendas.

### Conclusion. Why a focus on 1848 is important

There was a period when a focus on the year 1848 was largely absent from studies of nineteenth-century radicalism. Neville Kirk talked of 'between the mid 1840s and the late 1860s',[85] James Vernon[86] referred to the period 'up to 1867', while Peter Taylor wrote of 'the years around 1850'.[87] In all cases a direct reference to 1848 was absent. The origins of the focus lie in the continuity/discontinuity debate started by the Webbs. Following more detailed research, the emphasis on this question has shifted. For example, in 1985 Neville Kirk was able to argue for discontinuity on the grounds that Chartism declined in the 1850s,[88] independent working-class politics narrowed in focus and Chartist activists moved to support Liberals or Tories. However, by 1994 Kirk simply noted that 'the political and cultural independence which so marked the Chartist movement was greatly diluted during the mid-Victorian years'.[89] While there was argument about whether or not 1848 represented a decisive break in working-class radical ideas and organisation, there was no question as to the importance of 1848 as a key year for radicalism.

Studies over the past five years or so have begun to reinstate a focus on 1848. Edward Royle, largely following David Goodway's account of Chartism in London in 1848, has made a powerful case for the centrality of that year for understanding the nature of British radicalism. In a more limited way Miles Taylor has revisited the events of 1848 as they related very specifically to the political trajectory of Ernest Jones.

The argument of this book is that 1848 did not in itself mark a decisive turning point for working-class radicalism, but rather a defeat whose final implications were deflected for a further ten or more years, with the demise of national Chartist organisation not occurring finally until 1860. What it does represent is the highpoint of working-class activity after 1842 and the highest point of class struggle, arguably, until the explosion of new unionism in 1889. The period between February and August 1848 represented an opportunity for Chartist ideas on political education to be put into practice. A study of how this happened gives a vital insight into how radical ideas could, at the right time, lead directly to radical political activity.

### Notes

1 Jonathan Parry, *The Rise and fall of Liberal Government in Victorian Britain*, Yale, 1993, p. 172.
2 Miles Taylor, *The Decline of British Radicalism 1847-1860*, Oxford, 1995
3 Ibid., p. 107.

4   Lady Longford, *Wellington, Pillar of State*, London, 1972, p. 379.
5   Thomas Frost, *Forty Years Recollections*. London, 1880, p. 136, reprinted New York, 1986.
6   David Large, 'London in the Year of Revolutions, 1848', p. 201 in John Stevenson, ed, *London in the Age of Reform*, Oxford, 1977.
7   Margot Finn, *After Chartism, Class and Nation in English politics, 1848-1874*, Cambridge, 1993; Peter Taylor, *Popular Politics in early industrial Britain*, Bolton, 1815-1850, Ryburn, 1995.
8   See, however, Miles Taylor's important work on how Ernest Jones was caricatured in magazines like *Punch*, 2003, p. 112.
9   John Saville, *1848, The British State and the Chartist Movement*, Cambridge, 1987
10  Peter Taylor, 1995, op. cit., p. 133.
11  Gareth Stedman Jones, 'Rethinking Chartism', in Epstein and Thompson, Eds, op. cit.
12  Gareth Stedman Jones, *Languages of Class, Studies in English Working Class History, 1832-1982*, Cambridge, 1983, p. 178.
13  Gareth Stedman Jones, 'Karl Marx and the English Labour Movement', *History Workshop*, 42, Autumn, 1996, p. 31.
14  *Northern Star*, 26 August 1848.
15  Ibid.
16  David Goodway, *London Chartism, 1838-1848*, Cambridge, 1982.
17  *Northern Star* 15 April 1848.
18  Ibid.
19  Ibid.
20  Ibid.
21  Ibid.
22  Ibid.
23  Ibid.
24  Ibid.
25  Ibid.
26  John Saville, *The Consolidation of the Capitalist State, 1800-1850*, London, 1994, p. 69.
27  Miles Taylor, *The decline of British radicalism, 1847-1860*, Oxford, 1995.
28  Dorothy Thompson review of Miles Taylor in *The Times Higher*, 22 September 1995.
29  Margot Finn, op. cit.
30  Ibid., p. 61.
31  Ibid., p. 62.
32  John Saville, *1848* op. cit. ; *Consolidation*, op. cit.
33  *1848*, op. cit., p. 216.
34  Sir Arthur Helps, *A Letter from one of the Special Constables in blue, on the late occasion of their being called out to keep the peace*, London, 1848.
35  Colonel George Gawler, *Organised Special Constables, a very efficient bulwark against internal anarchy and foreign invasion*, London, 1848.

36 Colin Barker, *'The Mass Strike' and 'The Cycle of Protest'*, unpublished paper circulated to Alternative Futures Conference, Manchester Metropolitan University 1996, p. 10.
37 Ibid., p.10.
38 Ibid., p.10.
39 Dorothy Thompson, *The Chartists, Popular Politics and the Industrial Revolution*, Aldershot, 1986, p. 309.
40 David Goodway, *London Chartism*, op. cit., p. 74.
41 *Northern Star* 11 March 1848.
42 *Northern Star* 25 March 1848.
43 David Goodway, op. cit., pp. 68-69.
44 John Saville, *1848*, op. cit., p. 213.
45 *The Times* 2 June 1848.
46 David Goodway op. cit. p. 80.
47 See John Saville, op. cit., 1987, p. 162.
48 *The Times* 3 May 1848.
49 *The Times* 2 June 1848.
50 Ibid.
51 Ibid.
52 Ibid.
53 Ibid.
54 *The Times* 12 July 1848.
55 Ibid.
56 *The Times* 17 July 1848.
57 *The Times* 2 June 1848.
58 *The Times* 5 June 1848.
59 *The Times* 7 June 1848.
60 *The Times* 6 June 1848.
61 Terry Eagleton, *Ideology*, London, 1991, p. 34.
62 *The Times* 6 June 1848.
63 *The Times* 7 June 1848.
64 John Saville, *1848*, op. cit., p. 163.
65 *The Times* 26 July 1848.
66 *The Times* 29 July 1848.
67 *The Times* 17 August 1848.
68 *The Times* 4 August 1848.
69 *The Times* 19 August 1848.
70 *The Times* 17 August 1848.
71 Ibid.
72 *The Times* 26 August 1848.
73 *The Times* 19 August 1848.
74 *The Times* 27 July 1848.
75 Ibid.
76 Miles Taylor's work on Ernest Jones [2003] considers the period after June 1848 only in terms of Jones's imprisonment. Edward Royle [2000] does touch on the

defeat of revolutionary hopes in 1849 but does not focus on the latter half of 1848.
77  David Goodway, op. cit.
78  Dorothy Thompson, op. cit.
79  John Belchem, op. cit.
80  Henry Weisser, *April 10th, Challenge and Response in England in 1848*, New York, 1983.
81  John Saville, op. cit.
82  Marx and Engels *Collected Works* Volume 7, Moscow, 1977, p. 402-524; *Collected Works* Volume 38, Moscow, 1982, p. 77-183.
83  *The Reasoner* September 20 1848.
84  John Saville op. cit., p. 221.
85  Neville Kirk, *Labour and Society in Britain and the USA*, Aldershot, 1994, [Volume 1, *Capitalism, Custom and Protest 1780-1850*] p. 178.
86  James Vernon, *Politics and the People, a study in English political culture c1815-1867*, Cambridge, 1993.
87  Peter Taylor op. cit. p. 7.
88  Neville Kirk, *The Growth of Working-Class Reformism in Mid-Victorian England*, London, 1985.
89  Neville Kirk, op. cit., 1994, p. 197.

## Chapter 2
## The Chartist Meetings of 1848:
## discussing and acting on radical ideas and strategies

### Meetings and radical education

Key questions for any consideration of radical education in 1848 are how the debates and arguments within the rank and file of Chartism actually took place and how they eventually led to action. There are some important areas which must be addressed. Firstly, how did Chartists and Chartist sympathisers perceive the French Revolution of February and the subsequent developments which took place in Paris? A related but equally important issue is that of the medium or mechanism through which such perceptions were built up. Secondly, it is necessary to look at the ideas of rank-and-file Chartists and analyse whether, in the spring and summer of 1848, these ideas and those held by the Irish Repealers in particular were ahead of those of the national Chartist leadership. Thirdly, what were the driving forces of Chartist protest and militant activity? Were these based on a considered strategy or on a desire to confront authority and its symbols? Fourthly, how were they played out in the forum of radical meetings? Finally, there is the issue of a Chartist left in 1848 and how its ideas were developed and spread. There were top level disagreements between George Julian Harney and Feargus O'Connor. Harney was associated with a left-wing grouping, the Fraternal Democrats. One way of measuring how much such disagreements and the ideas of left groups were reflected at the level of rank-and-file Chartism is to consider how they were discussed in radical meetings. It is certainly reasonable in the context of the expectations raised by the events of 1848 to characterise Chartist discussion and ideas then as being influenced by socialist ideas. This characterisation, in turn, helps focus on the central point of these ideas why they held hegemony amongst ordinary Chartists in 1848.

## The importance of Kennington Common, April 10 1848

While there is considerable commentary on the Chartist meeting held at Kennington Common on Monday 10 April 1848, much of this focuses on the security arrangements made by the government to frustrate any Chartist plans to march on parliament. The success of these plans has led contemporary historians such as Gammage and, more recently, John Saville to argue that the day was a failure for the Chartists and a victory for the government. However, the frustration of Chartist hopes on 10 April had an impact not noted by historians, namely to increase the desire to meet illegally and to enter into a politics of armed conspiracy. Miles Taylor has argued that the government successfully sought to criminalise and depoliticise Chartism, with the trial of Ernest Jones playing a key role in this. Edward Royle has noted that after 10 April Jones was singled out for police surveillance.[1]

The idea of mass meetings was not abandoned after 10 April but given a harder edge.[2] In the previous chapter we covered the iconography of the day, another area not discussed by historians and which underlines its working-class and left-wing character. A few other studies do note some of the speeches made at the meeting – particularly those of O'Connor and Jones,[3] but none touch upon the dynamics of the meeting and its significance for such meetings in general.

The one area that is mentioned is O'Connor's meeting with the police at a public house on the edge of the Common where O'Connor agreed not to proceed with the march to parliament. What lies behind this is a series of untested assumptions. In his record of the day Thomas Frost noted that he breathed more freely when he heard the terms of the arrangement announced. He thought that a majority of the audience around him were similarly grateful for being released from the 'painful suspense' of not knowing the governments 'ultimate intentions'.[4] In other words, both sides were nervous of what might transpire until an agreement regulating the day's events was reached. The meeting could go ahead and the petition could go to the Commons but the march could not. As Weisser notes 'the very heights of the rejoicing indicated the depth of the fears'.[5]

Engels in Barmen wrote to Emil Blank in London on 15 April, arguing that the 'business of the procession was a mere bagatelle. In a couple of months my friend G. Julian Harney will be in Palmerston's shoes'. In the same letter Engels talked of the mood of the German ruling class and noted that 'the exaggerations, the lies, the ranting and the railing are enough to drive one out of one's mind. The most placid of citizens is a real enrage'.[6] It is difficult to think that Engels did not also have in mind the reaction of the British ruling class to 1848. Contemporary accounts of how people felt show that matters were not settled or closed and all kinds of possibilities weighed on people's minds.

The range and form of methods open to radicals in 1848 to convey opinions were considerable. Pickering[7] has noted the use of 'symbolic appurtenances, colours and modes of appearance' which 'performed several important communicative functions in radical political culture'. Certainly, the use of banners and placards in the protests of 1848 was considerable and, aside from the work of Paul Pickering, still awaits an historian. Public displays, however, could be constrained or banned altogether, as happened on 10 April and 10 June 1848. It was more common to interfere with meetings but even here it depended on how open the meeting was. Prothero has noted that 'radicals largely replicated forms of campaigning already established within the political system, the reason why public meetings, including outdoor ones were so prevalent in Britain was that parish, vestry, township, town, county meetings were established, legally and officially sanctioned institutions'.[8] Meetings could provide a visual spectacle in which ideas were communicated. The photograph of the Kennington Common protest makes this clear. Paul Pickering has underlined the importance of the banners that were carried at such events, although the photograph of the 10 April gathering shows relatively few, almost certainly because the photograph was taken well before the height of the protest. Reports in the *Northern Star* of the constituent demonstrations setting out from a number of meeting points north of the river, such as Russell Square, make it clear that a considerable number of placards and banners were carried. In an era before mass communication the street demonstration was also part political festival, designed to make a maximum impact on those watching as well as those participating. The sheer numbers involved, particularly at a time when such mass protest was a very new item of political life, sent a message to those involved and to the government that a powerful means of transmitting political ideas and leading them towards some form of political action was now at work. Therefore not surprisingly, the state in 1848 was unwilling to allow open-air meetings unlimited license.

The question of the strategy of the 'mass platform' was sharply posed in 1848 and has been much discussed by historians subsequently. The radical leader Henry Hunt is generally credited with shaping the strategy in the years immediately before Peterloo in 1819. John Belchem has described it:

> [T]he meeting, a legitimate extension of political activity, would be strictly "constitutional" a forum at which the distressed masses would enrol in an extra-parliamentary campaign of petitions and memorials to "save the wreck of the constitution" by the [?instauration] of universal suffrage, annual parliaments and the ballot.[9]

Of course, behind this strategy of mass meetings lay an implicit threat of revolutionary activity. 10 April 1848 represented a test for this strategy and one of which the participants were well aware. Thomas Frost noted that 'I have reason to believe that the vast majority of the tens of thousands who assembled on the following day went unarmed, at the risk of another Peterloo, rather than afford any pretext for a Whig Reign of Terror'.[10]

Prothero, seeing a necessary shift away from the mass platform strategy during and after 1848 has noted that social and convivial clubs 'with their own rented rooms or premises developed and were further bases of independence free of the masters control and pressure from landlords to drink too much...'.[11] For Prothero meetings in such contexts reflected a continuity of radical activity throughout the nineteenth century. In particular, he sees an 'enduring tone and ideology' in London radical clubs that survived from the National Union of the Working Classes in the early 1830s to the Land and Labour League in the 1870s.[12] Such clubs were the 'sites of small scale and informal collective practices that made possible wider temporary mobilisation and organisation'.[13] But in 1848 it was the mobilisation of radical opinion in huge open-air public meetings that still counted more than the closed meeting in a pub or club. However, as the mass meetings and processions continued, after 10 April they increasingly came into conflict with the government and the guarantee of constitutionality was lost. It may be argued, however, that unlike the 'gentlemen leaders' such as Hunt and O'Connor who fronted radical platforms, many of those who supported them always envisaged going in this direction.

## Sources for radical meetings in 1848

In 1848 the *Northern Star* was Chartist organiser and co-ordinator, but it also had to play the role of educator when methods of organisation and communication were restricted both by the law and by technology. The telephone had yet to be invented and the telegraph had just come into use. As a source the *Northern Star* has its problems for historians. 'Press of material' meant that reports were often omitted altogether. On the other hand there was no guarantee that reports of important meetings would necessarily be received. During the period of increased government repression, particularly after April 1848, there may have been considerable reticence in reporting what did take place and, certainly, the *Northern Star* could only hint at the many illegal activities carried on by Chartists. In more recent times much information in these circumstances and of such a character would have been transmitted internally for 'members only', but there is no evidence that the NCA either did or could operate in this way.

In spite of these reservations the *Northern Star* is still the best available source and for this purpose almost unresearched by historians. David Goodway's figures for Chartist localities or branches in London in 1848 show a maximum of 48.[14] However, a focus on active branches as reflected in reports in the *Northern Star*, suggests a maximum of seventeen, although these are rather more widely spread geographically than David Goodway's sample, which suggests that over half the branches were concentrated in the Marylebone and Tower Hamlets areas. These were clearly strongholds but Chartist organisation was to be found in most parts of London. The variation in figures reflected a considerable difference on the ground in respect of what branches and meetings actually represented. The partial reorganisation of the NCA in May had provided for a much more intricate organisational structure. This meant that the base unit was the class, which organised those in a particular street. A brigade brought together a number of units for an area and was itself then part of a wider district structure. For example, Tower Hamlets district met at the Whittington and Cat, Bethnal Green, while active brigades were named after radical heroes such as William Tell, William Wallace and Ernest Jones. In practice, while it might be expected that a Chartist district would send regular reports of its meetings to the *Northern Star*, this was much less likely for a brigade or ward branch. A report for a street class would hardly have been appropriate since anything of significance that had taken place there would have been reflected in the district structure.

It is also important to understand why meetings were reported in the *Northern Star* at all. The paper was the key Chartist organiser. If meetings were to attract public interest and attendance an appearance in the *Star* was essential. For other kinds of Chartist meetings this was less important. The *Northern Star*'s description of meetings could vary considerably. In most cases those which had gone badly or been ill attended would not be reported to the paper or were unlikely to be published in those terms. Although the *Northern Star* clearly aimed to tell the truth, there was little to be gained from printing a catalogue of defeat. This, no doubt, explains the significant drop in the number of meetings reported in the paper for the Autumn. For the earlier period, however, the emphasis was placed most often not on what was said at meetings but on how many attended them, with the word 'crowded' used frequently.

If *The Times*, by contrast with the *Northern Star*, was poor at understanding what really happened in Chartist meetings, there were also significant differences in how these were treated in *The Reasoner*. The *Northern Star* was recognisably a newspaper and stamped as such, with a large readership a considerable proportion of which was working class. It focused on political activity and protest and the tone of the paper was set by a front-page column written by Feargus O'Connor. There was little direct emphasis on cultural or social activities, but there was a national and international coverage of events of concern to what might be reasonably labelled the democracy. This latter aspect of the paper's coverage was provided by the day-to-day editor, George Julian Harney, who also wrote a column under the heading of *L'Ami du Peuple*.

The democracy, a term used in self definition by left-wing Chartists, referred partly to those who believed in the need for a considerable extension of political democracy and partly to the plebeian and proletarian classes who were held to have a democratic impulse in the sense of representing a popular and democratic voice. Like many concepts its meaning was ambiguous. In the mid nineteenth century to be in favour of democracy was to take a minority position since those in power certainly did not concede any extension to the limited form of Parliamentary representation. In Chartist understandings of democracy there was a tension between popular rule and a transition to a plebeian democracy, and an extension of representative democracy. From the Chartist use of the term may be traced both liberal and socialist positions on democracy. Marx and Engels themselves used the phrase 'the democracy' in an ambiguous way. On occasion it referred to a limited form of plebeian democracy, espoused not by workers but by artisans and small producers. At other times the phrase was used as an inclusive one, to cover all those, including radical workers, who were opposed to political reaction.

Under Harney's Editorship the *Northern Star* took as one of its key topics the prospects of 'the democracy' throughout Europe. In his journal *The Democratic Review* Harney clarified his understanding of the democracy as representing people on the side of progress and reform but not necessarily having a socialist character. By contrast, *The Reasoner* was a theoretical organ of secularism. It, too, had front-page leaders by a central figure such as G.J. Holyoake, but these rarely focused on strategy, tactics and lessons as Feargus O'Connor did.[15] *The Reasoner* carried only an occasional article on politics but it did carry considerable news of cultural and social activity on its back pages. This, moreover, was almost exclusively focused on London. *The Reasoner*, in 1848, had little impact outside of London except in terms of Holyoake's speaking tours. There was also no international coverage although there was support for the ideas of French Utopianism.

## Details of radical meetings

How meetings were reported in the key radical papers was an important element of how they were viewed generally by Chartists. Obviously only a relatively small proportion could attend a meeting during any one week. Many more, however, could read about it, or have details read to them, and form some sort of conclusion about the ideas that had been discussed. Most Chartist meetings above the local level were held in public houses. These were traditional meetings places for working-class people and also, before the growth of public society, were the only places, aside from Church premises, where any sort of gathering could take place. There were some radical meeting places, halls and coffee houses which were also used. While it has been suggested that temperance and drink were an important consideration in deciding where Chartists met, in practice, of the two meeting places specifically for female Chartists in London in 1848, one was a pub and the other was in the same street as the Whittington and Cat. As Dorothy Thompson notes,

> As the numbers of active Chartists declined, and fewer localities were able to maintain their own premises, the beer-shop offered an obvious meeting-place. If this trend coincided with the increasing influence over working-class women of the temperance movement, and with the withdrawal from work outside the home, it may well have accentuated, although it could not have caused, the move of the women away from politics.[16]

An examination of the most frequently listed meeting places in the *Northern Star* during 1848 indicates a large number of coffee houses. These included the Charter Coffee House in Strutton Ground, Mr Hopkinson's Providence Coffee House at Saffron Hill and the Republican Coffee House in Dover Road. Of the regular London meeting places around one-third were coffee houses. David Goodway's table of Chartist occupations shows seven coffee house keepers as opposed to nine publicans. The coffee house keepers, however, represented 6 per cent of the London total, while the publicans represented less than 1 per cent. David Goodway's argument that it was a 'striking feature of London Chartism that the localities met predominantly in pubs rather than coffee houses or halls'[17] therefore seems somewhat overstated. In general it may be argued that meeting in a coffee house was likely to be more conducive to discussion and debate than meeting in a pub. However, coffee houses had long been the subject of police interest precisely because they were meeting places for which no licence was required.

Few independent reports exist of what Chartist meetings places were like in 1848. If reports which survive from later periods, such as those of meetings in the 1860s and 1870s, are a guide then Chartist meetings in 1848 were not only crowded and noisy affairs, they were also extremely smoky and saw the consumption of much beer. According to W.E. Adams, who remembered the radical meetings places of central London from the 1850s[18] when they would have changed little from 1848, there was considerable variation in what meeting places were actually like. Of the John Street Institute he noted that 'a more useful centre of social and political activity did not exist in all London'.[19] However, in his sketch of a well-known debating room, the Temple

Forum in Fleet Street, he noted that 'It was held in a back room of the Green Dragon, small and ill-ventilated. The only time I visited the place, the debaters, whom I could scarcely see for smoke, were discussing a celebrated case of the day…'.[20] In these circumstances it would be surprising if significant numbers of Chartists, both women and men, were not put off. However, given the working and housing conditions of working people at the time, it is important not fall into the trap of believing that just because meeting places were less than ideal, real discussion and debate did not take place.

As might be expected, meetings were more frequent from early June and declined just as rapidly in the repressive political atmosphere from mid-August. Much of this increase was due to the alliance of Irish Repeal groups with Chartism. Only twelve meetings of any kind were reported in the first four September issues of the *Northern Star*. This reflected both a sharp downturn in activity and an awareness of the need for secrecy in the face of possible arrest. In addition, the *Northern Star*'s correspondent for the London Irish, Thomas Reading, was in fact a government spy.[21] Clearly there was no possibility of further reports from this source after the mass arrests began in mid-August. The *Northern Star* went through a number of editions, notably its Country and London issues, and its reports were varied to suit the audience. London meetings were reported in final editions but were often omitted if late news was to hand.

Most meetings were held on Sunday evenings, the number held at this time equalling the total of those held on other days. This, while it may seem odd to modern eyes, took into account that for many Saturday was still a working day, with Sunday being the day off and possibly 'Saint' Monday as well. The Kennington Common demonstration was scheduled for a Monday and this indicated that in London the practice was widespread in 1848. Saturday was not used for meetings since work in a number of trades went on into the late evening. There is, however, little indication of the practice of Saint Monday in the detailed studies of the London trades and working people that Henry Mayhew undertook in 1849 and 1850. Mayhew focuses on the Saturday night/Sunday hiatus in the labour process. He notes that

> The street sellers are to be seen in the greatest numbers at the London street markets on a Saturday night. Here, and in the shops immediately adjoining, the working-classes generally purchase their Sunday's dinner; and after pay-time on Saturday night, or early on Sunday morning, the crowd in the New-Cut, and the Brill in particular is almost impassable.[22]

On Sunday Mayhew noted that no costermonger, or street trader, 'will, if he can possibly avoid it, wheel a barrow'.[23] Public houses had to close by law from midnight on Saturday until 12.30pm on Sunday but there was no restriction on Sunday night opening, emphasising that it was Sunday when those in employment were free to attend Chartist meetings. In practice, as David Goodway's survey of London trades indicates, working hours were so long or irregular on other days that it was difficult for most workers to attend meetings.[24]

The evidence for the continuation of the practice of 'Saint Monday' in London in 1848 is thin. Neither Henry Mayhew nor Charles Dickens, the major social commentators of the period, makes any sustained reference to it. However, the fact that the Kennington Common protest was held on Monday 10 April, without anyone commenting that this was a working day and therefore represented not just a protest but also a strike for many of those participating, suggests that the practice may still have been so commonplace as not to merit comment. At the same time, there is no evidence from Mayhew that the alternative to Saint Monday, the Saturday half-holiday, was yet a significant feature of London working life. By the turn of the century it had become an increasingly strong feature of the working week of the factory worker in the north-west of England. At mid-century the impact of the Ten Hours Act on working hours was more important.

By 1848 what activities were permitted on a Sunday was a major source of contention between working-class people and the authorities. One element of this contention ended in the Sunday Trading Riots of 1855 but a good deal more of it became a process of struggle for licence and space between the authorities and workers. As new forms of working-class association became current after 1848, so did new forms of working-class leisure pursuit from the music hall to football, which fitted the limited amount of time available for such activities. Mayhew notes how, by the early 1850s, early morning Sunday markets were forced to close by police at 11 a.m. as religious services started. The 1848 Alehouses and Beershops Act shut beerhouses and public houses until 12.30 p.m. However, this was a tidying up and reinforcement of earlier law, rather than a new restriction. The battle for Sunday afternoon recreation was a major feature of the 1850s, but secularists already saw Sunday as the key day for meetings in opposition to religious services. Chartists and working-class radicals no doubt felt that, whether Saint Monday was observed or not, Sunday was the obvious day for meetings.

Meeting times varied between 7.30 p.m and 8.45 p.m. An examination of the starting times for meetings at the John Street Institution in central London for summer 1848 given in the *Reasoner* indicates that meetings could only start at 7.30 p.m. on a Sunday, the only official non-working day. In the week, because of long working hours and the need for people to travel to the meeting, starting times were set at 8.30pm or 8.45pm. While it is difficult to discover how long meetings lasted, and clearly this must have varied depending on their nature, it is likely that it was two hours or more. While the subject of each meeting was usually published it is of course difficult to determine whether the speaker was interesting or boring, whether those in attendance paid attention and what lessons, if any, they learnt from the meeting. Accounts by those who attended are few in number and most of these have focused on those which were of particular note. Beyond the reports in the *Northern Star* there is no historical record of what took place at routine meetings, although there were certainly a very large number in 1848.

For those meetings where speakers and topics were announced, most concentrated on the ideas and debates which underwrote the thought of ordinary Chartists. Meetings on the Labour Question (seen by many Chartists as central to the failure of the French Revolution), land colonisation, emigration, 'wealth and misery', 'the cause of misery and the means of speedily removing it' and 'labour's wrongs and labour's remedies' all focused on questions which Chartists wanted to hear about and discuss. This is reflected in the large number of occasions on which they were topics at meetings.

Not all meetings had a speaker. During the first eight months of 1848 especially, meetings were as likely to be general discussions or attempts to organise specific agitation. The purpose of meetings was not always clear, even when a specific topic had been advertised. Some meetings arose in response to internal debates within the Chartist movement. This explains, for example, the upsurge in discussions of Co-operation in the autumn of 1848. The sharp swing rightwards politically, which was a response to the defeats and repression of summer, also saw a significant increase in reports of branches of the National Land Company. Unlike secularism, which could maintain itself as a sect purely at the level of ideas and was therefore largely unaffected by events, Chartism ebbed and flowed with the mood of the wider workers' movement.

### The success and failure of radical meetings as an educational strategy in 1848

Models of radical meetings are not a feature of the secondary literature even in the burgeoning historical sociology/social movement theory area. In so far as there is a model it is that of 'closure', which posits a move from open-air public meetings in the early nineteenth century to closed and ticketed indoor meetings by the 1860s. Working-class participation in public meetings was increasingly controlled within the context of a more inclusive profile for Parliamentary politics, but in his recent book on artisan politics in Britain and France, Prothero has noted that 'the growth of indoor and ticketed meetings represented not a taming of popular politics but a recognition of its untameability'.[25] The vast majority of meetings in 1848 were open-air events in streets or parks simply because they were too big to be held indoors. More formal and exclusive meetings were held in pubs, cafes and halls and this dual pattern of outdoor and indoor meetings continued to be the pattern of radical politics for the rest of the century and beyond.

The success or otherwise of public meetings was the key to Chartist success in organising and focusing the vision of the Chartist crowd. The June outbreak in Bradford and the summer conspiracies in London therefore represented the failure of an inclusive meetings culture. In both cases relatively small groups, acting without the sanction of broader Chartist support, decided to challenge authority and were defeated.

The Bradford challenge was more broad-based and did succeed for a few days in establishing a kind of people's authority in the city. Yet the battle of the Chartists was not centrally with the local authority in Bradford. Indeed, in 1848 and for some years afterwards Chartist candidates formed part of the Liberal majority on Bradford City Council.[26] Rather than harnessing the power to change society the Bradford outbreak succeeded, in the long term, in dividing Chartist sympathisers, and a the opportunity of a third way of change, between a political riot and municipal reform, was lost. This third way involved mobilising large numbers to challenge authority through protest meetings, in effect an extension of the approach of the mass platform. As John Saville has pointed out,[27] Bradford of the 1830s and 1840s was a highly politicised town. It had a significant number of textile workers, many of whom were recent Irish immigrants who were brutalised by poor working and housing conditions. Population increase was significant, as was the increase in the size of the electorate for local, but not national, elections. There was also a clear split between the Tories, including some working-class Tories, who stopped the incorporation of Bradford until 1847, and the Liberals and radicals who won political control after this. To complicate matters it was the Tory dominated magistracy who in 1841 sanctioned the construction of a permanent military barracks two miles outside the town. John Saville notes that 'Bradford was a town which…epitomised the technology and class relations of the second quarter of the nineteenth century when industrialisation in the textile trades was making rapid progress'.[28] The events of 1848 and the defeat of a challenge by one of the best-organised Chartist groups in the country clarified class relations, and in particular ideas. Edward Royle sees class relations on a European scale changing as a result of the British Government's successful resistance to the Chartist challenge.[29] John Saville has noted that Chartists and liberals had, at least in theory, some key ideas and attitudes in common, in particular hostility to the landed aristocracy and the established Church. But they also disagreed sharply over an even more important and very practical issue: working hours and, particularly, the Ten Hours campaign. When it came to the Chartist challenge at the end of May, Liberals and Tories united against it. As Saville has again noted, 'Only when the turbulence was over and the relations between classes established on a more proper understanding of the rightful places of masters and men would the paternalistic liberalism of the worsted manufacturers and merchants once again be given full play'.[30]

Perhaps, as Koditschek has suggested, the problem was not so much that the Chartists were able to mobilise large protests but that the sections of society which they mobilised were not those capable of pushing through change. He argues that

> Ironically, the moments when Chartism posed its greatest political challenge were the moments when it represented not the organised politics of the voluntary association but the spontaneous, largely uncontrolled politics of the beerhouse, the mass rally and the radical festival and the street.[31]

In London the outbreaks of July and August were much more conspiratorial and again represented a sharp break with the strategy of mass popular mobilisation of people through giant meetings that had been tried on 10 April and 12 June. The frustration of both gatherings undoubtedly fuelled conspiratorial politics, but the crucial event was the arrest of Ernest Jones, the one Chartist leader who did have a strategy for an extension of the tactic of the mass platform.

Against this changing backdrop there remained, at least until the early autumn, a vibrant Chartist meeting culture which existed both to discuss how ideas and strategies raised in the *Northern Star* might be implemented, and also to act independently and make representations to the Chartist leadership about what direction might be followed. From May, however, the connection with the Chartist leadership, either in person or through the *Northern Star*, began to decline and decisions about strategy were left to individual Chartist branches and meetings. It was a democratic and plebeian culture where ideas and political education were at a premium. It was also one which was better able to discuss what to do than to actually put it into practice.

Colin Barker has edited a series of essays on major upheavals in society in the twentieth century.[32] These examine the social processes at work during times of revolt and change and many of the general points made are as applicable to 1848. Barker has noted in particular that in such periods 'learning processes speed up, long established patterns of loyalty break down and new allegiances develop. Political ties shift. In periods of days and weeks broad sections of the people make more advances than previously achieved in years'. He has also noted that:

> New hopes emerge. Previous habits of subordination and deference collapse. A new sense of personal and collective power develops...Normal everyday social relations are transformed. Old divisions between different groups of workers... between men and women are shattered and re-shaped by the development of new solidarities. Ordinary people find themselves performing tasks and assuming responsibilities from which society previously excluded them. New kinds of competence appear, new divisions of labour, new powers.[33]

In 1848 radical meetings were one of the structures through which ways of looking at the world and strategies for changing it developed. There can be no doubt of the immense importance of both indoor and outdoor meetings in a radical and working-class culture that remained, in the late 1840s, overwhelmingly oral and visual in its nature. It is possible that Chartist activists, defined as those that organised and spoke at meetings, may have both written and read the reports of Chartist meetings in the *Northern Star* and reacted to them. Indeed, during the summer of 1848 there was a dispute between the *Star* and the *Reasoner* precisely over G.J. Holyoake's written comments in the latter about the nature of some Chartist meetings in the north of the country. Holyoake, mirroring some post 1848 views of Chartism, had attacked the alleged bombast of O'Connor's supporters and, by implication O'Connor's leadership itself. The difference in leadership styles was important and it became a political question. Holyoake looked beyond O'Connor's style of the gentleman leader to a more a democratic and accessible leadership style which was typical if not perhaps of secularism, certainly of co-operation. However, for the vast majority of those active in support of Chartism in 1848 it is important to understand that it was not the written word but the radical meeting that provided their understanding and analysis of events.

Before the telephone, radio and television and when local and regional cultures were not integrated into a national concept of Britishness or Englishness political leaders seeking popular support had to tour the country and address public meetings. This was as true for Gladstone as it was for O'Connor and Holyoake. Holyoake almost exclusively addressed meetings in halls, partly because he was engaged in a battle with religious authorities about their availability and partly because they could accommodate the size of audience he attracted. O'Connor, as Gladstone, often addressed outdoor gatherings simply because the size of the crowd, and sometimes the location did not easily permit an indoor meeting. In 1848, however, O'Connor was busy first with the Land Plan and then in parliament and he did not tour the country. Holyoake, who was not yet directly involved in Chartist organisation, was free to engage in an extensive provincial lecture tour and it was during this tour that the dispute about leadership styles came to a head. Holyoake preferred rational argument and discussion whereas, he implied, O'Connor relied on demagoguery. However, such a position implied political changes. As Edward Royle has noted, with Holyoake 'the complacency of Victorian liberalism was already setting in'.[34]

Holyoake had clearly used his tour of the country to take issue with what he saw as the direction Chartism was taking under O'Connor's leadership, as the *Northern Star* was later to underline. In the summer of 1848 O'Connor was hardly in charge of Chartist policy. Holyoake wrote in the *Reasoner* of July 1848, after a meeting that he had attended in Hebden, that 'I think the Hebden winds O'Connor winds, or winds belonging to the late National Convention'.[35] In the 12 July issue he reported a lecture on 'Imperial Chartism' that he had given in Rochdale which had clearly occasioned critical comments from Chartists in the audience. Also visiting Stalybridge, a Chartist stronghold, several times during this period he noted that the Chartists would not debate with him about what the policy of radical reformers should be. The *Northern Star* in turn criticised Holyoake and he responded with what was probably his last public criticism of the Chartists in the *Reasoner* in August 1848. He wrote:

> The Star says I omit no opportunity of lauding the half Chartist Member for Oldham, or of having a slap at the whole Chartist Member for Nottingham...I am not the wholesale eulogist of the Member for Oldham, anymore than I am the wholesale censor of Mr O'Connor. So far from being disinclined to praise Mr O'Connor I wish I could always praise him, as he exercises great influence over the working classes...My lecture on "Imperial Chartism" which has excited the suspicion of the Star, is an argument against physical force reformation on the three-fold ground of Morality, Policy and Progress. In what respect do I differ from Mr O'Connor?...I will take this opportunity of repeating that personally I have great respect for Mr O'Connor. He has displayed more energy than all the Chartist politicians put together...yet I must be permitted to dissent from that incoherence and injustice of diatribe which is hurled at all who question his infallibility or differ from his opinions.[36]

Holyoake had, as can be seen, an ambiguous attitude towards the idea of what James Epstein has called 'the independent gentleman of the platform in which the relationship between the leader and his following was direct and unmediated, the champion and the people'.[37] On the one hand Holyoake admired the decisive leadership of O'Connor. Yet he was critical of its lack of democratic accountability. This was to be a constant theme in the discussion and assessment of radical leadership after 1848 and was one which was rarely satisfactorily resolved.

The huge range of meeting places, formats and subjects of discussion evidenced by Chartism in 1848 reflected a culture and a politics in a state of transition. Before 1825 many of the Chartist meetings held in 1848 could have been deemed to be illegal. By 1848 much of the hidden text of radical working-class ideas and thought was concerned with checking how far the right to hold organised meetings could be pushed. In a sense this was an extension of the politics of the mass platform, but it was also a vital prerequisite for the development of a different working-class politics which, whether it was the trade union branch, the benefit society or the co-operative society, depended on the ability to have regular legal meetings which were also part of a regional and national structure. In this sense at least some of those who participated in the meetings of 1848 were learning for themselves about the kinds of structures that could take forward radical ideas in the decades to come.

John Belchem and James Epstein, two of the most important historians of Chartism in the 1980s and 1990s, have looked at the question of the changes in meetings culture and the mass platform after 1848.[38] They have argued that a fundamental change was that 'the responsible individual replaced the assertive, previously riotous, free-born Englishman as the emblematic figure of popular politics'.[39] They suggest that underwriting this change was a 'self-selective language of acceptability, drawing aspiring new citizens away from the crowd into an enclosed culture of progressive improvement, party politics and constituency organisation'.[40] This was achieved 'on the respectable indoor platform, from which the unruly crowd was carefully excluded'.[41] For Belchem and Epstein these changes represented a closure both for radical meeting places and radical ideas in favour of the beginnings of an organised and Parliamentary political constituency.

Without question there is truth in this view. The impact of the defeat of 1848, changes in official Parliamentary politics and the beginning of the rise of organised labour clearly did make a difference to radical ideas and how they were communicated. Yet this is a one-dimensional picture focusing on new developments and changes without attempting to capture exactly what had happened to the old ways of thinking and organising. Perhaps not surprisingly these were not as inappropriate to changed times as Belchem and Epstein tend to suggest. There remained a considerable resilience in both the mass platform and in radical ideas opposed to Liberal politics.

For example, far from being redundant the organisation of Chartism was used as a model by Ferdinand Lassalle to set up a German workers organisation which went on to become the Social-Democratic Party. At least until

1914 this was one of the strongest parties of its type in the world. Further, as the work of Antony Taylor has shown – and Belchem and Epstein do accept – protests in London over access to open space for radical politics was something present in Chartism and the Social Democratic Federation and during the period between them. It was not an issue that was taken up or supported by official Liberal politics.

Perhaps the reality is that after 1848 a radical working-class movement which had been united diverged. In some cases the respectability of controlled and ticketed indoor events was preferred. In others open-air agitation continued as it had done before 1848. As might be expected, however, the division was rarely as clear cut as this. Secularists certainly organised large indoor meetings, which were ticketed and controlled, although certainly not in a sense respectable to Victorian bourgeois society. Yet secularist leaders like Bradlaugh also led and spoke at huge open-air meetings and protests. Likewise the rising labour movement, which relied on hard won organisation to sustain itself, certainly lived in a world of membership cards, tickets and indoor meetings. Yet the end result of many such meetings was often to organise mass open-air protests.

In reality the 'closure' of open radicalism after 1848 and the control of urban space was not a specific event but a contested process. Famously, music hall entertainment had, at least in part, replaced politics as a source of working-class interest by the final quarter of the nineteenth century. In the case of William Lovett's National Hall in High Holborn the transfer was a direct one as early as the late 1850s. Yet the Music Hall itself became the site for political subversion and the source of much official concern over how this might be controlled.

While Belchem and Epstein note that a rejection of open air radical politics was felt to be a prerequisite for the entry of a respectable working-class person into the official political nation, in reality the impact of this requirement was directly limited to a quite small group of such people as George Howell. A far greater number might move between official and unofficial politics depending on the context and issue. Belchem and Epstein do in fact concede:

> Unduly neglected by those historians, who regard the Liberal ascendancy as unproblematic, this radical alternative was to be carried beyond the Reform Bill agitation into an attempt to establish an independent labour politics in the 1870s…Shunned by Liberal gentlemanly leaders, the old open-access ways and means persisted as Chartist veterans, democ-soc republicans, the new socialists and Tory protectionists sought to mobilize outcast London.[42]

Of course, this mobilisation was as much a product of 1848 as the strategy of closed and ticketed meetings. The strategy of closure was not a given fact but a contested process that was sometimes successfully disputed.

The meetings of 1848 also marked a definitive change in working-class politics in other ways. They were the last time that conspiratorial or an inclusive meetings culture could draw any significant support. In the past 150 years the authorities have sometimes claimed that conspiracies have gone on in radical political life. From the jailing of Communists during the General Strike of 1926 to Harold Wilson's description in 1966 of seamen's leaders as a 'tightly knit group of politically motivated men' the government has often demonised radical opponents. 1848 was the first significant occasion on which such an operation was put in hand. In practice, however, the gap which existed between the social sphere of operations of the authorities and the social sphere of working-class political activists has narrowed hugely since 1848. Conspiracies, even if desirable, have not been an effective strategy in a world where increasingly everyone has known more or less what everyone else is doing. The fact that conspiratorial meetings did not work, not only because they could be effectively infiltrated by the authorities but also because they were not able to mobilise the kind of protests that could change things, was a further lesson learnt from 1848.

The strategies of mass mobilisation that were felt to be more successful in 1848 continued to be used in the decades following and even up to the present day. For example, the protests which won the ballot in 1867 were not significantly different in character to the large demonstrations of spring and summer 1848. They involved large numbers of organised workers at their core, with middle-class radical support much in evidence particularly at the leadership level, and they operated on the borders of legality.

### Understanding the radical meetings of 1848: theory and practice

It is important to grasp theoretically the impact of radical meetings in 1848. The work of the Italian Marxist Antonio Gramsci focused on how authority was maintained in western society, not so much by force as it was, for example in pre-1905 Russia, but by consent, albeit backed up by the implicit possibility of force. For Gramsci it was the hegemony in society of existing authority and the ruling ideas associated with it that prevented an effective challenge from below by organised working-class radicals. Gramsci situated the winning of such hegemony within civil society, and within this education had a particularly important role. However, in a recent commentary[43] Perry Anderson has argued that the key element for hegemony was not so much in civil society itself as in how it was linked to the state by some form of parliamentary democracy. It was precisely the legitimacy of the vote and the stake in the state that this seemed to offer ordinary people that underwrote the hegemony of ruling ideas.

In terms of 1848 this poses two key problems. Firstly, the vast majority did not have the vote and it must be questionable how far the hegemony of those in authority actually extended. This may explain why coercion featured so prominently in the summer months. Secondly, if the key purpose of radical meetings was to challenge for hegemony within civil society, it must also be questioned how far this was effective in terms of how extensive civil society actually was in 1848. In many ways it may be argued that civil society was only in the process of construction following the 1832 Parliamentary and 1835 Municipal Reform Acts.

Chris Harman, in his book on the impact of the events of 1968,[44] has underlined how analysis of the significance of what took place in 1968 has also coloured recent views of other periods of change, including 1848. He argues that while those who sought to minimise the impact of 1968 emphasised how easy it was for governments, through the mechanisms of civil society, to control revolt, in reality the real lesson was not how little but how much effort had to be put into this. In particular Harman, following the work of Tony Cliff, has argued that while the decline in the mechanisms of consent in civil society often leads to an apathetic working class, in 1968 the opposite was true. Atrophied mechanisms of consent failed to stir people into civic activity, but they also failed, when revolt sparked, to constrain people once they had decided to act.

Cliff has suggested that 'The concept of apathy…is not a static concept. At a certain stage of development apathy can be transformed into its opposite, swift mass action. Workers who have lost their loyalty to the traditional organisations…are forced into extreme, explosive struggles on their own'.[45] The mechanisms of civil society were under construction in 1848 and there was, ultimately in a number of instances, nothing to constrain Chartist militancy but force. However, as Harman has noted of 1968, 'the more farsighted representatives of the ruling classes saw the need to strengthen, or even create afresh, institutions for mediating between the state and the mass of workers'.[46]

But the very fact that most Chartists remained focused on the fight for parliamentary democracy and representation meant that there was some belief that electoral mechanisms could improve the lot of workers. As Harman again notes, 'bourgeois democracy was not simply an ideological abstraction or even a set of parliamentary forms. It was bourgeois democracy tied to certain concrete institutions…they translated ideology into bread and butter'.[47]

When it came to it in 1848, despite the use of special constables and troops and jail sentences handed down to leading Chartists, there remained what

Harman has called 'faith in the ability of electoral mechanisms to improve' the conditions of ordinary people. This may have been because while some meetings were prevented and some arrests made the experience of most was that they were able to protest freely. It may have been because there was a conscious comparison with the setbacks in the French and Irish revolutionary process, it may have been because in economic terms those who attended Chartist gatherings were less badly hit as the crisis of the winter of 1847-8 began to subside. Finally it may have been because of the skilfully ambiguous use by the Chartist leadership and Feargus O'Connor in particular of the concept of the freeborn Englishman. It suggested both that there were more democratic rights to be won and that England already had certain fundamental democratic rights that did not exist in other countries. Thus at the same time working people were free up to a point, but they could be much freer still.

While much of the debate at Chartist meetings and in the Chartist press in 1848 was about how much a democratic right to meet and protest actually existed in Britain compared to France, the whole issue of hegemony and winning a battle of ideas throws into sharp and rather different relief the Chartist strategy of the mass platform. Far from being, as John Belchem has argued,[48] the final and largely discredited use of such a strategy, 1848 may be seen as a way in which it was used to test the legitimacy or otherwise of parliamentary democracy. While the Chartists may appear to have done little to challenge for the hegemony of ideas with the middle class, it may also be argued that the very act of questioning how open the democratic system was posed a common interest with the middle class. In so far as the answer was in the negative, that meaningful democracy in Civil Society was lacking, and this did indeed seem to be the message of the Chartist trials, then the issue of winning hegemony peacefully through existing institutions did not fully exist. Many of the institutions of civil society where later generations of radicals could push their ideas, for example the post-1870 School Boards, did not exist or were not configured democratically.

A further way of understanding the role and importance of meetings during in 1848 is to see them as key framers of a melodramatic narrative which allowed ordinary Chartists to make sense of what was going on in their own terms. According to this analysis, argued particularly by Patrick Joyce and James Vernon but based on the work of the neo-Marxist linguist Frederic Jameson,[49] it was not so much what happened as how people thought it had happened and what mechanism they viewed it through. In this sense the meeting was an important event in itself with characteristics such as the speaker, venue and timing playing significant roles in building up a particular interpretation of 1848. Such an analysis has the benefit of focusing closely on what people thought and how they understood what was happening and, hence, shaped it. It has the weakness however of failing to grasp that people were motivated to support Chartism in 1848 because of *real* grievances and a belief that these could only be addressed through collective activity.

Finally it should be noted how participation in meetings of the kind organised by Chartists in 1848 fits into the categories of 'experience' suggested by E.P. Thompson. Thompson focuses on these categories, namely 'experience 1' and 'experience 2', as a way of explaining the differences which exist between how people are told the world is, through education and the press and how they actually find the world as they go about their lives. For Marxists in general there is a distinction between social being and social consciousness. Social being is the position in which people find themselves. For example they might be a shoemaker with a wife and two children living in a Clerkenwell slum. Social consciousness is how they understand their social being. They may regard themselves, for example, as fortunate to have employment in a skilled trade. On the other hand they may feel aggrieved that they have to work so hard and earn so little. In Marxist analysis social being determines consciousness but it can be seen from this example that this does not happen in an uncomplicated way. For Thompson the category of experience is to be found half in social being and half in social consciousness and therefore bridges the two.[50] People have direct experience of their working situation and the labour process and Thompson calls this 'experience 1'. They also try to understand and make sense of this experience, Thompson calls this 'experience 2'. He notes the objection, referred to above in the case of the shoemaker, that experience 2 varies so widely from person to person that not much can be made of it. This is not the point. Thompson underlines that events in the material world, for example a drop in the price of shoes, impact on social being. The shoemaker for instance earns less money. No matter how much the shoemaker may argue in his social consciousness that things are going well, or, alternatively can't get any worse, the drop in prices and wages will eventually cause him to reconsider his thoughts. Thompson notes, 'changes take place within social being, which give rise to changed experience: and this experience is determining, in the sense that it exerts pressures upon existent social consciousness, proposes new questions….'.[51] To return to our example, the shoemaker may read in the press that things are going well but his experience suggests otherwise. It is at this point that he may question what is happening and seek answers about it.

This analysis is problematic from a Marxist standpoint. While it can explain how material factors make people's views change and the reason they then seek an understanding of why this is, it might suggest that all experiences are as valid as each other and thereby undermine the material basis on which it claims to stand. To take an unlikely but not inconceivable example, the shoemaker, faced with a drop in the price of shoes, might have blamed this on the configuration of the stars or bad luck. This, would, of course, be valid in terms of her or his own experience, but it is clearly not an actually valid reason. However, whether the shoemaker had a coherent explanation of the reason for the price drop or not, the price would still drop and they would still be an artisanal shoemaker trying to sell shoes. In other words the objective world and the class relations within it would continue just the same.

Another way of looking at Thompson's categories of experience is to suggest that there is a distinction between what Marx called a class in itself and a class for itself. Irrespective of what the shoemaker thought they would still be a shoemaker, the former category. At some stage it would be possible for the shoemaker to develop a political consciousness of his status and attempt to change it for the better, the latter category. The transition itself would still be an educative and learning experience.

Attendance at a meeting was a key way of comparing the world as it was meant to be with the world as it was and then deciding what could be done about it. This final category may be labelled 'experience 3' or a move towards class-consciousness. Listening to the speakers and discussion at a radical meeting and perhaps even making a contribution was an important part of the process whereby layers of working people moved from a class in themselves to a class for themselves. An editorial in the *Spirit of the Age* noted of the Chartist trials that 'There is one right which the English people have always enjoyed more fully than any other people in Europe. We mean, of course, the right to grumble'.[52] In a sense it was precisely where such grumbling might lead and why it would lead there which was not only the stuff of Experience 3 in 1848 but also at the centre of Chartist meetings.

The Chartist meetings of 1848 addressed the kind of questions raised at the beginning of this section in terms of what could be practically done. In this the influx of militant sections of the London Irish to some Chartist events no doubt raised expectations as much as the activity of the police to restrict open-air meetings and protests lowered them. It was probably not therefore left-right splits in Chartism or whether Feargus O'Connor did or did not give effective leadership that was the key here. Rather it was the experience which the Chartist activists discovered as they tried to organise protest on a day to day basis.

Echoing a point made by Edward Royle,[53] it is also reasonable to ask why the enormous number of meetings and activity of 1848 failed to produce any real change at that time. It is not so much that workers were unaware of alternative models and experiences, although Chartists were clearly more aware than others, but that the immediate practicality of such models often failed to generalise. Terry Eagleton has noted that '[i]f people do not actively combat a political regime which oppresses them, it may not be because they have meekly imbibed its governing values. It may be because they are exhausted after a hard day's work...Ruling classes have at their disposal a great many...techniques of 'negative' social control.[54] The networks of ideas and activists and the sparks of revolt which can lead to mass protest and change more often lead either nowhere or to revolts which are contained without real change taking place at all.

From the impact of the economic crisis of the winter of 1847 to the first news of the French Revolution in February 1848, a ferment of radical ideas began to develop. Very often old ideas around the land, home colonisation and conspiratorial rebellion resurfaced. Conversely there was less evidence of the discussion of new ideas and solutions. However, any reading of George Julian Harney's *L'Ami du Peuple* column in the *Northern Star* was to grasp that new radical democratic ideas were developing and to understand that these ideas were leading in a leftward direction. It was Harney, after all, who was to publish the first English translation of the Communist Manifesto.

The question remains, however, of how radical ideas that were thrown up by the events of 1848 would be able to make an impact. Many hundreds of thousands of workers subscribed to a worldview that saw the enactment of the People's Charter as the way to a fairer society. How this worldview was harnessed to practical activity in order to do something about achieving this was another matter. In some cases, particularly early in the year, protests, while hardly spontaneous events, were clearly organised and led by local networks of activists, for example in Glasgow and South London. These protests were certainly not hostile to Chartism and may well have involved Chartists, but they were not controlled by the National Charter Association.

It took time for the NCA to relate to, and attempt to gain control over, the militants of 1848. Its foremost leader, Feargus O'Connor, who was engrossed at this time in developing the Chartist Land Plan, had no desire for organised Chartism to be at the head of the protests.[55] A new petition for the People's Charter was started and presented on 10 April 1848. In reality, however, most of the activists wanted to go far beyond petitioning and the ideas of those who protested were focused around what had happened in France and what was happening in Ireland rather than in the forms and ideas of Chartism which had been current ten years earlier.

The NCA, without O'Connor's support, launched a new form of organisation in May 1848. This had as a key purpose an attempt to turn it into a combat type organisation ready to confront the forces of the government. Its more detailed organisation allowed greater control over what Chartist activists at grassroots level were doing and thinking, but the wider parameters of ideas were still bounded by the *Northern Star*. Here a battle was underway between the 'old' ideas of the proprietor Feargus O'Connor and those of the editor, Harney.

The defeats, arrests and imprisonments of late summer and autumn no doubt led many to disown the ideas they had developed earlier in 1848, or at least not to speak of them openly, but once possibilities had been opened up it was not so easy to forget about them again, even if the language used to describe them had to be cautious in tone. Indeed it could be argued that this blocking was not broken until Ernest Jones's Manchester speech in late 1850 when he repeated some of the phrases and ideas he had been arrested for in July 1848 and the authorities took no action. The moment had passed but it was a signal that the ideas developed then were still very much alive amongst Chartists two years later.

The lessons and ideas which developed from the experience of 1848 were those of the 'Charter and Something More'. The phrase was used in 1848 but it was not codified into a Chartist programme until the St Martins Lane London Conference in March 1851. The interregnum reflected the fact that the turmoil of 1848 opened up a period related to the battle of ideas which was not finally resolved for several years. The reality was that the NCA followed, rather than led, this battle because of the impact of the defeat of 1848. Harney was able to publish a theoretical journal of left Chartist ideas, *The Democratic Review*, in 1849 and 1850 but no Chartist leader was able to speak from a platform to rank and file Chartists about the ideas contained in it. Because the NCA had been set up to organise Chartism without any direct link into the chief organiser of Chartist ideas, the *Northern Star*, there was a break at key moments in how the vision of Chartist supporters was turned into action.

In an essay on Chartism politics and organisation in 1848[56] John Belchem has argued that the Chartists followed a strategy of the 'politics of protest',[57] where the 'interaction between the protesters and the authorities is recognised as all important'.[58] As Belchem admits, far from being a hangover from early radical tactics this particular strategy is a familiar one in modern forms of protest. Belchem also notes that above all 1848 was a year when the politics of radical organisation were hotly debated. He refers to the 'quality, intensity and complexity of the debate which was to produce a fundamental redirection of radical endeavour in the ensuing years';[59] primarily this was a turn towards a popular front style alliance with middle-class radicals but also to the organisational precursors of the First International. However, as noted above, when it came to making organisational forms effective there was a considerable gap between rhetoric and reality. Belchem notes that 'Many agitators were still content to rodomontade about the power of the platform, indulging in thrilling oratory and ominous threats, without ensuring that their audience actually enrolled in centrally co-ordinated ongoing organisation'.[60] The spontaneous protests of February and March, which had been outside the control of the NCA but had been characterised and caricatured as Chartist by the press, had impressed on the Chartist left just how serious the gap was between the ability to mobilise protest and the ability to organise and direct it. Thus it was leaders associated with the left such as Harney and O'Brien who were keenest not to go ahead with the protest on 10 April, much as the Bolsheviks had tried to counsel caution during the July days of 1917.

The issue posed by changes in the format and to an extent the content of radical meetings in 1848 was whether these would be open mass meetings or closed conspiratorial meetings. The impact of events on 10 April 1848 dictated that the latter strategy would win out and this had significant implications for the development of radical education during the year. The debates and arguments of the Chartist movement moved from public arenas to back rooms of public houses, and with this move the battle of ideas moved significantly in favour of the government.

**Notes**

1  Edward Royle, *Revolutionary Britannia*, London, 2000, p. 115.
2  On the strategy of the mass platform, see Belchem, pp. 110-116.
3  David Goodway, *London Chartism 1838-1848*, Cambridge, 1982, p. 141.
4  Henry Weisser, *April 10th, Challenge and Response in England in 1848*, London, 1983 p. 115.
5  Weisser ibid., p. 133.
6  Friedrich Engels to Emil Blank, 15 April 1848, *Collected Works*, Volume 38, London, 1982.
7  Paul Pickering, *Chartism and the Chartists in Manchester and Salford*, Basingstoke, 1995, p. 167.
8  I Prothero op. cit., p. 203.
9  John Belchem, *Popular Radicalism in Nineteenth-Century Britain*, London, 1996.
10  John Frost, *Forty Years Recollections*, London, 1880, reprinted New York, 1986, p. 136.
11  I Prothero op. cit., p. 299.
12  I Prothero op. cit., p. 302.
13  I Prothero op. cit., p. 300.
14  David Goodway, *London Chartism 1838-1848*, Cambridge, 1982, pp. 13-15.
15  Barbara Blaszak in her *GJ Holyoake and the Development of the British Co-Operative Movement*, Lampeter, 1995, has suggested that Holyoake had 'mid-Victorian' ideas, p. 96.
16  Dorothy Thompson, *Outsiders, Class, Gender and Nation*, London, 1993, p. 99.
17  David Goodway op. cit., p. 59.
18  W.E. Adams, *Memoirs of A Social Atom*, London, 1906.

19 Ibid., pp. 313-4.
20 Ibid., pp. 315-6.
21 David Goodway, op. cit., pp. 87-8.
22 Henry Mayhew, *Mayhew's London*, edited by Peter Quennell, London, 1984 edition, p. 33.
23 Ibid., p. 96.
24 David Goodway op. cit., Part 4, *The Trades*
25 Iorweth Prothero, *Radical Artisans in England and France 1830-1870*, Cambridge 1997.
26 Derek Fraser, *Urban Politics in Victorian England*, London, 1976.
27 John Saville *1848*, Cambridge, 1987, p. 144.
28 John Saville ibid., p. 144.
29 Edward Royle ibid., p. 187.
30 John Saville ibid., p. 150.
31 Theodore Koditschek, *Class Formation and Urban Industrial Society: Bradford 1750-1850*, Cambridge, 1990, p. 513.
32 Colin Barker, *Revolutionary Rehearsals*, London, 1986.
33 Ibid., p. 225.
34 Edward Royle, ibid., p. 192.
35 *The Reasoner*, 5 July 1848.
36 *The Reasoner*, 16 August 1848.
37 James Epstein, *The Lion of Freedom. Feargus O'Connor and the Chartist Movement 1832-1842*, London, 1982, p. 92.
38 John Belchem and James Epstein, 'The Nineteenth Century Gentleman Leader Revisited', *Social History* Vol 22/2, May 1997.
39 Belchem and Epstein op. cit., p. 176.
40 Ibid., p. 177.
41 Ibid., p. 177.
42 Ibid., p. 191.
43 Perry Anderson, *The Antinomies of Antonio Gramsci*, New Left Review No.100, 1977.
44 Chris Harman, *The Fire Last Time*, London, 1998.
45 Tony Cliff, *On Perspectives*, in *Neither Washington or Moscow*, London, 1983, p. 234.
46 Harman op. cit., p. 351.
47 Harman op. cit., p. 352.
48 John Belchem, '1848 Feargus O'Connor and the Collapse of the Mass Platform', in James Epstein and Dorothy Thompson eds. *The Chartist Experience*, London, 1982.
49 See Patrick Joyce, *Democratic Subjects, the self and the social in nineteenth-century England*, Cambridge, 1994; James Vernon, *Politics and the People, a Study in English Political Culture 1815-1867*, Cambridge, 1993; Fredric Jameson, *Marxism and Form*, Princeton, 1971.
50 See E.P. Thompson, *The Politics of Theory*, p. 406, in R. Samuel ed. *People's History and Socialist Theory*, London, 1981.
51 E.P. Thompson, *The Poverty of Theory*, London, 1979, pp. 200-207.

52  *Spirit of the Age*, 30 September 1848.
53  Edward Royle, op. cit., p. 173.
54  Terry Eagleton, *Ideology*, London, 1991, p. 34.
55  See John Saville, op. cit., 1987, p. 162.
56  John Belchem, ibid., 1982.
57  See Sidney Tarrow, *Power in Movement*. Cambridge, 1994.
58  Belchem op. cit. p. 270.
59  Ibid., p. 270.
60  Ibid., p. 273.

## Chapter 3
## The Impact of Defeat on Radical Ideas in 1848

Analysis of the significance of the events of 1848 has not entirely kept pace with the development in social and socialist historical method and approach. Much work remains focused on political history. For example, Miles Taylor, in a recent study of the 1840s and 1850s,[1] has argued of 1848 that 'the Chartist leadership responded to the defeat of the movement, and the loss of the mass following, by rejoining and becoming reconciled to the mainstream of radical and liberal politics'. For Gareth Stedman Jones there were no 'simple rules of translation from the social to the political'. Hence he has argued that 'the nineteenth century shift in popular politics from Chartism to Gladstonian Liberalism did not occur because the country had become in some Marxist or sociological sense less class defined'.[2] In doing so he not only implied that there was no real link between material circumstances and ideas, but also overlooked the developing study of dialogics which explores precisely these links.

### The youth: young radical activists in 1848 and after

The events of 1848, certainly as understood by most general histories of the period and more particularly by active radicals in the fifty years afterwards were hidden from history and almost wiped from the historical memory of the working class, except as a reminder that supposed revolutionary agitation would not work.[3] G.J. Holyoake noted in 1905 that:

> The 10 April 1848, known as the day of the Chartist Terror – still spoken of in hysterical accents – …shows the wild way with which sober, staid men can write history…The 10th April 1848 has for more than half a century held a place in public memory. The extraordinary hallucination concerning it has become historic, and passes as authentic.[4]

The impact of 1848 on the future of radicalism, in terms of how future radical activists experienced the events of the year, is one way to test their lasting importance and impact. For Joseph Cowen Jnr., who was nineteen years old in 1848, a key radical figure of the later nineteenth century and Liberal MP for Newcastle, it was precisely the impact of 1848 in the north-east that made him a Chartist. On 29 October 1849 Cowen told a Newcastle Chartist meeting that 'he must avow himself a Chartist. He knew the Chartists had committed excesses but that did not affect the justice of their claim.[5]

For W.E. Adams, born in 1832 in Cheltenham Spa, aged seventeen in 1848, and from 1863 the long-standing editor of the *Newcastle Weekly Chronicle* owned by Cowen, 1848 remained an abiding reference point. Referring to Cheltenham he wrote in *Memoirs of a Social Atom* that '[i]t came to pass that the insignificant atom who writes this narrative, having all the effrontery of youth, took a somewhat prominent part in the Chartist affairs of the town. The first important business in which he was concerned was the National Petition for the Charter which was set afloat immediately after the French Revolution of 1848…The animated scenes at our meetings where the petition lay for signature are still fresh in the memory'.[6] Adams also recalled that 'even at that time I was a "Chartist and something more"'.[7]

Charles Bradlaugh the future Secularist leader, born in 1833, was fifteen in 1848. Significantly, his first real engagement with Chartism appears to have been with the Sunday Trading Bill riots in Hyde Park in 1855. In 1848 Bradlaugh, then religious, was introduced to a 'little group of earnest men [freethinkers]' and began the process of his conversion to secularism.[8]

George Howell was also born in 1833 but unlike Bradlaugh he was already involved with Chartism in 1848. He was an apprentice shoemaker in Wrington, Somerset from 1847 and was introduced to political discussion and radical newspapers by his fellow workers. His really formative political experiences date, arguably, more from the period after 1855 when he arrived in London than from 1848. Even so, it was 1848 that introduced Howell to the Chartist milieu that was to provide the starting point for his political development in the 1860s.

Thus the impact of 1848 on this next generation of radicals differed between those who were actively involved in that year and those who became active in the 1850s. In both cases Chartism was still the dominant frame of reference for working-class politics. However, those who were active in 1848 had experience of a working-class movement at its peak with the potential to change the world. Those who became active afterwards saw Chartism on its way down. Hence both Bradlaugh and Howell, unlike Adams and Cowen, were definitively post-Chartist political activists and leaders. There was a distinct generation of 1848 who carried a vision of politics formed in that year into later decades.

## The specific impact of 1848 on radical ideas and education

1848 saw the conclusion of a sustained period of trial for the tactics and strategy of the mass platform. The mass platform was used again successfully in the Reform League campaign of 1866-7, although the tactic had been seen to run its course with only limited success in the 1840s. John Belchem has suggested that after 1848 'radicalism lost both its confrontationalist stance and its resistance to meliorist alternatives and cultural assimilation…1848 represents the end of an era in popular radicalism'.[9] At one level this was true. There was to be no significant repeat of the pattern of protest of 1848 in the 1850s. However, the successful strategy pursued by the Reform League was based once again on the mass platform strategy of demonstrations which tested the legal boundaries of collective protest. It may be argued that not only was the mass platform of 1848 different from that used at Peterloo, although the basic model remained the same, but that its failure in 1848 was because the state felt able to define the legal boundaries of protest in a way it did not in 1866-7.

The significance of the events of 1848 and their impact on radical education saw a maelstrom of ideas and strategies which coalesced around three key mental maps. Firstly, it was thought that revolution was a possibility and this appeared imminent in France. It was also argued that popular constitutionalism could progress little further, given the power of state repression now facilitated by rail travel and the telegraph. This led to a third conclusion: that the options perceived to be open were either for some kind of revolutionary conspiracy, or to develop a post-Chartist platform focused on other means, whether co-operation or the social programme of 'Charter and Something More', which would appeal to a wider range of constituencies than 'pure and simple' Chartism.

1848 may therefore be seen as the year when radical strategies and ideas were both broken and, in embryo, remade. John Saville has argued that in 1848 '[t]he government had overwhelmed the radicals by physical force, and they had triumphed in ideas'.[10] It was clearly true that the government had triumphed in ideas amongst the middle class. This was a temporary victory, but sufficient to win the test of strength for the government in 1848. They made little headway in challenging the ideas held by the working class except in the important negative sense that they underlined the point that, however attractive the ideas of Chartism and radicalism were, they were not immediately achievable. If a government victory in 1848 took certain ideas and strategies off the radical agenda, however, it clearly added the search for others.

## The success and failure of Chartism in 1848 and its impact on radical ideas and education

More than for any other year until 1870 radical education in 1848 meant the opportunity to apply in practice the ideas, theories, strategies and tactics learnt in the various educational forums in previous years. The ebb and flow of ideas during the year was considerable. The obvious conclusion to be drawn was that whatever strategies and ideas were applied – primarily a mixture of the extra-constitutionalist mass platform and lessons, real or constructed, from the French Revolutions of 1789, 1830 and 1848 – they did not achieve what was hoped for and perhaps, in some quarters, expected. In particular, if revolution in France and insurgency in Ireland inspired radical activity in Britain, they also dampened it down as the forces of the old order regained control in both countries. From these experiences of advance and retreat lessons were drawn and new understandings reached which led some Chartists towards the politics of a democratic and social republic and others towards single issue, if all embracing, strategies such as co-operation and the land.

Yet the difficulties experienced by Chartism and Chartists in 1848, in making sense of what was going on and discovering ideas which could progress their cause, did not arise from a specific failure of Chartist strategy or its pursuit of anachronistic ideas. Engels recalled in his 1895 introduction to Marx's *The Class Struggles in France* that:

> When the February Revolution broke out, all of us, as far as our conceptions of the conditions and the course of revolutionary movements were concerned, were under the spell of previous historical experience, particularly that of France. It was, indeed the latter which had dominated the whole of European history since 1789 and from which now once again the signal had gone forth for general revolutionary change. It was, therefore, natural and unavoidable that our conceptions of the nature and the course of the 'social' revolution proclaimed in Paris in February 1848, of the revolution of the proletariat, should be so strongly coloured by memories of the prototypes of 1789 and 1830....[11]

It is not particularly good historical practice to criticise the Chartists for failing to break out of ways of thinking and acting that even those who had made a revolution had not shrugged off. As Engels again noted: 'in 1848 there were but very few people who had any idea at all of the direction in which this emancipation was to be sought'.[12] Against this however, with the hindsight of almost 50 years, Engels offered important qualifications which have a central bearing on whether or not the Chartists could have succeeded in 1848. He noted that

History has proved us...wrong. It has made it clear that the state of economic development on the Continent at that time was not, by a long way, ripe for the elimination of capitalist production...how impossible it was in 1848 to win social transformation by a simple surprise attack'.[13]

There are two points to be made here. Firstly, while, as Engels noted, economic revolution was to hit France, Russia and other countries after 1848, Britain had already been in the process of economic revolution for at least fifty years. It is possible to argue, therefore, that the state of industrial development and the size and nature of the working class in Britain at that time was at least comparable, and probably in considerable excess of that of Russia in 1917. By these criteria revolution was possible in 1848.[14] Engels' other test is more problematic. Revolution came to Russia in 1917 with the Russian bourgeoisie in deep crisis and with a series of earlier struggles from 1905 and before to build on. There is little evidence that the events of 1848 in Britain built on any particular lessons from 1839 or 1842, although they repeated many of the same strategies.

The NCA was formed in July 1840 as a response to the events and defeats of 1839-40 and it suggested that the main lesson learned by Chartists in this period was that they needed to be better organised if they were to secure the Charter. This way of thinking appears to have continued because the key reaction of the NCA to the French Revolution of February 1848 was to reorganise itself.

However, ideas – sometimes alternatives to a focus on the Charter, from the Land Plan to Co-operation – were discussed in the NCA. It was also possible to characterise different periods of it's existence from the kind of ideas that were discussed at particular times. Before its formation a rapid escalation of strategies and tactics had been tried from petition to armed insurrection. After it had been formed it stayed aloof from the 1842 general strike. The NCA did not support the idea that a direct exercise of workers' power could advance the process of political change until after 1848. In the five years between 1843 and 1848 when the possibility of winning political change seemed remote, the focus switched to discussion of ideas about the land. In 1848 it may be seen to have followed a policy of 'People or Popular Power' and, in reaction to the defeat of that year it very clearly adopted the left-turn which was the Charter and Something More. The ideas held by organised Chartists changed as economic and political fortunes changed in much the same way as those of political parties in the twentieth century. Certainly the position of a static set of ideas originating in the late eighteenth century and still in place fifty years later – the argument advanced by Gareth Stedman Jones – does not fit the reality of the situation.

It may be argued that it was above all the leadership of Chartism which carried the responsibility for drawing lessons from past activity and of suggesting strategies for future action. Certainly Feargus O'Connor, and in 1848 and from the left, George Julian Harney, did write on these lines in the *Northern Star*. However, they had no direct link either to the NCA Executive or to Chartist branches with which to turn their general political line into specific political actions. Indeed the reason why certain lines of action and strategies rather than others were followed by Chartists at the grassroots still requires further research. The NCA was the first working-class party. Although it did not fully develop the mechanisms of control and direction which are such a familiar part of socialist and Communist parties of later years, as James Epstein has argued it represented a considerable leap forward for working-class political organisation, even if this was not sustained after 1842.[15]

The British bourgeoisie,[16] while certainly not politically stable in 1848, had a degree of self-confidence and consciousness that it could overcome the Chartist challenge. This was not the case for Tsarism in Russia in 1917. It may be argued, therefore, that while revolution was a possibility in 1848, and the middle class was probably more persuaded of this than the direct protagonists, specific circumstances and strategies meant that actual revolution was never on the agenda.

However, perhaps because it represented over six months – from February to September – of sustained political activity against a backdrop of revolution in France and unrest in Ireland, 1848 drew in many ordinary people to political activity and thought. For these people the experiences of 1848 suggested lessons that remained with them. Sometimes these lessons were about the possibility of change and hence the radicalisation of a section of Chartists to the left. On other occasions the lessons were about the difficulty of change. As Colin Barker, an historical sociologist, has suggested of the general lessons to be learnt from upheavals like that of 1848:

> Capitalism continually reproduces a working class whose daily experience teaches that it cannot rule society. The 'muck of ages' – the learned necessity of subordination to the rule of an alien class – contains us all within the bounds of class society. It may be that 'power corrupts', but powerlessness corrupts even more, so that socialism appears an impracticable dream...It is precisely the function of social revolution to permit the breaking – in practice – of this subordinate consciousness.[17]

1848 opened up a Pandora's box of ideas and possibilities that continued to have an impact for many years afterwards. At the same time those who had not been active in that year or, like Bradlaugh, had not been directly involved in the events but came to Chartist politics in the 1850s, picked up a very different view and experience of what Chartism and radical politics meant. They had not experienced the high points of 1848 but only the difficult times that came afterwards. Their view of what was possible and how it might be achieved was adjusted accordingly.

The events of 1848 are the crucial starting point. It was during the first eight months of that year that ordinary people came on to the political stage as participants in demonstrations and meetings. Through a close reading of radical papers like the *Northern Star* and a critical analysis of *The Times* it is possible to construct a picture of what the rank and file of the Chartist and radical movements were actually thinking and saying at the time. Not only does this provide an important factual counterweight to the arguments made by Gareth Stedman Jones and subsequently developed by others including John Belchem that radical ideas in 1848 had not changed substantially since the late eighteenth century, it also allows us to test the differences and similarities between ideas which appeared on the written page and ideas as they were expressed in people's thought in practice.

In particular, those who participated in the events of 1848 did not have models to draw on except those which were available from previous experience of British extra-Parliamentary action and those which had been reported back, either directly or in the radical press from France. There was certainly no model of successful urban insurrection available in 1848. The first such insurrection did not arise until the Paris Commune of 1871.

What happened in 1848 raised the possibility of change in the perspectives of ordinary people but they also frustrated the hope of change. Recent work by John Belchem and Antony Taylor[18] has begun to focus on the politics of space in the Chartist and post-Chartist movement. While it is important not to mistake or confuse the public expression of discontent with the material reasons and basis for that discontent – the former could be constrained, the latter continued at some level until they were addressed – there is no question that the battle for public space was a key, and so far little explored, element of 1848.[19] In 1848 there was no specific right to public assembly or demonstration. John Saville has noted:

> The great and outstanding merit of English law, in periods when the propertied classes have found themselves, or thought they have found themselves, threatened, has been its extraordinary flexibility. For the nineteenth century, A.V. Dicey's *Law of the Constitution* summed up what his contemporaries believed to be a correct interpretation: "At no time has there been in England any proclamation of the right to liberty of thought or freedom of speech".[20]

In practice, rights to assembly and demonstration were subject to negotiation as events unfolded between the Chartists and what forces the state could muster. The state focused its efforts in two key areas. Firstly, it tried and succeeded in connecting at least some of the leaders of Chartism with the many unofficial demonstrations and protests which took place. Secondly, it was determined to close down the public space that Chartists had for meetings. The 10 April gathering at Kennington was not allowed to cross the Thames and a huge array of forces guarded London on that day. Subsequent protests in June were prevented by a show of armed force. Finally, public meetings themselves were undermined by the threat of arrest and the hurried beginning to a series of Chartist trials in the summer. The state was determined to underline that protest from below would not work and that there did not exist the space, either political or physical, for it to do so.

While the state could, if only at key locations, stop public expressions of protest, it found it much more difficult to influence the underlying ideas held by ordinary people. A show of force could convince people that the ideas they held about reform were not immediately practical, or at least that to demonstrate support publicly for them was not a sensible or practical way forward in the short term. It could not, however, persuade people that the ideas themselves were wrong. It had no direct communications mechanism for this, nor did it have a reliable group of people who could argue against the ideas of Chartism and reform. It had none of the familiar mechanisms of civil society that modern governments use to influence opinion.

In 1848 the state was narrowly based but John Saville has suggested that it was 'solidly' based and that while it contained only a small bureaucracy, with twelve men responsible for directing strategic operations, it was able to deal with threats to its stability in an efficient manner. To an extent this is a matter of historical record. There was no revolution in either mainland Britain or Ireland in 1848 and the state was able to contain challenges to it. What is much less clear from the historical record is how easily this containment was carried through, how the government felt about this and how it was perceived by those involved on the Chartist side. However, the ability of the government to arrest and imprison leading Chartists such as Ernest Jones suggests the likely line of response. Edward Royle suggests a different perspective in referring to Holyoake's July 1849 lecture 'Why have we had no revolution in England?' Holyoake's points included the difficulty of organising revolutionary activity in London and the question of whether provincial towns would follow London's lead.[21]

Narrowly or more solidly based, the state was able to win the support of the middle classes in 1848 because the alternative of revolution appeared worse. However, the middle classes, who had had a political stake in local government since the 1835 Local Goverment Act which opened the way for middle-class control of local councils, and often had commercial interests as well, were far from content with the status quo. The same equation may be made for sections of the working class who acted as special constables or remained quiescent in 1848. The Ten Hours Act had underlined a degree of flexibility in the system, but this did not translate into positive support for the political status quo.

Radical ideas could still flourish in a world where negative acquiescence rather than positive commitment to the government was the order of the day. In this arena the government had a much more limited ability to intervene decisively. *The Times* could and did suggest alternative strategies based on a programme of moderate reform but it did not reach beyond a middle-class readership. The Christian Socialists, beginning in 1848 but growing after it, were able successfully to launch workers' co-operatives and the London Working Men's College, but these remained very much a minority strand in the working class.[22]

The mental map and worldview of Chartists and radicals in 1848 remained largely undisturbed by the government. The 'liberalisation' of the state, the construction of 'modern' political parties and civic structures were not yet sufficiently developed to cause much of a change in thinking. The suffrage had not been extended. There was no way for most to participate in democratic processes. Trade unions were still usually unrecognised and security of employment remained very closely related to economic fluctuation.

This led to the impact of 1848 being very much a deflected defeat for radical ideas. What was defeated was the idea that radical plans and proposals could be given immediate practical effect. The expression of radical ideas themselves remained unchallenged. Eventually the gap between what could be achieved and what was wanted and required had to be bridged. This was a process taking many years and through the development of institutions like trade unions and working men's clubs. It involved middle-class radicals developing voluntary organisations which could include working-class radicals and activists. This worked most effectively where, as in many northern towns, liberals had control of the local council and were able to promote what Koditschek has referred to as 'new agencies of local governance'. In the meantime there was less confidence about radical ideas and particularly in their open expression. However, no coherent replacement for them was on offer.

### The experience of defeat in 1848

While the theory of deflected defeat can account for the specific and peculiar nature of the delayed defeat of Chartism in that year, it cannot point to the developments, particularly for radical ideas and education, which flowed from 1848 and had a decisive impact on Chartism in the years that followed.

The failure of Chartism to force change in 1848 was most commonly ascribed to material factors. The Chartists have been held to be too early in the development of industrial capitalism to have succeeded and too unclear about what kind of society or state they wanted. David Goodway has noted that 'while the Chartists were therefore linked with indissoluble bonds to their predecessors, their relationship to later metropolitan radicalism is utterly different. A profound hiatus exists around mid-century...'.[23] Another view, however, is that the Chartists could have achieved more if the Chartist left – those like Ernest Jones and G.J. Harney who did want revolutionary change – had been more decisive and better organised. While the views and tactics of the Chartist left were highly influential in the aftermath of April 10 and right up to the repression of August, the left never met to consider its ideas and approach. Nor was there any newspaper which argued a left-wing Chartist approach consistently. Such newspapers came into existence only after 1848. This left the ideas of Feargus O'Connor with an abiding influence over the wider Chartist movement. Indeed Royle points to an 1849 article by Harney where he surveys the failed revolutions of 1848 and agrees that gradual reform is the only way to achieve change.[24] However, Harney was to change his view again not long afterwards.

From the summer of 1848 to the Chartist Convention of 1851 there was a hiatus in Chartist political activity. The memory of the repression of 1848 was still fresh and many Chartist leaders were in jail, not least the most important figure of late Chartism, Ernest Jones. The search for explanations of what had happened in 1848 and alternative strategies to Chartism was underway by the autumn of that year. The correspondence of the Chartists prisoners at Kirkdale gaol, which focused on the need for education and propagation of ideas, is well known. The figures for the upsurge of interest in co-operation also provided an important clue as to the direction of post-1848 radicalism.

In his hugely influential history of the Rochdale Cooperative Society G.J. Holyoake noted that in 1848 'Neither revolutions abroad, nor excitement nor distress at home, disturbed the progress of this wise and peaceful experiment'.[25] The figures for membership of the Rochdale Co-operative Society in this period suggest another story. They are as follows:-

| 1845 | 74 |
| 1846 | 80 |
| 1847 | 110 |
| 1848 | 140 |
| 1849 | 390 |
| 1850 | 600 |
| 1851 | 630 |

Clearly there was a considerable turn towards co-operation after 1848. By 1850-51 when Chartism was again campaigning around the 'Charter and Something More' the rate of recruitment had dropped again. A similar point can be taken from the figures for active Secularist groupings during this period: in 1848 their numbers declined. Secularists did not have a great deal to say directly about the activity of spring and summer although no doubt many participated as Chartists. Afterwards, with a sharply increased interest in the issue of ideas, the milieu of the secularists, the number of Secularist groups shot upwards. In London the number of Secularist groups rose from eight in 1848 to thirteen in 1850.[26]

The nature of the mental worlds of the Chartist activist and supporter from 1848 was also an important question. The failure of Chartism to achieve change in 1848 probably did not amount to decisive proof in the mind of many Chartist activists and sympathisers that change could not be won. It was what happened in France that was more important. After all, in France there had been a revolution and, while by 1849 it was clear that 'reaction' was winning the battle against social democracy in that country, it took several more years and much discussion and analysis from the Chartists to come to the conclusion that the 1848 French Revolution had ended in failure. The impact of 1848 was again delayed but for those active in that year the impact was unquestionably that however desirable decisive change in the political system might be it was not on the immediate agenda. Marx and Engels had come to the conclusion quickly after 1848 that real change would take a succession of battles lasting twenty, thirty or more years. This was the conclusion reached eventually by many Chartist activists. However, since these activists also had to survive on a day to day basis they began to look for more immediate and piecemeal changes and other ways of retaining their independence. Of these, in 1848 and immediately afterwards, the Chartist Land Plan was the key focus.[27]

If we take Christopher Hill's criteria for the experience of defeat[28] we can see just how partial the defeat of 1848 was and how this shaped the climate for radical ideas and strategies in the period afterwards.

For Hill there are two aspects to the experience of defeat. There is defeat in practical terms. Radicals may be persecuted by the state, lose their income and position and generally be marginalised in society. This did not apply, on the whole, to the generation of 1848. Certainly, as John Saville has noted, a number of important leaders were convicted at political trials and endured several years in prison in harsh conditions. However, in the decades that have followed 1848, such treatment from governments professing a commitment to justice and democracy has been, unfortunately, quite commonplace. Moreover, Feargus O'Connor continued as an MP, untroubled by the state, and G.J. Harney, one of the two leaders of left Chartism, also remained at liberty. In the 1850s, far from being marginalised many Chartist leaders were able to make their way to positions of significance within the system, either politically or industrially based.

For Hill there is also the question of defeat at the level of ideas. He sees two aspects to this. For many defeat led to silence. There is no question that this was an important aspect of the post-1848 radical environment. For those who did remain active the main focus was on lessons, explanations for what had happened and new ideas and directions to stop it happening again. This was a profoundly educational question.

### The politics of deflected defeat after 1848

In socialist theory it was Leon Trotsky who was credited, after the 1905 Russian Revolution, with developing the theory of permanent revolution.[29] This argued that Russian society would not need to move from its then proto-capitalist level of development through advanced democratic capitalism to socialism. In fact the movement could be made in one bound, particularly if the move towards socialism was in an international setting. The key point for this study is that once a process of change was underway, there was no necessary limit or stopping point that it had to observe.

Later theorists, having observed a series of revolutions, for example in Eastern Europe in the late 1980s or Africa in the 1960s and 1970s that overthrew dictatorial regimes but did not then proceed to socialist societies, have developed Trotsky's theory into one of deflected permanent revolution. This theory focuses on the ability of those in charge of a revolutionary process at a particular point to halt its development so that they can retain control rather than be swept away as it progresses further.

There was no revolution in Britain in 1848. However, the theory of deflected permanent revolution can, in this instance, be looked at in reverse. It is possible to understand the actual experience and impact of the events of 1848 on Chartist and radical working-class thought and activity after 1848 by using a theory of deflected defeat.

There can be no question that 1848 represented a series of substantial defeats for Chartism. Not only was it unable to repeat French or Irish events[30] in the major cities of the British mainland, as some hoped it might, but also mainly due to harsh government repression by the end of the year it was in a state of crisis with a significant section of its leadership in jail. It might have been expected that this would be the end of Chartism. Indeed radical middle-class writers at the time and later historians of a similar persuasion made considerable efforts to claim just this. Starting with Theodore Rothstein,[31] and then Reg Groves,[32] a different analysis has shown that this was not true. Organised Chartism on a national scale did not end until the Spring of 1860. The reality is that Chartism was able to deflect the impact of the defeats of 1848 in ways which were to an extent similar to those used to prevent revolutions running a full course in the 1970s and 1980s.

For example, in the Eastern European revolutions of 1989-90 the former state apparatus, represented by those who had run it, was able to retain a level of support which both prevented the revolution going its full course and allowed it to continue to exercise influence over government. As with Chartism after 1848, they were greatly helped in this by the lack of a clear alternative to the old system, either at an organisational or an intellectual level. The key point here is that while the regimes were defeated their ideas, usually somewhat modified, continued to attract support and the impact of the defeat, far from leading to a sudden collapse, has been years of decline and change.

Likewise, after 1848 there was a slow decline in Chartist support, with some significant rallies and new areas of interest rather than the sudden collapse that might have been expected. As with the twentieth-century examples of deflected revolution, there was also a modification of Chartist ideas so that these now appeared under another label, for example suffrage reform, while retaining many of the characteristics of Chartism.

Centrally, there were limits to the ability of the state to continue to coerce Chartism after 1848. It was able to do this most effectively for key locations, events and personnel but it did not have the apparatus to do so permanently. It had to hope that its display of force was sufficient to act as a long term reminder about what it could do if it chose. In the years that followed there were many confrontations between Chartists and other working-class radicals and the state but none ended as they had in 1848. The fact that the state was not prepared to use such repressive tactics again underlined just how exceptional it felt them to be. The impact on the mental world of Chartist activists and supporters is hard to judge precisely. Certainly the level of repression and imprisonment of key activists had a severe dampening impact on anyone who sought direct confrontation with the government during the 1850s. However, the perception that the government was undemocratic and unrepresentative and that Chartist politics were generally the way to change this remained. The construction of a worldview, either on behalf of the Chartists or the government, where organised labour was included within the political system and political radicals tolerated and occasionally also incorporated into official politics began to emerge from the impact of 1848 but took years to become widespread.

While all kinds of alternative ideas and strategies began to develop after 1848, there was no group which was able to exercise the kind of authority that the Chartists had maintained. The *Northern Star* remained in place as the only national working-class paper and the NCA was still headed by Feargus O'Connor. It should also be taken into consideration that with the National Land Company the Chartists themselves had developed a powerful parallel strategy to that of winning political change.

The state won the battle of physical force in 1848 and temporarily persuaded many of the middle class of the danger of Chartist ideas but it was not able to win over significant sections of them to support its project. Indeed, it is doubtful if the British state, after 1848, knew exactly what its project was. It came under increasing pressure, to which it gradually gave way, to reform, change and generally democratise its procedures and practices. This took time, and the Reform Act of 1867 and the Education Act of 1870 must be considered as notable signposts. In the meantime there were very few openings inside the political system that might persuade important radical middle-class figures to support the state's case. There remained, too, very little chance in the 1850s for working-class activists who wanted to move beyond Chartism to argue that there were other avenues open for change.

This raises the further question, however, of what caused the collapse of national Chartism in 1860. By that time alternative strategies for change had begun to develop successfully. In particular, both the co-operative movement and the trade unions had not only begun to make a mark in some areas but, as importantly, had also begun to be recognised by some employers and government representatives as powers which had to be consulted and whose views should be taken into account. The early 1860s are littered with meetings between post-Chartist leaders and government ministers over foreign and domestic issues. Such people had not even been allowed over to the north bank of the Thames on 10 April 1848, let alone allowed inside Whitehall offices.

There was also the question of the Chartist analysis of events. Despite the arguments of Gareth Stedman Jones, recently echoed by John Belchem and others,[33] Chartist thinking did progress significantly after 1848. Indeed much of the work below is concerned with how new ideas and strategies were worked out in the context of a continued effort at radical education in the

1850s. By far the most important of these was the programme and strategy of the 'Charter and Something More'.

John Saville has described the 1851 Chartist programme which stood for the 'Charter and Something More', as the blueprint for a socialist state and the most advanced working-class ideas of the nineteenth century.[34] It underlined that a section of the Chartists, notably the left, partially under the influence of Marx and Engels, had learnt lessons from what had happened in 1848 and determined that social and economic as well as political change must be on the Chartist agenda. By 1858 the 'Charter and Something More' had been abandoned, even by the leading Chartist figure of the 1850s Ernest Jones. It was an advanced programme but its influence among the working class was uncertain and it was infrequently campaigned for as part of a political strategy which might achieve change in the short term.

The support of many Chartist sympathisers by the 1860s had therefore moved not to the 'Charter and Something More' but to something rather less than the Charter demanded and implied a further extension to the suffrage, building on the Act of 1832. Some of the processes whereby Chartism, which the state felt offered a challenge to its existence in 1848, moved away from the ideas of extra-parliamentary activity towards a focus on reform within the parliamentary system are considered below. The state conceded, under huge and organised pressure, to further reforms in 1867. These processes were the mechanism by which the deflected defeat of Chartism finally occurred, as its national independent organisation and weekly paper collapsed. It should however be noted that the twelve years which it took Chartism to die after 1848 also ensured that Chartist ideas, both pre- and post-1848 would continue to be the currency of much of the left and the labour movement until the new strategies of statist reform and syndicalism began to emerge in the 1880s and the 1890s.

A pattern of waves of radical education may be detected in 1848. As the political challenge of Chartism declined so the emphasis on radical education began to increase. In a sense this is the reverse, or perhaps a counterpart of, the theory of 'Really Useful Knowledge'. While 1848 marked a clear and decisive defeat for the forces of Chartism, undercurrents of radical ideas continued. In fact, from the autumn of 1848 the increased interest in such ideas may be seen as a retreat into areas of radical education and thought. The government either would not or could not easily intervene to curtail or prevent these. At the same time the decline in radical political activity meant an increased availability of personnel to organise radical schools and to teach in them. The radical schools which sprang out of the activity of 1848 may be seen as the product of defeat and also as the beginning of the warrening process of civil society. But they were also the beginning of the remaking of radicalism, especially of radical ideas that had been unmade by 1848.

This is not to argue that radical education, ideas and language had a completely autonomous role in society. While Gareth Stedman Jones has argued that his long essay 'Rethinking Chartism' was an attempt to 'bring to the fore the politics of Chartism, freed from the a priori assumptions of historians about its social meaning...applied a non-referential conception of language to the study of Chartist speeches and writings',[35] more recent work has criticised such a model for its one-dimensionality. Steinberg has noted that '[a] group's sense of agency, its members' shared consciousness of the moral precepts that justify their actions, and their vision of a desired future are all constructed through the fighting words that accompany their repertoire of instrumental action. A dialogic analysis of ideology, identity and interest demonstrates how contests over social meaning are both part of the struggle and a power dynamic that shapes other aspects of conflict.[36]

The implications for the developments considered here of such theoretical disputations are significant. Stedman Jones has argued, for example, that Engels based his theory of class struggle and class formation on a model drawn from the pre-1848 Chartist movement. He suggests that 'the decline of Chartism could partly be attributed to the limitations inherent in an ideology, which was dominant within it, that was incapable of articulating the new pattern of class relations in the factory districts of the North.[37] Yet Marx himself, writing about the defeat of the French revolutionaries in 1848, noted that 'what succumbed in these defeats was not the revolution. It was the pre-revolutionary traditional appendages, results of social relationships which had not yet come to the point of sharp class antagonisms – persons, illusions, conceptions, projects – from which the revolutionary party before the February Revolution was not free, from which it could be freed not by the victory of February, but only by a series of defeats'.[38]

## Conclusion

Clearly there was a recognition of the impact of the defeats of 1848 on the shape of the working-class movement and a renewed battle for the ideas and strategies to which it would adhere. In terms of the content of radical education, the growth of a moral agenda or economy can be seen. At the most basic level an emphasis on secular education underlined this. However, a focus on cooperative knowledge, on job vacancies and wage rates, and on the mechanisms for gaining an extension of the suffrage suggest that radical education helped to frame an alternative, working-class view and understanding of the world, with very different priorities to either Manchester school Liberalism or paternalistic Toryism.

## Notes

1. Miles Taylor, *The Decline of British Radicalism 1847-1860*, Oxford, 1995, p. 99.
2. Gareth Stedman Jones, *Languages of Class*, London, 1982 p. 242.
3. Edward Royle, op. cit., 2000, p. 135.
4. G. J. Holyoake *Bygones Worth Remembering*, London, 1905, Chapter VII., *The Tenth of April, 1848 – Its Incredibilities*, pp. 73-5.
5. Nigel Todd, *The Militant Democracy*, Tyne & Wear, 1991, p. 31.
6. W. E. Adams, *Memoirs of a Social Atom*, New York 1967 Edition, p. 170.
7. Ibid., pp. 151-2.
8. Hyptia Bradlaugh Bonner, *Charles Bradlaugh, A Record of His Life and Work*, London, 1906.
9. John Belchem, *The Chartist Experience* op. cit.
10. John Saville, *1848*, Cambridge, 1987, p. 163.
11. Frederick Engels, *Introduction to, Karl Marx, The Class Struggles in France*, Moscow, 1979, p. 11.
12. Ibid., p. 14.
13. Ibid., p. 15.
14. For a discussion of this issue between John Saville, John Charlton and the author see the letters pages of *Socialist Review*, May 1997.
15. James Epstein, op. cit., pp. 220-236.
16. For a useful analysis of the British bourgeoisie in this period, see T. Koditschek, op. cit., p. 517. He notes that 'yet by 1850…amidst a stable climate of economic growth and prosperity, the liberal ideal of a voluntary progressive consensus seemed…a sober fact.…the challenges of Tory paternalism and proletarian collectivism had faltered'.
17. Colin Barker [ed] *Revolutionary Rehearsals*, London, 1987, p. 219.
18. John Belchem, *Popular Radicalism in Nineteenth-Century Britain*, Basingstoke, 1996; John Breuilly, Gottfried Niedhart and Antony Taylor, *The Era of the Reform League, English Labour and radical politics, 1857-1872*, Mannheim, 1995; Neville Kirk, op. cit., 1998, p. 87.
19. See Edward Royle, op. cit., 2000, p. 125.
20. John Saville, *The Consolidation of the Capitalist State 1800-1850*, London, 1994, p. 77.
21. Edward Royle, op. cit., 2000, pp. 148-151.
22. See John Saville 'The Christian Socialists of 1848' in Saville [Ed] *Democracy and the Labour Movement*, p. 152.
23. David Goodway, *London Chartism*, Cambridge, 1982 p. 13.
24. Edward Royle, op. cit., 2000, p. 192.
25. G.J. Holyoake, *Self Help by the People. The History of the Rochdale Pioneers*, London, 1893, p. 19. This was the tenth edition of the volume, first published in 1857.
26. Edward Royle, *Victorian Infidels*, Manchester, 1984, p. 301.
27. See Malcolm Chase 'We wish only to work for ourselves: the Chartist Land Plan' in Malcolm Chase and Ian Dyck [Ed] *Living and Learning*, Aldershot, 1996.
28. Christopher Hill, *The Experience of Defeat*, London, 1994.
29. Leon Trotsky, *The Permanent Revolution*, New York, 1969, Edition.

30  See John Saville, *1848*, Chapter 1, pp. 27-50, Cambridge, 1987.
31  Theodore Rothstein, *From Chartism to Labourism*, London 1929.
32  Reg Groves, *But we shall rise again*, London, 1938.
33  Belchem op. cit.
34  John Saville, *Ernest Jones, Chartist*, London, 1952, p. 45.
35  Gareth Stedman Jones, *The Languages of Class*, London, 1982, p. 21.
36  Marc Steinberg, *Fighting Words*, London, 1999, p. 236.
37  Stedman Jones, *Languages of Class*, op. cit., p. 18.
38  Karl Marx, *Class Struggles in France*, Moscow, 1968, p. 27.

## Chapter 4
## The Battle of Ideas, 1848-51: locations, influences, results

### Introduction

Beneath the headline view that Chartism failed in 1848 matters were not so simple. There had in fact been revolutions in many European countries in that year. While the Chartists had been unsuccessful their very existence was a reminder to the government that the potential for revolt remained. The Chartists themselves, while clearly defeated with many front line leaders in prison, did not at this stage believe that the defeat would be long lived. A revival was expected, if not in months then certainly before many years had passed. The left-wing Chartist grouping, the Fraternal Democrats, argued that that the revolutions of 1848 were not finished and indeed could not be because now ordinary working people had entered on to the stage of history they would see the battle for political and social rights through. The past in Marx's phrase 'weighed like a nightmare'[1] on present thinking, influencing both the government and the Chartists. As Chartist strength waned into the 1850s, the government was able to feel more relaxed about threats of revolution, and with this confidence came openings to reform which further blocked off any revolutionary hopes. But this was not the case in the years immediately after 1848.

The Great Exhibition of 1851 was a demonstration of the power of the developing British imperial project. Yet the government remained worried about the possibility of working-class disorder at the Exhibition site in Hyde Park. This was not such an idle worry since Hyde Park in the later 1850s and 1860s was the scene of major working-class challenges to government policy. The government was also worried that the mere presence of the Chartists in London, and the continuing possibility of revolt, would scare off visitors to the Exhibition. Troops were put on stand-by and around the country committees were set up to encourage workers to visit the Exhibition for reasons of pleasure rather than revolution.

The Bishop of Oxford had made an attempt to draw the organised working classes, along with middle-class radicals, into the arrangements for the setting up of the Exhibition. Yet the presence of even moderate Chartists such as Lovett and Vincent had caused the authorities to refuse to deal with the Bishop's Committee. It subsequently dissolved itself. Even radicals like Charles Dickens were very critical of the Exhibition. The whole affair underlined how difficult it would be to construct an alliance of working- and middle-class radicals that would be able to exert any pressure from within the system.[2]

At the same time there was a move by the authorities, particularly at local level, to close off the public spaces in which radicals operated, by a mixture of policing and privatisation. Again this was not achieved overnight. However, as the weight of numbers supporting working-class radicalism declined, or perhaps more accurately, pursued diverse projects, the finance available to run buildings became more limited. In Manchester the Owenite Hall of Science became the public library. Martin Hewitt has shown how, after 1848, the local authority, and in particular the police, were able to restrict gradually meeting places and spaces for working-class radicals.[3] This suggests, however, a very different picture to that painted by those who argue that radicals voluntarily closed down public open air meetings.

The most well known post-1848 structure of the type mentioned above were the Christian Socialists. Initially co-operatives of working tradesmen were set up, mainly in London. Later these became Working Men's Colleges. There were other institutions which had their origins in the post-1848 period – in particular, in some areas, retail co-operative societies. There was, of course, tension in these structures between middle-class sponsorship and working-class independence, and this was more broadly reflected in the battle of ideas about what society was and how it could be changed that started in this period.

Enormous effort was also put into educational endeavours, broadly defined. The British Library catalogue covering the period 1849-1851 records, for example, an increase in the number of titles listed as 'manuals' from 72 to 93 and the number of titles listed as 'guides' from 95 to 158. There was also a small but significant increase in titles relating to secular education from 2 in 1849 to 8 in 1850 and 6 in 1851. These changes, reflected in the British Library catalogue only at a general level, suggest a thirst for knowledge and understanding following on from the events of 1848. However, they also pointed to the beginnings of middle-class radical investment in secular schools.

Whether these secular schools were within the milieu of radical working-class politics or simply radical compared to the view of existing middle-class thought varied from area to area. In London, middle-class secular schools were associated with radical politics. In Manchester and Glasgow this was rather less the case. This underlines a key point about the post-1848 period.

With the retreat, although not the final defeat, of Chartism there was now a growing unevenness about radical politics from area to area. Martin Hewitt, in his study of radical politics in post-1848 Manchester, has noted that: 'we need to seek different patterns of decline in which the relative importance of the processes at work varied from place to place'.[4] This means that there is considerable evidence of working-class radical schools being set up after 1848 in London. Elsewhere, where the working-class movement after 1848 found it harder to maintain its independence, such evidence is lacking.

### Radical Education in London after 1848: the battle of ideas begins

New Series of Secular School Books...the efforts at length being made to develop and extend secular instruction is creating a wide demand for trusty and honest guides.... *The Reasoner*[5]

Secular schools are rapidly rising in London and are destined to extend themselves over the country. Genuine secular education is rare. Mr Fox's Bill did not propose it, though it would have involved it in many places.
*The Reasoner*[6]

By the beginning of the 1850s the rise in the provision of secular schools, certainly in London and to an extent elsewhere, was such that *The Reasoner* was able to write with confidence about them. Yet these schools had their origins only two years earlier in the events of 1848.

Between February and August 1848, as David Goodway in particular has shown,[7] London was the venue for numerous demonstrations and meetings, both in and out of doors. The character of these meetings was overwhelmingly working class and politically radical. Against this wider picture of the ferment of radical ideas and political activity it is also possible to focus in detail on what was happening to the provision of specific radical education in schools for young people.

London in 1848 was a city in transition to the huge urban area it is today. In fact, as Goodway has noted, it remained relatively compact, with most development north of the Thames. He also points out that

in many significant ways London remained a pre-industrial city, exuberant, chaotic and semi-rural...But fundamentally, London life had been undergoing...a radical transformation, becoming increasingly sober and orderly... Londoners by the Chartist decade were less intoxicated, brutal and debauched, more tractable, self-improving and self-disciplined.[8]

It was in this milieu and geographical area that most evidence for radical schools could be found. While the geographical area of the city was compact, movement around it, often on foot, was widespread. It should certainly not be assumed therefore that radical schools' catchment areas were simply their immediate environs. The son of the Secularist publisher Arthur Dyson regularly walked considerable distances to school from his home in Shoreditch High Street. It may be argued that there was an identifiable radical artisanal and working-class community in London in 1848 and that the radical schools detailed below existed, in aggregate, to serve the children of this community. However, Edward Royle's view of the Secularist milieu in London at this date suggests that far from their being a cohesive radical community, organisations and societies were in fact in transition from a low point during the frenetic activity of 1848, rising sharply in the years immediately afterwards as the impact of defeat set in.[9] Organisationally this was also the period between the demise of the Owenite Rational Society branches and the rise of Secularist organisation which eventually led to the formation of the National Secular Society.

A map of the locations of radical schools in 1849 shows them to be located at:

- The John Street Institute, Fitzroy Square (off Tottenham Court Road) WC1.
- Birkbeck School, London Mechanics' Institute, Southampton Buildings, Chancery Lane, WC2.
- Birkbeck School, City Road, Finsbury, EC1.
- Ellis's Academy, George St, Euston Square, NW1.
- Stanton's Day School, City of London Mechanics' Institute, Gould Square, Crutched Friars, EC3.
- Mutual Instruction Society, Circus St, New Road, Marylebone, NW1.
- Finsbury Mutual Instruction Society, 66 Bunhill Row, EC1.
- Soho Mutual Improvement Society, 2 Little Dean St, W1.
- Eclectic Institute, 72 Newman St, Oxford St, W1.
- 242 High Holborn, WC1. The National Hall under the proprietor ship of William Lovett.

These locations may be seen to represent the geographical spread of artisanal and radical working-class London after 1848 but before the spread of the railways led to the development of new suburbs. In fact it would be possible to tour on foot all of the locations mentioned within an hour. They also mirror quite closely some of the major radical meeting places of the period. These included:

- Hall of Science, City Rd, EC1.
- Finsbury Institution, Bunhill Row, EC1.
- General Secular Reformers Society, Leather Lane, Holborn and High Holborn, WC1.
- Metropolitan Institute, John Street, WC1.
- South London Secular Society, Blackfriars Road, SE1.
- Society of Materialists, Paddington and Marylebone, NW1.
- Society of Free Inquirers, Euston, NW1.

Although the actual numbers of places provided are known only for William Lovett's Holborn schools, the overall total of places in central London must have been in the high hundreds if not over a thousand. The desire for education of children, certainly from a parental standpoint, may well have been strong given the huge changes underway in the nature of life and work in London. The concern that education should be secular and outside of official control was considerable given the extent of the activities of the state and its agents in London in 1848. Parents were unwilling to trust an official apparatus that had imprisoned radical leaders and constrained the freedom of assembly and protest with the education of their children. The demand for state education, when it came from the quarter of working-class radicalism in the 1851 Chartist Programme, was couched very carefully in terms of government finance but local democratic control of schools.

The importance of the protests of 1848 for radical education and ideas has been discussed. The meetings and protests of the year were certainly the most significant aspect of radical education at this time. There was also, however, an important growth in the provision of radical education for young people, particularly based in some of the radical working-class communities of inner London.

The defining characteristic during 1848 of the schools set up in this area was not their overt radical politics but their commitment to secular education. That there was also a commitment to radical politics more loosely defined is evidenced by the fact that all the schools were mentioned in the *The Reasoner*. While direct radical politics were not necessarily wholly appropriate to younger pupils the commitment to progressive educational teaching methods and content was.

The numbers of pupils involved is difficult to judge precisely because no records for the schools are extant beyond references in the radical press and biographies. It seems clear, however, that the schools were not simply the kind of private school which catered for the sons and daughters of the well-off members of the radical middle class. Neither were they the kind of working-class private elementary schools analysed by Philip Gardner.

Each school was tied to a specific radical educational project and through this to wider radical political objectives. William Lovett's School at the National Hall in High Holborn was a conscious attempt to advance his belief in progress through education as against the more direct Chartist activities of 1848. William Ellis's school, one of a number funded and organised by him, was directly aimed at influencing the development of secular schools. The school at the John Street Institution, Fitzroy Square was a further development of the activities of what was one of the best known and most well used radical meeting venues in central London. The Chartist Convention had met in the building in the Spring.

The schools were not transient affairs thrown up by the events of 1848 merely to disappear shortly afterwards. All continued to exist into the 1850s. Their longer term impact is difficult to judge, but their direct rootedness in radical political culture and their permanent status represented a significant landmark for radical education.

Summarized below are details of the key central London schools which were mentioned in *The Reasoner*.

### The National Hall School

According to William Lovett in his autobiography the day school at the National Hall in High Holborn 'so long postponed' was finally opened in 1848.[10] In fact two separate schools were opened catering for 300 pupils in February of that year. A 'generous friend', the radical political economist William Ellis, who also funded the Birkbeck Schools, provided all necessary equipment and paid the salary of the teacher. The school prospectus read that 'the object in forming this school is to provide for the children of the middle and working classes a sound, secular, useful and moral education – such is best calculated to prepare them for the practical business of life – to cause them to understand and perform their duties as members of society – and to enable them to diffuse the greatest amount of happiness among their fellow men'.[11] Lovett noted that the 'small payment' made by pupils was not sufficient to keep the school on a firm financial footing without assistance from his middle-class benefactor Ellis.[12] A report in *The Reasoner* for August 1848 noted that the pupils of the school had visited the 'Collection of Curiosities, illustrative of the Religion and Customs of the North American Indians' which was then showing at 6 Waterloo Place, Pall Mall. The report also noted that the 'behaviour of the children [120 in number] was orderly and indicative of pleasure and the whole proved that the sons of working men are as capable of appreciating knowledge as those who hitherto seemed destined for it,'[13] According to Lovett's autobiography the School was still operating in 1857 when the National Hall was forced to close in favour of a Music Hall. In his biography of Lovett Joel Weiner notes that 'About 300 children attended the two National Association schools between 1848 and 1857. Many were part-time pupils; others left after a few months to work full-time or because the parents could not afford to pay the low fees required'.[14]

Lovett noted that 'For the first eighteen months of the establishment of our school I could not devote much time to its superintendence being employed...in the service of Mr Howitt'.[15] This was an issue of some importance because who exactly should teach at the schools, and hence how they were positioned in terms of radical politics and education, was the source of some controversy.

Brian Simon recounts how Francis Place told William Lovett that he would 'never even have one school'[16] and tried to enlist his help in the Anti-Corn Law agitation. In fact Lovett secured the backing of William Ellis and Place did offer his support as a guardian of the school. In his autobiography G.J. Holyoake suggests that it was Place who agreed that he should offer himself to Lovett as a teacher at the National Hall school.[17] However Lovett did not respond to Holyoake's offer and suggested that it had been Place's job to do so. Holyoake noted of the episode that:

> ...so strong was his prejudice against me, who had been imprisoned for heresy, that he who had been incarcerated for sedition was unable to be civil to me. I told him that if it should appear to the promoters of the school that my being a teacher of it would be detrimental, I should myself object to my own appointment. Heresy in theology proved a much more serious thing than heresy in politics; and that avenue of employment was closed.[18]

Positioning the school as secular but not radical provided real problems for Lovett. When the second schoolmaster Lovett had engaged resigned in 1851 precisely because the school was secular, Lovett was unable to find another teacher and had to take on more of the teaching duties himself.

An interesting assessment of the school's first year of performance was provided by Lovett in his evidence to the Select Committee on Public Libraries. In response to the question, 'Are the schools and other parts of your institution in a flourishing condition at present?' Lovett responded, 'We are not so flourishing as I could wish; we have a debt of about £300 which is rather an obstacle in the way'.[19] The significant debt built up in a year, and even with middle-class financial backing, underlines the fine line that existed between keeping fees low enough to attract large numbers of working-class pupils and failure due to insolvency.

Lovett's autobiography provides an account of the problems and issues which developed in not only opening, but sustaining a school outside religious or charitable control. There were problems with finding suitable teachers, with finance and with determining what appropriate subject matter to teach the pupils. The impact of Lovett's political trajectory on his ability to influence radical education was therefore of significance. It was precisely because Lovett was able to distance himself from mainstream Chartism that he was able to gather the financial support to run the schools. In addition, his own political position laid more emphasis on the importance of an individual's education. The position of much of mainstream Chartism was that while educational provision was important this had to come through state funding and local democratic control rather than a reliance on individual activists and middle-class patronage.

David Goodway has suggested that Lovett's National Association was a marginal group on the fringes of Chartist activity and this applied equally to the successor People's [International]League which Goodway labels as 'ultra-respectable'.[20] Yet it was Lovett and the group around him who had written the People's Charter and the organisations that Lovett was involved in throughout the 1840s, while clearly not enjoying significant support amongst rank and file Chartists, did attract a section of well known radical figures. Even so, as events demonstrated, Lovett was too conservative politically for both William Cooper and G. J. Holyoake.

While Lovett focused on formal educational provision, there also remained a strong radical educational tradition developing through the mechanism of radical culture, with ideas being discussed in workplaces, pubs and meetings, often from items read out from radical working-class papers such as the *Northern Star*. Such a culture could, as the autobiography of W.E. Adams indicates, successfully induct a young activist into the Chartist milieu. Lovett's activities, however were aimed at an even younger age group.

Two paths can be seen coming together in the activities of William Lovett. One was the desire for knowledge to be found amongst working autodidacts and activists, and the belief in knowledge and schooling as a good thing. Secondly the idea was also prevalent amongst a small section of radical-middle class activists such as Joseph Cowen Jnr., that if a practical route to reform and change, particularly one focused on education and knowledge, could be funded and encouraged then, at least, some of the energy built up around Chartist activity could be put to good effect. Both 1848 and its immediate aftermath was an important meeting point for these paths to reform, from above and below. The activities of the Christian Socialists and middle-class patrons of Co-operation, where these existed, followed similar routes.

However, neither the convergence of the paths or their destination was in any sense stable. It remained an open question as to whether working- or middle-class interests, which were not the same, would gain the upper hand. In terms of self-improvement it remained a matter of how far the limited example of the work done by William Lovett could suggest a wider example of change, or how far it was seen as limited to individual example or experiment.

In the wider context of 1848 the activities of Lovett and William Ellis suggested a notably different trajectory for radical politics and ideas to that normally accepted by historians. This viewed the radical middle class and working class as expressing a joint interest in the French events of February and March, with the former breaking sharply in concern at the Chartist demonstrations of Spring 1848. The new middle class in control of the northern cities alternated between attempts to include the working-class within a new municipal structure and repressing their activities by the use of the police. In Bradford, which received a municipal charter in 1847 and where Liberals then overwhelmingly controlled the new council, police work absorbed 49.6 per cent of the entire budget for 1847-8.[21] However, between 1849 and 1854 at least four Chartists were elected to the council and this represented a turning point where some elements of the middle class and some sections of working-class radicalism sought a rapprochement. Koditschek notes the 'emergence of a more pragmatic and genuinely inclusive entrepreneurial liberalism, but [also] the appearance of a comparable shift from absolutist engagement to opportunist pursuit of limited objects on the part of both the most respectable and best organised sections of the workers'.[22]

## The John Street School

The John Street Institution was already a well known radical and Chartist meeting place and a school opening there was bound to receive considerable publicity. The school, for boys, opened on Monday 25 September 1848 and was conducted by Alfred Derviche Brooks under the 'superintendence' of Thomas Cooper.[23] How important this superintendence was is difficult to judge. Cooper, in his autobiography, mentions lecturing at John Street during this period but there is no reference to the school. Subjects taught included reading, writing, arithmetic, grammar, geography, history, mathematics, vocal music and an introductory knowledge of the inductive sciences[24]. Fees were set at 6d a week and the hours were from quarter past nine until 3pm with a half hour break. Weekly advertisements for the school appeared in *The Reasoner* and as the school got underway these began to give some detail as to the aim of the school. It was 'purely SECULAR' and had as its object to 'give children a comprehensive practical education'.[25]

## The Birkbeck Schools

In October 1849 *The Reasoner* noted that '…the Birkbeck School was opened in the Lecture Theatre of the Institution on the 17th July 1848, where every facility is afforded for the highest mental development of the boys from the age of seven years upwards…the course of education is purely secular'.[26] The school was run by Mr Runtz. A further Birkbeck school was opened at City Road, Finsbury under the direction of Mr Cave. The son of the secularist publisher Arthur Dyson walked their each day from his home in Shoreditch High St until his death from typhus aged 9 in 1849.[27] William Ellis opened a considerable number of other Birkbeck schools in London during the 1850s, most of which survived until the impact of the 1870 Act made itself felt.

It was significant that the first of the Birkbeck Schools was opened in 1848. In their curriculum, location and appeal they spanned the gap between middle-class radical schools-where these existed, Chartist and secularist schools, and educational activities which developed on a less formal and much less well-funded basis. The two schools opened in the 1848-9 period in Holborn and City Road were ideally situated to pick up on the radical artisanal working class whose politics and income levels suggested the possibility of interest in such schools.

The biography of William Ellis by Ethel Ellis makes considerable play of his links to William Lovett as early as the mid-1830s, when Lovett was involved in drawing up the original People's Charter. She suggests that the remarks about education in this document and the 'New Move' on education by Lovett and Collins in 1840 were both heavily influenced by the ideas of Ellis. Ellis's concern was to steer Chartism towards a more practical reforming strategy.[28] He, of all the middle-class radicals who tried to influence Chartism,[29] was perhaps the most interesting because he backed a successful practical venture, the creation of secularist schools. His background and money was made in insurance, but he had a wider reforming interest and, crucially, one that was reinforced rather than broken by the events of 1848. Indeed, it seems that they were the spur which led to Ellis's decision to move from influencing the ideas of what might be described as the right wing, or more moderate Chartist constituency which focused on self rather than collective improvement, to actually funding schools. Initially the schools themselves were located in a relatively limited area of northern central London, closely matching the pattern of artisan and working-class location. During the 1850s they spread out and there were some early provincial locations, notably in Edinburgh from 1850.

### The City of London Mechanics Institute School

A report in *The Reasoner* of February 1848 noted that the 'public generally are respectfully informed that it is intended shortly to establish a Day School to be conducted by Mr J Stanton'.[30] The same Mr Stanton was also responsible for running a mutual instruction society at Circus St, New Road, Marylebone.[31] The City of London Mechanics' Institute had been a branch of the Owenite Rational Society until 1846 and maintained strong links with Owenism and secularism, particularly through the lectures of Holyoake.[32]

In 1848 Secularist organisation was in transition from old branches of the Owenite Rational Society to the secular societies of the 1850s. Organisational continuity seems to have been an exception. *The Reasoner* itself was London based and focused, although the lecturing tours that Holyoake undertook in the Provinces formed the basis of secularist organisation in later years. Certainly, however, no mention is made in *The Reasoner* of 1848 of radical schools and other independent educational venues outside London. From this a number of key points can be seen to flow.

Developments in London during 1848 were not the end of radical education but rather the beginning of a new phase of its provision, which continued in various forms for the remainder of the nineteenth century and beyond. It had taken between ten and fifteen years of radical Owenite and Chartist organisation to set up the basis for the kind of schools which were started during 1848. While that organisation began to change or decline after 1848, the network of schools continued. They drew radical activists out of mainstream political activity and into the project of running radical independent working-class schools. The decline of the wider organisational framework of radical politics muted the political content of the education. The schools, however, remained as a legacy of the strength of radical organisation in the years to 1848.

It is surprising however that there is no evidence of similar schools existing in other urban areas of radical strength, in particular, perhaps, Manchester and some surrounding towns, Newcastle upon Tyne and some towns of the Midlands such as Wolverhampton. It may be that radical organisation had greater strength and influence in depth in London in 1848. In Manchester, where the radical inheritance after 1848 was much more easily subsumed into a general middle-class radicalism, the independent profile of working-class radical politics was simply not high enough to provoke the demand for radical schools.[33] An alternative, if related, explanation is that in 1848 London was an exception and it was only the example of the sustained existence of radical educational ventures in the capital that provoked the idea and the actuality elsewhere.

## Combined & Uneven Development; Parent Culture; Class and Secular Schools

There is no question that by the early 1850s in London and in other locations there had developed a genuine working-class constituency for secularist schools. William Ellis made the point in his 1851 volume The 'Conditions of well-being' as taught in the Birkbeck Schools and as they ought to be taught everywhere.[34] The aim of this pamphlet was to popularise the success story of the Birkbeck Schools. Ellis wrote that

> It is well known to us all that there has been a growing demand of late years for improved secular Education. A powerful body, not long organised, is now occupied both in urging on this demand and in endeavouring to bring forth a supply to meet it. An effort of a more silent kind is being made to test how far the parents of the day are prepared to appreciate a really useful Education for their children. If placed within their reach…There is a large and increasing number of London parents alive to their duties and intelligent enough to hasten to avail themselves of schools calculated by their improved discipline and instruction to facilitate what they conceived to be the faithful discharge of these duties.[35]

Ellis refers in the first instance to the efforts of the Lancashire Public School Association to generalise secular education. The LPSA, however, was considerably more middle-class and less radical in its structure and intent than the Birkbeck schools. Ellis infers that the work of the schools spoke for itself, in addressing the needs of London parents.

There were however difficulties, as the reports of the Edinburgh School made clear. These revolved around the issue of what kind of working-class pupils the schools should endeavour to attract, how much they should pay in fees, and how often they should pay. The Edinburgh School which was opened on 4 December 1848 attracted an average attendance of 32 boys in its first month. By October 1849 this had risen to an attendance of 160 of whom around 50 were girls. The first Annual Report, published in April 1850, provided an interesting insight into the teaching methods employed when it noted that 'In the organisation of the school, the teacher has endeavoured, as far as possible, to combine the advantages of the monitorial and simultaneous systems, without carrying either of them so far as is customary with their exclusive partizans'.[36] Subjects taught included social economy, physiology and phrenology, which suggested a degree of radical endeavour well beyond most provided schools of the time.

However, the content of the teaching itself, as appendices to the second report published in 1851 made clear, was far from what most Chartists would have found acceptable. A model lesson on social economy, for example, agreed that wages were too low, but suggested that the answer to this was that workers increase their productivity so that profits could increase and employers could then pay higher wages. Even in the 1850s this was not a radical argument, although the recognition of low pay in the first place was.

A further problem arose with attendance. As payment was on a weekly basis, when parents found themselves short of cash, pupils were withdrawn and allowed to return when financial times were better. However, this meant disruption to lessons and the running of the school. A switch was therefore made to payment of fees on a quarterly basis. This had the effect of excluding pupils from poorer parents and led to a drop in pupil numbers of around thirty. The second report noted, however, that the pupil base had become younger and with more girls as a result.

The Birkbeck Schools are of interest because they are on the cusp between radical education for working-class pupils and middle- class education. They were clearly aimed at working-class parents and children and they did provide, for the time, a radical education. However they were limited, both by the central involvement of middle-class radicals and by cost. In practice they reached only a section of those interested in radical working-class education.

However, the fact of their existence underwrote a much wider network of mutual instruction societies and radical schools run directly by radical workers. The 1850s was to see a battle for the content and role of radical education. These schools and societies provided an important part of this battle.

### 1849-51: From Green to Red, the Charter & Something More

1848 was a defeat for the Chartist movement and a serious one. The man who was to become the main leader of post-1848 Chartism, Ernest Jones, was imprisoned, as were many other second rank activists. Of the key Chartist leaders only Harney remained both out of prison and focused on rebuilding the Chartist movement.

The period immediately after 1848, up to the adoption of the programme of the 'Charter and Something More' programme in 1851, has attracted relatively few secondary commentaries. Gareth Stedman Jones's work on the language of Chartism may be seen as a negative commentary on the development of Chartist ideas after 1848, but Stedman Jones does not directly explore these.[37] Kate Tiller has written on Halifax Chartism after 1848 but provides only a couple of pages about the immediate post-1848 period. Writing about the northern Chartist stronghold of Halifax in 'late 1848' she has argued that Chartism had 'lost it momentum. Degrees of disillusionment and forms of response varied'.[38] It is maintained that an organisation of the strength of the Chartists 'could not be dissipated overnight'.[39] Indeed crisis of organisation, 'fluctuation, renewal and reorganisation' as Tiller puts it[40] were regular features of Chartism. There was no indication at this stage that 1848 had marked a decisive turning point. The upheavals of 1848 had demonstrated a strength of the Chartists analysis, namely that the majority of people were excluded from the political process. It had also suggested ways in which mass protest could influence this situation.

The crisis came when a decision had to be made on what to do next. As Tiller notes, '...force was to have been the Chartists ultimate sanction. Now it had failed a bankruptcy of tactics existed'.[41] There was a wider underlying problem. By late 1848 an upturn in economic conditions was underway which was to last for a number of years. The fact that young workers could now pick up jobs in the mills as Tiller again notes 'sapped sources of political urgency'[42] and led to immediate signs of Chartist decline. It was not possible, for example, to continue to fund the Chartist hall. Yet while the defeats of 1848 and the return of something like economic prosperity might explain why support was not forthcoming for a fresh Chartist challenge, it should also have been the case that regular work and income started to provide the basis for an increase in working-class consciousness and combativity.

For Mark O'Brien there is no necessary direct link between an economic upswing and a decline in radical consciousness. As he notes of the 1850s, 'the improvements which did occur for workers...cannot be considered to have been so substantial as to have provided the basis of the end of the Chartist movement'.[43] For O'Brien however there is also a sense in which capitalism triumphed after 1848. Class struggle declined and eventually ceased altogether and workers found that improvements could be obtained by pressure within the existing system, through using trade unions, for example. This is a less than satisfactory explanation, not only because it ignores the fact that the decline of class struggle was far from a smooth or easy matter, but also because it overlooks the significant number of workers who continued to hold radical ideas of one kind or another.

### The Involvement of Marx and Engels in radical education after 1848

The influence of Marx and Engels on the development of radical ideas after 1848 was probably the decisive change from the period before 1848. They had become refugees in England after 1848, as reaction swept the rest of Europe. Their position was by no means secure; but they tried to influence and organise the community of émigré radicals and revolutionaries who were now in London and also the leader of left Chartism in this period, G.J. Harney. Engels wrote regularly for Harney's *Democratic Review*, while Marx was an occasional visitor to the Harney household. Engels' regular letters on Germany and France in the *Democratic Review* formed one of the central bases for an understanding of what had happened in Europe after 1848. By their appearance in what was in effect the theoretical journal of the left-wing Chartists, Marx and Engels were able to have an important influence on a key debate in Britain. This point has often been lost on historians who assume that because the final works which came from these articles, such as the *Eighteenth Brumaire of Louis Napoleon*, were neither published nor read in Britain, the ideas and arguments themselves were unknown to the Chartists. This was not so. The post-1848 environment, amongst both the emigre community in London and the surviving Chartist centres was a maelstrom of ideas. In this context the influence of both Marx and Engels on the left of the Chartist movement after 1848 was considerable. However, just as they had to fight for their ideas and strategies in the émigré movement in London, so they did with the Chartists. Harney and Jones certainly listened to Marx and Engels but they also listened to Louis Blanc and others. For their part, writing at the end of 1850, Marx and Engels saw a debate amongst the Chartists. They wrote: 'The main bone of contention between the two Chartist factions is the land question...O'Connor and his party want to use the Charter to accommodate some of the workers on small plots of land...the revolutionary faction of the Chartists opposes this demand for parcelling out with the demand for the confiscation of all landed property.'[44]

The defeat of the French Revolution of 1848 and the increasing repression of the left also had a significant impact on the ideas of British radicals. The more advanced French radicals such as Louis Blanc and Victor Considerant found a ready market for their ideas in Britain after 1848, particularly in the form of tracts or pamphlets. Blanc published a regular monthly journal from London, while Considerant's *The Last War* was published simultaneously by James Watson in London, Abel Heywood in Manchester and John Melson in Liverpool.[45] Defeat and the discussion it sparked amongst working-class activists also inspired British radical support for violent revolutionary action in Europe, often as an alternative to attempts at change in Britain.

Much Chartist energy after 1848 was spent in collecting money, not just for Chartist prisoners but for their families as well. They often had no other means of subsisting and the impact of Government repression in 1848 on the second rank of Chartist leaders must have been considerable. However, prison also acted, in the cases where conditions were less harsh – generally where the Government had agreed that the offences were of a political nature – as a debating forum about the future of Chartism. The notable surviving example is the discussion between George White and others Chartist prisoners at Kirkdale jail, which focused on the need for pamphlets and political discussion and education to take Chartism forward.

The political terrain and landscape had changed after 1848, however, and in ways with which Chartists struggled to come to terms. The political expectation was that the revolutionary events of 1848 would, sooner or later, repeat themselves. Economic developments undercut this expectation, but in ways that could only really be grasped in hindsight. Eric Hobsbawm establishes the start of what he refers to as the 'great global boom' to the years around 1850. In a sense, therefore, this explains why left-wing Chartist ideas were still able to flourish and appeal in the period. However, during the 1850s the British economy expanded at an unprecedented rate. As Hobsbawm has noted, 'never...did British exports grow more rapidly than in the first seven years of the 1850s'.[46] The expansion of the economy also meant an expansion in the number of workers. In the 25 years from 1820 to 1845 the number of cotton workers grew by around 100,000. In the 1850s alone the increase was 200,000.[47] As Hobsbawm has noted, the 'political consequence of this boom was far reaching. It gave the governments shaken by the revolution [of 1848] invaluable breathing space and...wrecked the hopes of revolutionaries. In a word, politics went into hibernation'.[48]

While Hobsbawm may have exaggerated the picture, his grasp of the general trend is correct. The boom of the 1850s created a large new workforce, but not one that was as concerned about unemployment or – although labour remained cheap – absolute poverty. It was a challenge for those brought up on the ideas and economy of the pre-1848 period to relate to this change. A note of caution is needed, however, about how rapidly the change took place. Neville Kirk's study of wages of mill workers in the north-west after 1848[49] shows that while there may have been more stability to workers wages in the 1850s, the level of increase was not significant.

In terms of radical education, the changes did mean a vastly expanded potential market for schools and an ability to pay for them. At the same time, however, it also raised a serious question over whether the old forms of radical education were now relevant.

### The Charter and Something More

In the face of the failure of its strategies of petition and armed revolt, the retreat of the left on a European-wide scale, and repression at home the Chartist movement could have collapsed or turned into a rump. In fact it did not do so. It suited elements of middle-class radicalism, for example Christian Socialists like Charles Kingsley author of the novel *Alton Locke*, to use this argument for their own propaganda. In fact by 1849 Chartism had begun the process of renewing itself and had done so by moving sharply to the left.

As a document the 'Charter and Something More' was not promulgated until a meeting in London in March and April 1851, but the years of 1849 and

1850 were spent exploring and debating moves to the left in Chartist ideas and politics, and also changes in strategy and tactics. Repression and imprisonment had created an urge to review what the possibilities of Chartism were and a desire to spread the ideas of the movement more widely, often through educational mechanisms such as discussion groups and pamphlets. The new Programme of the Charter and Something More addressed directly the issue of how to win working-class support for Chartism. It noted that:

> A political change would be inefficacious, unless accompanied by a social change; that a Chartist movement unless accompanied with social knowledge, would result in utter failure; that we cannot claim or received the support of the labourer, mechanic, farmer or trader, unless we show them that we are practical reformers; that power would be safely vested in Chartist hands; that we know their grievances, and how to redress them....[50]

This concept, that the Chartists had to address the concerns that the working class really had and show how they could be taken up and resolved, somewhat undermines the claims of Gareth Stedman Jones in *Languages of Class* that the Chartists were unable to break out of a late eighteenth century radical ideology. Stedman Jones has argued that 'after 1848, in the period of "Charter socialism", when Chartists were demanding "the Charter and Something More" nothing is more striking than the basic continuity of their analysis...a language of natural right still predominated'.[51] It is clear from the 1851 programme that Chartists did seek to relate directly to the ideas of the more advanced sections of the working class around them.

The following paragraph demonstrates the widening appeal of the Charter and does so in a very modern way. Lenin referred to revolutionaries as tribunes of the oppressed and revolutionary movements as the festival of the oppressed but fifty years before the 1851 programme had noted that:

> The Chartist body should...stand forward as the protector of the oppressed – each suffering class should see in it the redresser of its several wrongs – it ought to be the connecting link, that draws together on one common ground, the now isolated bodies of the working classes, self-interest being the tie able to bind them to each other.[52]

While some of the ideas behind this may have been taken from the French revolutionaries of 1848, it underlined the forward looking nature of Chartist ideas at this time. It was this that led John Saville to suggest that the 1851 Programme was the most advanced political programme of the nineteenth century, not bettered until the rise of social democratic organisation fifty years later.[53]

Where the advanced ideas of the 1851 Programme came from is unclear; it has received some attention from commentators and is essential for a consideration of the impact of radical education after 1848. Kate Tiller has noted that the Halifax Chartist community, to which Ernest Jones returned after his release from prison, had an impact on the ideas of the 'Charter and Something More'. However, Jones had not been out of prison for many months before the spring 1851 conference. Marx and Engels had influence, particularly through the key Chartist leader of the 1849-50 period, Harney. Harney was also impressed by the ideas of a number of continental revolutionaries between which, often to the fury of Marx and Engels, he often failed to distinguish.

For Miles Taylor, Jones's heart was never in the 'Charter and Something More'; rather he preferred a focus on the agenda of 1846 'at the heart of which lay the land and the church'.[54] Taylor argues that at the heart of the new programme was a 'largely rural agenda', which ignored industry and saw Jones speaking out against trade unionism.[55]

Despite this the development of the programme for the Charter and Something More did represent an important and progressive development for Chartism. Yet recent secondary work has tended to overlook the opening to the left it represents, perhaps precisely because it did not in fact characterise radical politics in the third quarter of the century, fading by the end of the 1850s.

John Foster's classic account of radical politics in Oldham, South Shields and Northampton[56] sees the period after 1848 as one of stabilisation of the capitalist state where working-class politics shifted to the right. The left turn of 1851 is not mentioned. Neville Kirk's book on the rise of working-class reformism[57] does tackle the issue, but in terms of battles of ideas between the Chartist left and right and for Chartist influence in the newly developing layers of the working-class. He clearly believes that the left had some success, but does not account for how this hard won influence was then frittered away. More recent work by Neville Kirk[58] retreats from this analysis and leans towards the view of John Foster. Kirk supports the concept of political liberalisation after 1848 but does not see the process of accommodation of working-class ideas and organisation as a settled question in this period. However, Kirk very much falls in with the trend in recent works since he overlooks the significance of the leftward turn in ideas represented by the Charter and Something More.

The sheer breadth of the headings for the subjects covered by the 1851 programme underlined the attempt by Chartists to address the changed situation after 1848. There were twelve sections including those on the land, the church, education, labour law, the currency and the army and navy. Chartism, as an organisation had to retreat from the strategies that flowed from many of the ideas of 1851 during the 1850s, but the ideas themselves were to remain in common radical currency during the remainder of the nineteenth century

## Conclusion: radical education and ideas after 1848

Gareth Stedman Jones has argued that while radical and Chartist ideas after 1848 remained firmly focused in the late eighteenth conceptions of the French Revolution, the working class had moved on. At one level there is truth in this. After 1848 the development of organised labour in trade unions began to take off and artisan labour declined. Both developments had been in place before 1848. The issue at stake was the trend and the speed at which they took place.

Richard Johnson has argued that the kind of really useful knowledge which was appropriate to radical workers in the 1830s and 1840s did not find such ready support after 1848. The question that needs to be answered, therefore, was whether radical education and radical ideas did in fact find support after the defeats of 1848 or whether the trends leading to radical support for the 1870 Education Act were now starting to become dominant features.

In an editorial published in issue 24 of *The Red Republican* on 30 November 1850 G. Julian Harney noted that instead of the following issue being No.25 of the paper it would, instead, be the first issue of *The Friend of the People*. Harney had already noted in issue 11 of *The Red Republican* that the name had put off some newsagents from carrying it, including some that were associated with Chartism. However, Harney's decision to change the name of the paper was made for more complex reasons than just an organised boycott and witch-hunt of the paper.

Harney was concerned that although the paper was reaching 'the organised trades' including new layers of workers who had 'hitherto never given a thought to politics', some were put off by the title. He argued that this restricted the paper's role as a propagator of radical and left-wing ideas. He noted that 'it would be of little use…that this journal should continue to be supported by those only who are already Red Republicans. It is necessary that it should circulate amongst those who have yet to be converted to the Republican faith'. Harney assured readers that *The Friend of the People* would be no less 'red' but would carry articles designed to appeal to those who were new to democratic politics.[59]

The change and the reasons for it were significant. Firstly, it focused on an emerging constituency for radical ideas, namely that of organised labour. Before 1848 Chartism had related to this area only sporadically and then rarely to workers with specific grievances, as *The Red Republican* had done with the typesetters during their 1850 strike. Secondly, it recognised that there was now a new generation of workers who knew little or nothing of Chartism in 1838, and perhaps had not been particularly involved in the events of 1848. They too had concerns which could be focused and advanced by Chartist ideas.

Richard Johnson has drawn attention to the need to investigate further how it was that state education became something that was seen as inevitable by a layer of radical working-class leaders and actvists after 1848.[60] As early as 1851 Ernest Jones' programme for the Chartist Convention, which was written under the influence of Marx, had called for education to be 'national, universal, gratuitous and to certain extent compulsory'.[61] This can be seen as the origin of a statist approach to education espoused by radicals, which froze out the concept of really useful knowledge as it had existed in the 1830s and 1840s. Yet this is not how it was seen at the time. Chartists wanted state funded education to take away provision from religious groups and factory owners. They recognised that they did not have the means to construct an alternative national education system, however well they could succeed locally. While state funding was demanded the aim remained to control the funds locally, very much on the basis actually laid down by the 1870 Education Act and later abolished by the 1902 Act as too radical.

Johnson has emphasised that there was an expectation among the working class by the time of the 1870 Education Act that the government should provide education where the demand for it was not otherwise being met.[62] Yet, as Phil Gardner has demonstrated, this was a view which met opposition from significant sections of the working class.[63] Johnson has referred to post-1850 education holding a range of assumptions quite different to those which had been held by radicals before 1850 but it might be more appropriate to focus on why the assumptions of working-class radical activists changed while those of many working class people did not.

The implication of Johnson's argument is that there was a definitive split in radical working-class attitudes towards education before and after 1850. This seems a crude distinction and an excuse for the failure to examine empirically how such attitudes changed. Johnson has suggested however that the very concept of tradition was responsible for creating such splits.

Richard Johnson has suggested four key reasons for the decline of really useful knowledge and independent working-class education after 1848. Firstly the nature of the new working class in the world of highly mechanised factory production systems did not allow the space for workers either to run or to attend radical educational activities. Secondly, the rise of the factory school also meant that education aimed specifically at young workers began to develop and thus created the division between child and adult in education. Thirdly, the working class simply did not have the resources to sustain meaningful, radical initiatives on a national or even a regional scale. Both time and money were scarce resources. Lastly, Johnson argues that working-class radicals and particularly radical leaders began increasingly to focus their energies on the need for the state to provide at least a basic education from above. They demanded that this education should be democratically controlled on a local basis. The locality remained where radicalism and radical education could still make an impact. This pressure for state provision was a definitive mark of post-Chartism. The Chartist position had been that political power was required before any real progress on education could be made.

The rise of radical education *after* 1848 underlines that a more complex picture in fact prevailed than Johnson has allowed. The nature and composition of the working class did not create insurmountable difficulties in the production of really useful knowledge. The demand for some kind of really useful knowledge was thrown up by the nature of the work process itself. While really useful knowledge changed in character in the 1850s and 1860s it did not disappear. At the same time while the working class had changed it was not the undifferentiated mass which Richard Johnson imagined it to be. There was probably as much, or as little time and resource to provide Really Useful Knowledge in 1838, as there was in 1868. The issue was how such scarce resources could be most usefully employed, which strategies and ideas were appropriate and were felt to fit circumstances and, most importantly, had a real chance of success.

The rise of an institutional basis for labour, in the form of co-operatives and trade unions, suggested a specific form to post-1848 really useful knowledge that was not there before. This knowledge was opposed to middle-class political economy but it was not necessarily opposed to capitalism as such. Furthermore the demand for the provision of education by the state was not a negation of the viability or possibility of the working class being able to produce really useful knowledge but an understanding of its limitations, an appreciation developed over a long period and formed on the basis that capitalism had not, as had been hoped, been overthrown or destroyed. In practice, and this is where Johnson's arguments on the post-1848 period are at their weakest, really useful knowledge did continue for both children and adults. Indeed it was the radical ideas which were around in the 1860s that influenced and shaped the activists who were responsible for the rebirth of independent working-class politics in the 1880s.

There remains the question of a model of radical education and working-class demand for radical education after 1848. Prothero's survey of French and English artisanal radicalism during the first sixty years of the nineteenth century has argued that while governments often successfully curtailed or suppressed forms of working-class expression, the desire for this expression remained and simply found new outlets.[64] The most indirect form of this was the radical dinner where toasts and speeches were made to commemorate a radical figure or event. Funerals too could become political occasions, even when the person concerned was only indirectly related to radical politics.

Applied to radical education it would seem clear that a demand for the kinds of really useful knowledge which had been discussed before 1848 was likely to continue to exist after 1848. Most working-class leaders of this period remained self-educated. WE Adams for example, working in Cheltenham after 1848, was responsible for organising radical meetings with speakers such as Thomas Cooper, Ernest Jones and James Finlen.[65] He then picked up his understanding of what the 'more' was in the Charter and Something More by reading columns by W.J. Linton in the *Red Republican*. Later, when he moved to London, Adams recounts in detail how he read a morning paper when walking from his residence in Kennington to Fleet St every day. While self-education, within the context of a milieu of radical working-class organisation and ideas remained a feature of radical education after 1848, there was a trend towards the institutionalisation of the process of acquiring really useful knowledge as the organisational strength of trade unions and co-operative societies began to grow.

Table 1: The *real* Language of Chartism after 1848

British Library catalogue, incidence of words by title reference

|      | *Suffrage* | *W. Class* | *Labour* | *Strike* | *Land* |
|------|-----------|-----------|----------|---------|-------|
| 1850 | 9 | 1 | 9 | 2 | 68 |
| 1855 | 1 | 1 | 10 | 1 | 61 |
| 1859 | 6 | 0 | 16 | 2 | 55 |

|      | *Social* | *Democracy* | *France* | *Revolution* | *Labour* |
|------|---------|------------|---------|-------------|---------|
| 1847 | 30 | 1 | 157 | 35  | 12 |
| 1848 | 58 | 6 | 180 | 179 | 22 |
| 1849 | 32 | 3 | 113 | 66  | 10 |
| 1850 | 33 | 1 | 135 | 88  | 9 |
| 1851 | 25 | 2 | 125 | 47  | 9 |

**Commentary**

A search of the British Library catalogue by title and key word does not of course provide a definitive insight into Chartist language after 1848. Chartism was still predominantly a oral and visual culture, and even where it was written, this tended to be in pamphlets, newspapers or ephemeral publications that the British Library does not tend to keep in its collections.

However, a search by key word can give a very good idea of the kind of language that was in general use, and referrent to political radicalism. 1848 provides a benchmark year when the use of words with radical overtones was at a peak. As might be expected titles which refer to 'France' or 'Revolution' were especially common at this time.

By contrast directly 'political' words such as 'socialism' and 'communism' are poorly represented for the years 1849-1851. A forgotten classic of the semi-pornographic genre that Ernest Jones argued W.M. Reynolds was representative of, *The Merry Wives of London*, provided a fascinating tale about the 'socialist girl'. However, references to titles with these words number only two or three for each year. The exception is for works related to Christian Socialism, showing, perhaps, not that the ideas of Kingsley and Maurice were widely popular amongst radical workers, but that they placed more value on getting into print than some.

Other words with direct 'political' connotations such as 'red' and 'republican' are also rare. The two are clearly linked in Harney's paper of the same name, which is in fact one of the handful of entries for either word in the BL catalogue for the years 1849-1851.

In reality, the higher incidences of words relate to generic type phrases. For example, titles with the word 'social' number 32 in 1849 and decline slightly to 25 in 1851. The reference is largely to work published in, or about France. Surprisingly, perhaps, given the modern day connection between the two words, 'democracy' gets only a handful of mentions in each of the three years. However 'France' has a large number of references with a peak of 135 in 1850, again, with works very largely focusing on the question of the 1848 revolution and its aftermath. Not so surprisingly, 'revolution' found 88 references in 1850, although not much more than half that the following year.

The headline conclusion is that the impact of the French events of 1848 dominated English radical thought in the years 1849-51 in a way which has not previously been fully understood or investigated. The physical defeat was a big restraining factor on radical activity, but the ideas thrown up, particularly by the left-wing currents in the revolution, moved into the currency of English radical political discussion in the years that followed. Again, this challenges Gareth Stedman Jones's argument that Chartist ideas had not changed significantly since the French Revolution of 1789. It underlines a working-class radicalism that was consumed by the experience of current revolutionary events and their defeat, rather than one that looked back sixty years.

This analysis of the usage of radical words in the general printed milieu can be related to the use of language in the radical and Chartist press. It can also tell us something about the process of radical political education after 1848. As can be seen with Marx and Engels dismay that Harney mixed their own ideas indiscriminately with those of other exile leaders, while radical language was a common discourse, in marked contrast to Stedman Jones's claim that the language of the late eighteenth-century still prevailed, it did not necessarily imply an attachment to a political strategy or organisation. Nevertheless, the common use of left-wing terms which are still recognisable on the left 150 years later, after 1848, does suggest an important breakthrough in radical ideas and education. However, as the working-class movement failed to fully recover from the defeats of 1848 and some advance within the system became possible, as the 1850s wore on the use of radical language declined. The old pre-1848 terms and ideas had become much less important, but they were by no means replaced by the left-wing ones in use in the few years immediately afterwards. The 1850s saw a renewed battle of ideas and words, and of debates about what radical education meant.

## Notes

1. Karl Marx, *The Communist Manifesto, Red Republican*, November 1850
2. See JA Auerbach, *The Great Exhibition of 1851*, London, 1999, Chp. 5.
3. Martin Hewitt, *The Emergence of Stability in the Industrial City, Manchester 1832-1867*, Aldershot, 1996, pp. 268-9
4. Ibid., p. 302.
5. *The Reasoner* 12 June 1850.
6. Ibid., 19 June 1850.
7. David Goodway, *London Chartism 1838-1848*, Cambridge 1982 Part Two
8. Goodway op. cit., p. 3.
9. Edward Royle, *Victorian Infidels, the origins of the British Secularist Movement 1791-1866*, Manchester, 1974.
10. William Lovett, *Life and Struggles of William Lovett*, London, 1967 ed, p. 279.
11. Ibid.
12. Ibid.
13. *The Reasoner* 2 August 1848.
14. Joel Weiner, *William Lovett*, Manchester, 1989, p. 120.
15. William Lovett, *Life and Struggles* op. cit.
16. Brian Simon, *The Two Nations and the Educational Structure 1780-1870. Studies in the History of Education*, London, 1960, p. 267.
17. G.J. Holyoake, *Sixty Years of an Agitator's Life*, London, 1892
18. Ibid., p. 177.
19. *Select Committee on Public Libraries*, 22 May 1849, 2765.
20. David Goodway op. cit.

21 Theodore Koditscheck, *Class Formation and Urban-Industrial society, Bradford 1750-1850*, Cambridge, 1990 p. 562.
22 Ibid., p. 564.
23 *The Reasoner*, 20 September 1848.
24 Ibid., 13 September 1848.
25 Ibid., 6 December 1848.
26 Ibid., 3 October 1849.
27 Ibid., 17 October 1849.
28 Ethel Ellis, *Memoir of William Ellis*, London, 1888, pp. 46-7.
29 Others included Joseph Sturge and Alderman Livesey.
30 *The Reasoner* 2 February 1848.
31 Ibid., 26 January 1848.
32 Edward Royle, 2000, op. cit.
33 J Breuilly, *Labour and Liberalism in Nineteenth-Century Europe. Essays in Comparative History*, Manchester, 1991.
34 William Ellis, *The Conditions of well-being as taught in the Birkbeck Schools as they ought to be taught everywhere*, London? 1851.
35 Ibid., p. 36.
36 *Edinburgh School First Annual Report*, 1850, p. 4.
37 Gareth Stedman, *Languages of Class*, Cambridge, 1982.
38 Kate Tiller, *Late Chartism in Halifax*, in James Epstein and Dorothy Thompson, *the Chartist Experience*, London, 1982, p. 318.
39 Ibid.
40 Ibid.
41 Ibid.
42 Ibid.
43 Mark O'Brien, '*Perish the privileged orders': A Socialist History of the Chartist Movement*, London, 1995, p. 122-3.
44 Marx and Engels *Collected Works*, 1849-51 p. 515.
45 Victor Considerant, *The Last War*, London, 1850.
46 Eric Hobsbawm, *The Age of Capital*, London, 1995, p. 30.
47 Ibid.
48 Ibid., p. 31.
49 Kirk, op cit., 1984
50 John Saville, *Ernest Jones, Chartist*, London, 1952, Appendix
51 Gareth Stedman Jones, op cit., pp. 155-6.
52 John Saville, 1952, op. cit.
53 John Saville, op. cit., p. 45.
54 Miles Taylor, op. cit., p. 140.
55 Miles Taylor op. cit., p. 145.
56 John Foster, *Class Struggle and the Industrial Revolution*, London, 1974.
57 Neville Kirk, *The Growth of Working Class Reformism in Mid-Victorian England*, London, 1985, op. cit.
58 Neville Kirk 1998.
59 *The Red Republican*, 30 November, 1850.
60 John Saville, *Ernest Jones*, op. cit.

61 Richard Johnson, Really Useful Knowledge, op. cit.
62 Ibid.
63 Phil Gardner, *The Lost Elementary Schools of Victorian England*, London, 1984.
64 I Prothero, *Radical Artisans in England and France 1830-1870*, Cambridge, 1997.
65 See Owen Ashton, W. E Adams, op. cit., p. 53.

## Chapter 5
## The Breaking and Making of Radical Education and Ideas in the Late 1850s

It was the period from Ernest Jones's *Evenings with the People* in 1857 to the publication of the *Beehive* and the *National Reformer* in 1860-61 which saw a shift from a Chartist politics to a post-Chartist politics based on the rising power of organised labour and co-operation. Some have argued that this period represented the birth of a 'grey' and intellectually unadventurous 'labourism' in the British working-class. Perry Anderson, for example, has argued that 'the main tradition of late 19th and 20th century Labourism took its cast from anti-capitalist ideas beyond those of Paine, yet remained 'transfixed' in a parliamentarist framework...The class E.P. Thompson described was revolutionary in temper and ideology, but not socialist. After the mid-century metamorphosis, as sections of it became socialist, it ceased to be revolutionary'.[1] However, while a grand narrative approach to the development of the British working class is important, Anderson, unlike Thompson, has been unwilling to grapple with the detail of the strategies and ideas discussed in the developing labour movement after 1850 and to understand why some ideas and strategies proved more popular, if not more successful, than others. Debates about what role education should play in the development of the working class and what strategy would achieve an extension of the franchise reflected a maturing of a long-running debate in the working-class movement. The maturity also bred a reformist political perspective, although this process was by no means inevitable. The left had failed to relate effectively to the changing forces in the working class and to argue coherently its case beyond the limited milieu of the meeting room, pub and small outside meetings. It may be argued, however, that various changes by the government and in the economy during the 1850s made the task of the left all the more difficult.

Leading activists of the later 1850s such as Ernest Jones, G. Harney and G.J. Holyoake had a lengthy experience of defeat. By contrast, generation of leaders from Charles Bradlaugh to George Howell, while well aware of those defeats, had more confidence in their ideas and strategies, and, crucially, more confidence that they could force change from the system than the earlier generation. It was this difference above all others, which meant that the new generation of radicals coming to the fore in 1860 spearheaded a successful fight for further extension of the franchise, rather than the more limited aims of the educational strategy.

### Midnight in the Century, November 1858-March 1859

The specificity of the approach adopted in this study can be judged by a survey of the crisis of radicalism in the later 1850s. An examination of changes which took place from the second half of 1858 to the later months of 1859 show how developments in radical politics and thinking could be, at times, critically time specific. Gradual changes, ebbs and flows of the process of class struggle and the battle of ideas between radical workers and the radical middle class, took place on a broad historical sweep. It is important, however, as John Foster has noted of the period after 1848, to identify what was different or new about the period and tease out the implications of what the differences were.[2]

> The years 1858 and 1859 were the precise time when Chartism passed from being an active national movement to a set of ideas and strategies which remained important in the consciousness of workers, particularly at the level of memory, but which had little practical impact on the day to day development of radical working- class political life.

During this period both of the key radical papers of the post-1848 period faltered. As a result, the landscape of radicalism changed. The *People's Paper* ceased publication entirely in November 1858. Although Ernest Jones was able to replace it almost immediately by the little studied *Cabinet Newspaper*, this did not have the national presence, impact or reputation of the *People's Paper*. The *Cabinet Newspaper* became the house journal of surviving Chartist fragments rather than a journal that could determine a national radical strategy. At the same time Holyoake, worn out by years of radical activity and seeking new political directions, stepped down as editor of *The Reasoner*. Thereafter it never regained its previous impact as the leading organ of radical freethought. The trends which caused the crisis in radical ideas and organisation in 1858 and 1859 had been present in 1848. However when they cohered ten years later they were to cause a decisive shift in the worldview and map of working-class radical politics.

In his *Memoirs Of a Social Atom* W.E. Adams noted of Ernest Jones in this period

...he kept the old flag flying till he was almost starved into surrender. When near its last gasp he was in the habit of addressing open-air assemblages on Sunday mornings in Copenhagen Fields, now the site of Smithfield Cattle Market. I walked from a distant part of London through miles of streets to hear him... The old fervour and the old eloquence were still to be noted. But the pinched face and the threadbare garments told of trial and suffering. A shabby coat buttoned close up round the throat seemed to conceal the poverty to which a too faithful adherence to a lost cause had reduced him. A year or two later even Ernest Jones had to confess that Chartism was dead.[3]

Adams also painted a sharp picture of what happened to those Chartist leaders who were unable to make the transition to the new forms of radicalism which developed at the turn of the decade. He describes 'Some time about 1865 I was standing at the shop door of a Radical bookseller in the Strand. A poor half-starved old man came to the bookseller, according to custom to beg or borrow a few coppers. It was John Arnott'.[4] He had been the General Secretary of the NCA in the 1850s. Adams concluded of this episode that 'Chartism was then, as it really had been for a long time before, a matter of history'.

Meanwhile G.J. Holyoake's hold on *The Reasoner* had been much reduced because of long term illness. Of this McCabe wrote:

Worn with anxiety, vexation and many labours Holyoake had a serious collapse in 1859. He was ill throughout most of the year and was badly disfigured with acute eczema...He returned to work early in 1860 not wholly recovered... During the earlier part of 1860 he worked with difficulty and made frequent use of Turkish baths – a new importation which he did much to popularise.[5]

A crisis of both policy and personnel had combined to create a situation where there was no longer a national radical political organization nor a central organ of radical opinion. The *National Reformer* and the *Beehive* were to fulfil this role from 1860 onwards. However, for a period of something over a year there was a major hiatus in radicalism. Even the working-class benefit journal which had been advertised in the final issues of the *Union* to make its appearance in December 1858 did not in fact appear until March 1859.

While this period saw the dissolution and splintering of established radical working-class politics it also contained, paradoxically, the seeds of a new working-class politics. Throughout 1859 and 1860 the building workers were on strike, at first in pursuit of a nine hour day and then against an attempt by employers to break the union. While the nine hour day, which was often argued in terms of the need for more time for education, was not won, the employers were unable to break the Operative Builders Union following huge support from other trades unionists. One result was the formation, in 1860, of the London Trades Council. According to Margot Finn, 1858 was a key turning point in radical politics because it was the time when newly organised sections of the working class began to make their impact[6]. On this reading the six months from the Winter of 1858 to the Spring of 1859 was when this transition occurred. This was underlined by the fact that although the Working Men's College had been in existence since 1854 it chose January 1859 to launch the first issue of its magazine. As old ideas and forces collapsed, new ideas and organisations were already being constructed. The impact on radical education was of the greatest significance.

The year 1859 saw the publication of J.S. Mill's *On Liberty*, Charles Darwin's *The Origin of Species*, Samuel Smiles's *Self Help* and Karl Marx's *Critique of Political Economy*. The impact of each of the texts varied enormously, but their year of publication underlined the process of breaking and making of ideas that was underway. As old working-class organisational forms, and the ideas associated with them, began to fade, so the ideas for a new generation were coming into the public arena.

To trace the discontinuities and continuities in the later months of 1858 through 1859 and into the new decade of the 1860 must be to construct a map of what happened to radical ideas and radical education as Chartism subsided and new, often labour-orientated, forms of organisation began to develop. The general picture was that really useful knowledge became both much narrower and more specific and at the same time much more general. With the growth of organised labour there was a focus on information related to how unions were organised, what wage rates should be and what political economy had to say about these subjects and about working hours. This development was also mirrored in co-operative societies, which sought equally detailed knowledge about the conditions of their existence. At the same time there began the development which led to the educational work done by the Reform League, particularly through the efforts of former building worker George Howell. Radical activists, both middle and working class, now focused on the narrow issue – compared to the Charter – of manhood suffrage and the precise tactics and strategies that would be required to win reform in this area. At one end the broadest form of really useful knowledge dovetailed into the radical tail of the Liberal party which was now under construction. At the other end it fed into the detailed arguments about wages, prices and profit which Marx raised in the First International and which preoccupied the surviving groups of Chartists and Owenites.

These changes in the nature of really useful knowledge both required and reflected changes in the nature of radical education and the way such education was organised. The hardest change to map is what John Saville has referred to as the spirit and psychology of the working-class movement.[7] As the focus of ideas narrowed to the suffrage, or organizing a trade union branch or cooperative society rather than looking for sweeping changes in the national political structure, so the way in which those ideas were expressed changed. In practice this meant that nearly all of the advanced ideas expressed by Ernest Jones under the heading of 'The Charter and Something More' were lost to the vast majority of radical workers. There was a reversion to the ideas of pre- 1848 Chartism.

Radical workers were more cautious about the language they used and they were less likely to take risks with political organisation. It was a time for keeping heads down and warrening the political and economic system from end to end. This slow and methodical work did not lend itself to grand theories or fine sounding pronouncements. Thus it was that when Marx came to write the rules of the First International five years later he moderated his language considerably, noting that workers were not yet ready for the old boldness of language in either written or verbal forms.

To be able to pinpoint precisely the changes which led to the very different spirit behind papers such as the *National Reformer* and the *Beehive* compared to the *People's Paper* is difficult. One change was the sudden birth of working-class journals which focused centrally on insurance, benefit or building societies. Such societies had existed in something more or less like their modern form from the late eighteenth century,[8] but it was only in the period immediately after the collapse of organised Chartism that the space opened up for them to become a central feature in the radical working-class landscape. Where Chartism had offered the prospect of a fairer society, the societies offered some degree of security in the present unfair one. Such a change of perspective again clearly had an impact on ideas. Radical ideas were not forgotten but they became very much secondary.

Another change which can to a limited extent, be pinpointed, was the time when leading radical activists decided that they could not continue in the old way. W. E. Adams wrote in his memoirs, of 'that type of revolutionist that is never happy except in revolt'[9] when discussing the decline of the radical movement in this period. The development of the small groups and sects who, by pursuing their own shibboleths on currency and the land, were able to keep going in the 1860s and 1870s was already underway. Adams is more specific still. He noted that 'Our little band of propagandists kept the flag flying till the end of the fifties. Then, as the more active among them left London for the provinces, the Colonies or the United States, the movement quietly died out'.[10] Adams charted a situation where the best radical activists despaired of progress from the established radical organisation and began to look for new directions.

An alternative perspective is laid out by Leventhal in his biography of George Howell and by Ashton in his study of Adams.[11] This is that the radical debating clubs of Fleet Street and its surrounds, although representing a retreat from any form of radical mass influence, allowed radicals like Adams and Bradlaugh to meet and discuss issues with most of the leading radical figures of the previous twenty years. On this basis they then proceeded to construct the radical movement of the next twenty years. The problem is that it would appear that the lesson they learnt from discussions and meetings was that what was required was a narrower focus rather than a renewed attempt to win the demands of the Charter. It was the lessons of the highspots of Chartism which needed to be passed on to a new generation, not the demoralisation of leading figures at the movement's low point. Therefore a key indicator of the importance of the specific period 1858-9 for the working-class movement and the ideas it held was the almost complete disappearance of the 1851 strategy of the 'Charter and Something More' and its reappearance, in altered form and context, as the policy of the supporters of Bronterre O'Brien.

**The road to 1870. The educational franchise and the 'extreme sections'**

The argument about which way the post-Chartist radical movement should go in the late 1850s had education at its centre. One group of radicals wanted an educational strategy to achieve political change. This was an important movement, although one with quite limited support. For the majority of radicals education was not simply about the ballot. Many did not agree that there should be a connection and this was reflected in the radical press which, for a brief period around the final demise of Chartist hegemony over the working-class movement, played a central role in developing the discussion on radical strategy. Meeting halls and discussion clubs, particularly in London, also took up the argument on the question of the way forward for radicalism in the late 1850s.

The main question for radical political education in the later 1850s was how to develop and build a new generation of activists and what structures and ideas would facilitate this. The aim was not only to carry on radical political organisation but also radical education itself. Here the two way relationship between them became clear. Without some form of radical political organisation it was impossible to provide a coherent national radical education. Without radical education, however, there was a much reduced chance of new politically trained activists developing who could run the radical political organisation.

The educational strategy of the late 1850s represented a narrowing of the perspectives of Chartism and an accommodation to the ideas of the radical middle class. *The Reasoner* reprinted an article from the *Newcastle Daily Chronicle* on 'The Educational Suffrage' which was subtitled 'brains as well as bricks', It noted in part that:

> ...Manhood Suffrage is an ultimate aim. Its advocates will always demand it as a right, but the reasonable part of them will not refuse any concessions in the meanwhile. If the debt cannot be paid in full they will accept instalments. The producing classes demand an extension of the franchise- for whom? Not for the ruffian debased by drunkenness and brutalised by immorality whose freedom beyond the prison walls is only an accident. Not for the man so grossly ignorant of his duties as a citizen as to sell his franchise for a glass of ale.[12]

There were several elements here which help give an understanding of the educational strategists. Firstly, there was the introduction of a clear reformist strategy around the question of the ballot where previously there had been majority resistance to any movement away from the Six Points of the Charter. Following the joint Chartist/Reform Conference of February 1858, the impression that working-class radicalism under Jones' leadership was prepared to make concessions to middle-class radicalism on the suffrage was current although this was not in fact the case. Jones stood by the Chartist programme while lending support to Manhood Suffrage as an interim measure. Interpretation of the significance of this point became central. There were other significant points to the statement. The idea that concessions could be gained on the ballot certainly reflected a growing feeling that some reforms were now on the agenda. Additionally the division between 'advocates' and others taken to be the 'reasonable part' reflected the first attempt at a new politics of reform, splitting those prepared to 'play' the system against those trying to beat it. This division into respectable and unrespectable reformers was further driven home by the rest of the article. The idea was that while it was desirable to extend the franchise it would not be at all desirable to give it to those sections of the working class, the unskilled and uneducated perhaps, who spent their lives in drink and crime. It was the division between respectable and unrespectable that was central to the educational strategy, the division between the 'intelligent and unintelligent' which at root had a class basis. However for the later 1850s and, indeed up until the Education Act of 1870, even the broadest of arguments for an educational strategy was a failure. It would be wrong to suggest that the educational strategists achieved nothing. But they did not materially alter the situation in respect of their main aim – limited reform towards manhood suffrage.

This failure was above all because the educational strategy as a way of reforming the suffrage was only one of many such schemes. Moreover it was one of the few which suggested a comparatively complex formula for extension of the suffrage not directly related to the vote itself. Other schemes based on householder or ratepayer suffrages appealed to the same constituency. Since the main point of reform for many radical reformers, although never for the educational strategists, was how many extra working-class men any reform would allow to vote, those schemes which allowed such calculations probably had greater currency. With the educational strategy the extra numbers admitted to the suffrage were indeterminate. The ambiguity of the educational strategy in respect of this central point may well have appealed to a minority of radicals but suggested that it was unlikely to be taken up seriously by those who might have carried it forward in its own terms: radical Liberal MPs and Peers.

The debate on the educational strategy to achieve electoral reform continued and, to a degree, had intensified by 1860. Holyoake came to lean quite heavily on the arguments of J.S. Mill and the advanced wing of radical liberalism. Mill shared some of the same premises as Holyoake about progress towards the ballot, particularly that such progress could be expected to be limited in the short term. Grugel has noted that the franchise was the 'single issue which dominated domestic politics from the late-1850s until the mid-1860s'.[13] The franchise was the index against which all other radical politics was measured. Grugel has suggested that Holyoake 'provides the historian with an example of a significant and new element of the Victorian political spectrum- the working class liberal'.[14] In fact his only source for this argument is the brief summary of working-class liberalism to be found in John Vincent's classic study.[15] There remains a great paucity of research in this area and, particularly, the process by which working-class radicals like Holyoake became liberals, in so far as they actually did. Barbara Blaszak has noted that Holyoake 'perceived the 1850s as a time of increasing tolerance and good feeling among the classes and consequently a time of progress', holding radical assumptions about self-help, class collaboration, laissez faire and free trade.[16]

Grugel has suggested that Holyoake 'did articulate many of the attitudes towards franchise reform of that sector of British society which was to be taken within the pale of the constitution, namely the labour aristocracy'.[17] If this was the case, then the labour aristocracy must have been focused much more closely on education and ideas than other studies have previously revealed. Alternatively, Holyoake may not have been fully representative of the labour aristocracy. He certainly disputed this point and regarded himself as a representative of working men. The measures he proposed may have advanced the interests of the labour aristocracy, but this was not Holyoake's stated intention. It can be argued that Holyoake represented at least some of the skills and crafts which have been associated with the labour aristocracy.

If this point is accepted it throws a rather different light on its composition, ideas and aims.

Grugel's argument that 'Holyoake cannot be considered as a working man by any socioeconomic standards he was a petty bourgeois'[18] cannot be sustained either, as Grugel has admitted, by Holyoake's perception of himself, or by his position in the class structure. He was, like a whole layer of former Chartists, a full-time political activist because he was unable to obtain other employment. When not engaged on political agitation, Holyoake worked as a freelance journalist and author, invariably for papers or people who sympathised with his political beliefs. Grugel is on stronger ground when he suggests that Holyoake's view of franchise extension ran parallel to, and sometimes connected with, the limited position of reforming MPs in Parliament. However, Grugel's suggestion that it was the leadership of men like Holyoake which persuaded the organised working class to follow the route of gradual reform rather than revolution is far too simplistic. Holyoake's influence extended, even at occasional peaks, to only a comparatively small section of the working class, albeit a section which carried some political weight. Indeed Blaszak has noted that in the Birmingham election of 1868 'G.J. Holyoake Esq, as he called himself, was as far removed from the working class as the Liberal candidate John Bright'.[19]

It is useful to examine here what the origins of Holyoake's specific interest in franchise reform were. Grugel has made a number of interesting, if limited, suggestions. Holyoake had stood for Parliament in 1857 and this act had forced him to come forward with a liberal/radical political programme, but it was the events around Palmerston's attempt to attack supporters of Orsini, the man who had tried to assassinate Napoleon in 1858-9 which really drew Holyoake into the Parliamentary political process. Holyoake provided much of the propaganda for the campaign in early 1858 to prevent repressive measures proposed by Palmerston from going through Parliament. It was of great significance, given the defeats of the Chartist years, that the radicals won. Palmerston's bill was defeated and the Government resigned. Grugel notes that 'Impressed with their success Holyoake, Ernest Jones and some middle-class radicals founded the Political Reform League [PRL] to 'build public pressure for domestic reform'.[20] This is a very simplistic account of the formation of the PRL but the essential point is correct. As had happened on a number of occasions after 1849, support for the causes of foreign radicalism had, in turn, inspired activity at home. However, Holyoake's reform agenda stretched rather wider than Grugel's account allows. Holyoake had begun to move away from a specifically secularist agitation, a fact that caused a crisis in that movement and the rise of Bradlaugh's leadership. In the Fleet Street House he had the means for the production of effective propaganda and this underlined the beginning of Holyoake's transition from an outsider to someone who was, at least partly inside the official political system. He became a leading figure in the co-operative movement and gradually began to develop informal relationships with leading figures of middle-class radicalism and liberalism.

It was not, however, just Holyoake's campaigning and propaganda activities that led to his importance, albeit of a limited scope. It was the development of an organised working-class constituency which had moved beyond Chartism and could relate to the more limited radicalism now put forward by Holyoake. Grugel has argued that between 1859 and 1861 Holyoake was ill and that from 1861 to 1864 he turned his attention to 'freethought co-operation, the affirmation bill'.[21] Perhaps this was so, but this was also a period of transition when Holyoake tried, through a variety of measures, to construct a reformist perspective. If anything his illness may be seen as a product of and an assistance to this attempt by allowing a break in his activities. The context of the growth of organised labour meant that a perspective of forcing small changes from the system, something that Holyoake had done well in the campaign for an unstamped press, was now supported by people who had real means, both industrially and financially, to do something about them.

## An Argument for Complete Suffrage, 1860

The development of what could be termed a working-class-liberal alliance also provoked a reaction. WE Adams, himself an eminently respectable working-class radical who was a skilled printer by trade, had, even by 1860, challenged the position being put forward by Holyoake. He had been an early student at the London Working Men's College and had now become an important radical figure in Manchester. Adams published a pamphlet entitled 'An Argument for Complete Suffrage'[22] and his criticism of the concept of educational suffrage sparked off a lengthy debate about the issue in the pages of *The Reasoner*.

In his autobiography Adams noted that *An Argument For Complete Suffrage* sold very few copies.[23] But its importance can be measured by criteria other than that of sales. Adams, who went on to be the editor of the *Newcastle Weekly Chronicle* for forty years, had then placed a marker for a position which, while post-Chartist, refused to give up independence and be submerged in radical liberalism. If Holyoake's minimum programme of franchise reform could at least look for a position in working-class liberal politics, Adams's maximum programme suggested that working-class politics, while it might take liberalism as its starting point, still desired to go further, or in different directions.

The arguments which Adams expressed in *Complete Suffrage* raised the general question of which way a reforming strategy should develop in the post-Chartist period. Adams took as his starting point the 1832 Reform Act. He argued that this should have been seen as only an 'instalment' of reform. However no further change had occurred for almost 30 years. The context of the attack on both liberal reformers and Holyoake was set at the beginning of the pamphlet. Adams wrote that 'so little thought there is now of the whole debt being paid that popular Reformers accept with complacency a six-pound qualification and reported Friends of the People invent ingenious schemes of educational enfranchisement'.[24] The pamphlet then proceeded to go into more detail on these issues. As John Saville has noted, Adams was not a socialist.[25] He did not object in principle to private property. He did not, however, see why property should play any role in 'legislation'. This cut him off from the most radical of middle-class liberals and their schemes for franchise reform.

Adams reserved his most powerful arguments for the educational franchise. He wrote that 'Education for all is an inevitable consequence of the enfranchisement of all. But we have to deal with a palpable injustice as it may stand tomorrow. While bad laws are made who suffers? Is it the scholar solely?'[26] Adams' argument was that educated and uneducated alike had to exist under the same law, therefore there was no reason why the educated should have the monopoly in making laws. He went on to consider the question of education further. Firstly he attacked the universities which were 'the great seats of learning: yet what sane man would transfer the prerogatives of government to either Oxford or Cambridge?'[27] He also suggested that 'in our own days great criminals have been recruited from the higher ranks of education'. This led Adams on to an attack on the whole philosophy of educationalism. 'The aptitudes of men...are inherent by no means acquired'[28] he noted and in doing so distanced himself completely from the Owenite political and philosophical background that had done much to influence Holyoake's thought.

Finally, Adams raised some important practical questions both about what the nature of an 'educational test' for the franchise would be and what, in any case, it meant to be educated. Both were intensely political questions which could only have come from someone like Adams who had been a leading Chartist and a student at the Working Men's Colleges. Adams's challenge to Holyoake was certainly made from a position of some radical authority. Of the test Adams queried

> Is it a scientific or literary test or is it a test of political knowledge...the test of political knowledge the only one it is even plausible to propose will certainly not be ventured on by the present, governing classes because it is just the political thinker of the working class who most clearly discerns the preposterous

pretensions of those who persuade themselves and us that they are born to govern'.[29]

Here Adams hit at the heart of Holyoake's scheme. The whole philosophy behind it was that respectable layers of the working class, defined not necessarily by skill or job but by knowledge, were those who could safely be enfranchised. Adams' argument suggested, on the contrary, that these were precisely the most dangerous to enfranchise on their own, from the point of view of existing authority, because they were capable of forming an alternative governing class.

Adams also had a secondary argument about the nature of education itself. He suggested that 'in the circle of every man's acquaintance we doubt not that there are men who cannot put together a decent English sentence or speak properly a lengthy English word who yet on political questions are deep thinking far seeing men…'.[30] This was an alternative argument, namely that an educational test would actually exclude people who by any standards, were quite capable of exercising careful political judgement.

The final section of the pamphlet put the case for manhood suffrage. Adams pointed out that it was really up to those who denied the suffrage to justify who they excluded from it and why. He suggested that 'not a single objection has been urged against Manhood Suffrage which is not of equal force against every other form of franchise'.[31] In the last paragraph Adams returned to his core position. This, centrally, was about which route was now open for reformers and what reform would now mean.

Adams's arguments in the pamphlet were more advanced than the old Chartist position which Ernest Jones had defended in 1859. Jones was concerned to develop a coherent and practical strategy for the advancement of manhood suffrage. He was not opposed to the extension of suffrage to women in principle. He was doubtful that it could be on the immediate political agenda. Adams, on the other hand, was concerned to lay down a yardstick for future post-Chartist radical politics. In theory Adams' maximum position was close to that previously held by Holyoake along with several of the more radical middle-class reformers. They had spent some of the 1850s attacking Jones for his refusal to include female suffrage in the Chartist programme. Now their position had been revealed not as one of principle but of tactics. At the sign of possible movement towards manhood suffrage they had dropped it. This was the basis for the exchange which took place between Holyoake and Adams in *The Reasoner* during the Spring of 1860.

Holyoake had originally outlined his views on the extension of the suffrage, not in *The Reasoner* but in the Liberal paper the *Daily News* on 20 February 1860. Only later on 4 March did he reprint the article for a radical working-class audience in *The Reasoner*. If, as Grugel has suggested, Holyoake was ill in this period, it is also clear that he used his period of illness as a way of reassessing and reorganising his ideas on key issues such as the franchise. Holyoake's argument was raised in 'relation to the pending reform bill' and it was developed in this context as well. It was an attempt to enter into a debate between radical liberal politicians and to push a possible extension of the franchise further than it might otherwise have gone in the direction of the working class. It was also undeniably a good time to make such an intervention. The Liberal Party was in the process of formation and therefore particularly open to external influence.

The nub of Holyoake's scheme was that the 'intelligent operative', 'by virtue of his intelligence' should be admitted to the franchise. This, of course, raised the question of how 'intelligence' was to be proved. Holyoake had worked out a detailed scheme for this. He suggested that a test could be conducted around books such as Brougham's 'Political Philosophy' and the Dean of Hereford's 'Lessons on Industrial Phenomena'. All those prepared to declare that they had read these books would then be eligible to undergo a formal examination supervised by the Society of Arts. This would consist of three evenings. On the first two, lecturers would explain the contents of the books and questions would be taken. On the third evening potential voters would be required to answer 'verbally or otherwise' from three to six questions out of twelve. Those who successfully did so would receive a certificate which would give them eligibility to vote.

The test proposal appears, and no doubt appeared to many radical workers at the time, to be somewhat forbidding. However, in a sense the issue was not the severity of the test but the very possibility of its existence. Holyoake simply noted that 'Probably a Majority of those who now actively seek the franchise would be content with it when they knew they could get it'.[32] In his *Daily News* article Holyoake was concerned specifically with the mechanism, the franchise of fitness, whereby he could extend the suffrage. However, in a series of open letters to Lord John Russell, published at the same time under the title *The Workman and the Suffrage*, Holyoake expanded on the reasons for his advocacy of the educational test. Holyoake was a constituent of Russell and, on obtaining the vote in 1857, had given it to Russell at the following election.

In his first letter Holyoake quoted from an article 'Reform in Parliament' which had been published in the *Westminster Review* of 1 January 1859. The article suggested that 'the real problem of which no real solution has perhaps yet been published is by what enactment can skilled artisans be admitted to vote without swamping them and us by an unintelligent mass whether of peasants or of town population?'[33] This was undoubtedly the implicit theory behind Holyoake's proposals on the franchise, but he, of course, was very careful not to state so clearly or openly who he thought should be included or excluded from the suffrage. Indeed, at the beginning of his second letter, Holyoake simply noted that 'what is wanted is an expansive suffrage which shall be open to the worthy and shut out the unfit'.[34]

In this second letter Holyoake was however prepared to explain in some detail the precise trade-off which he believed his franchise could bring about. He wrote:

> My reason for thinking some such arrangement as this would be acceptable to the people generally is that it would be unsatisfactory to extreme sections on whose behalf I write who go farther than any other party in politics. To them the "six points of the charter" seem tame and restricted. They hold principles of democracy which imply that womanhood as well as manhood is included in humanity. They would not stop at the establishment of the aristocracy of men [which is all that the charter proposes] as the final effort of political justice. They admit the reasonableness of women being ultimately admitted to some direct voice in the affairs of the state. They do not see why parliament should not include colonial representatives...But they are not so mad as they seem: while they would advocate the principle they think intrinsically right they would go with the strongest party likely to carry the most practical measure in that direction – holding that conviction is not honesty but obstinacy when it becomes an obstruction and that it is fanaticism when it refuses instalments of its own truth.[35]

Who exactly the 'extreme sections' were that Holyoake claimed to be speaking for remains unclear. They were not necessarily Chartists and indeed much of Holyoake's earlier position on universal adult suffrage can be seen in the statement. There is no evidence that the demand for colonial representatives in parliament was ever raised directly although, of course, it is entirely possible that it was an idea in common currency amongst radicals who were much exercised by issues of international politics. The general tactical purpose of the statement is clear. Holyoake held himself out as a model of reasonableness compared to the 'extreme sections' but implied that, were his measure to be accepted, he had the power to persuade these sections to acquiesce in it.

Above all for Holyoake the issue of the franchise based on fitness was a question of balance. On the one hand he had to reassure the middle classes that an extension of the suffrage would be useful and would have the support even of the 'extreme sections'. On the other, he had to sell the franchise to radicals as an idea fully in line with radical thought. For this latter reason he went on to discuss the 'advantages of the kind of self-acquired suffrage I would suggest'.[36] The concept of self-acquisition focused on the franchise as something that radicals could win for themselves, rather than being conceded from above by the State. Holyoake provided numerous reasons in support of his scheme. He began by facing the issue of what the radical 'extremes' would say about the measure. His first reason, therefore, was that '[a]ll demagogues, advocates and agitators would accept it because they are all in favour of popular knowledge'.[37] He followed this with the point that '[a]ll persons and partisans likely to give the government trouble if excluded would be satisfied with the opportunity of an intelligence franchise, cease agitating in a discontented spirit and commence to study and qualify themselves'.[38] Holyoake here gambled that the possibility of a stake inside the system which the franchise offered would reduce the appeal of opposing the system from the outside.

He then moved on to look at more specifically educational reasons for the franchise. He felt that 'teachers instructors, lecturers and clergy of all denominations' would 'probably be in favour'[39] because it would provide a recognition of their efforts in the field of popular education. At the same time Holyoake noted that it would give political importance to educational mechanisms such as Mechanics' institutions, Working Mens' Colleges and improvement classes.

Finally, Holyoake returned to his earlier arguments. The franchise would, he suggested, 'shut out the mob' without offence. It would be a select franchise without insulting exclusiveness…propery could not be endangered by it, hereditary timidity need not be afraid of it'.[40] This was Holyoake's message to the middle class namely that his franchise would certainly not threaten their current position and, indeed, might on balance strengthen it. To reinforce the point further, he noted that 'There is hardly any probability with the widest extension of the franchise that any working man would be elected this generation'.[41] Once such statements are considered it becomes easier to see why radicals like Adams were prepared to attack Holyoake so forcefully and why, correspondingly, Holyoake began to find favour with advanced liberals.

Holyoake himself agreed in his *Daily News* article that his franchise was aimed at 'an intelligent portion' of 'the people'. Who were these people? Holyoake suggested that they consisted of all those who work for a weekly wage while he noted that Bright referred to those who 'dwelt in a cottage'.[42] Holyoake had gone a long way towards radical liberalism in his proposals on the suffrage. Even so, he remained more radical than the most radical of the liberal leaders such as Bright and Mill. It was in this context that two weeks later, on 7 March 1860, Holyoake reviewed Adams's pamphlet. It was not, of course, an argument that Mill or Bright would have engaged themselves in. He declared that it was 'thoughtful, well written'.[43] Holyoake argued that Adams had confused his desire to move towards manhood suffrage, with the aid of an educational franchise, as an attempt to replace manhood suffrage with an educational test. Holyoake resented this suggestion and noted instead that Adams appeared to 'sneer at education'. Holyoake argued that 'deep and wide cultivation is still the glory and the best security of public liberty'.[44]

Adams sent a swift response which appeared in *The Reasoner* of 6 April 1860. He argued that he did not undervalue education 'as an instrument of social benefit'.[45] He went on to suggest that being educated neither qualified nor disqualified somebody from the franchise. The core of Adams's objection to the franchise was that once in operation it would become a replacement for manhood suffrage rather than a step towards it, whatever Holyoake's intentions might have been. Adams noted that 'when you enfranchise a man because of his education you count his intelligence above his manhood'.[46]

The core of the argument developed from these positions. While Adams opposed an educational franchise, it was what such a franchise symbolised that really led to disagreement. Adams suggested that 'compromises will always find advocates enough in the world without believers in a great principle condescending to abet them'.[47] He also argued that by supporting the educational franchise Holyoake was crossing the divide between working-class radicalism, which supported the franchise, and middle-class radicalism, which did not. Adams went on to argue that in any case education in politics would not come through any form of franchise, but when it was the 'right of all'. Finally Adams concluded that Holyoake's franchise would help to create an 'aristocracy of schoolmen'.[48] This attack so stung Holyoake that he replied immediately underneath Adams letter. He argued that in practice Adams was opposing the possibility of some extension of the suffrage. The franchise of fitness, Holyoake suggested, would read not 'school men' but 'working men'.[49]

Adams replied further in *The Reasoner* of 6 May 1860. He noted that it was only with regret that he was replying to Holyoake's earlier 'spiteful appendage'.[50] Adams distanced himself from the 'obstructive folly' of those Chartists who had supported Feargus O'Connor. This was an important point. Adams did not oppose Holyoake because he opposed change or because he wished to stick to the letter of the Charter. He wanted change, but the change was very different from that desired by Holyoake. He focused again on whether Holyoake was actively supporting a position of liberal reform, noting '[i]t is one thing...to refrain from obstructing measures of partial suffrage and quite another to abet and concoct them'.[51] Adams' policy of neither opposing nor supporting change short of what was desired can be seen to be very different from Holyoake's pro-reform position. Adams went on to underline the logical contradictions in Holyoake's policy, arguing that while Holyoake's aim was to reach working men by the fitness franchise, 'working men to be reached at all must first be schoolmen'.[52] The educational franchise was self-selecting and exclusive. It was quite the opposite of the inclusive franchise the Chartists had always sought. Adams emphasised the exclusivity of the strategy by noting that those 'who successfully gained the vote as a result will be recognised not because they are men but because they are scholars'[53]. He then returned to his substantive argument. Even if discrimination in favour of the already educated was allowed a more serious objection would still apply. Namely that 'every diversion of force in favour of a fancified fitness is a loss to the popular party'.[54] Adams went further and accused Holyoake of 'defection' from the fight for the suffrage, a defection which furthermore must be counted as a 'considerable one'. The charge of disunity had always been a powerful one amongst Chartists and radicals and, while Adams himself had stood aside from Chartism in the 1850s, the accusation here was of a broader nature. It was alleged that Holyoake was going beyond the bounds of 'generally agreed radical focus on the suffrage'. Adams went on to criticise the 'energy expended on private schemes of doubtful value'. He argued that Holyoake, by advocating an educational franchise, was diverting support away from the 'acknowledged legitimacy' of the 'great principle' of the Charter and manhood suffrage.[55]

Holyoake was provoked by Adams's criticism into a further response in his weekly letter. Holyoake argued that some progress on the franchise would be better than none and that 'A Clause which would equally apply to the six millions to be left unenfranchised can hardly be denominated a private scheme'.[56] The importance of the argument between Adams and Holyoake was to underline the centrality that education had to working-class arguments about the suffrage in the late 1850s and early 1860s. Its practical implications were more limited. Holyoake's role in Secular politics was overtaken by Charles Bradlaugh as the *National Reformer* replaced the *Reasoner* as the paper of Secularism. The Reform League framed the ideas and arguments that informed the battle for the 1867 Reform Act. While both Holyoake and Adams played a role in the Reform League, it was the latter's views on the suffrage that held sway. The extension of the suffrage in 1867 led, indirectly, to the 1870 Education Act, not the other way around.

### 1857-1860: From the educational strategy to a labour aristocracy?

Holyoake's proposals for an educational franchise won support amongst some sections of radical workers and, more particularly, amongst some influential activists and leaders. For example, Joseph Barker writing in an early issue of the *National Reformer*, itself a title which suggested a specific frame of mind and way of doing things, noted that 'We are in favour of the addition of a fitness franchise'. However, like W.E. Adams, Barker was a controversial and uncertain figure in the radical cause.[57] 'The clause suggested by Mr Holyoake through *The Reasoner* some weeks ago and since drawn up in due form, we endorse with all our hearts'.[58] At the same time some sections of the radical middle class also supported the scheme. *The Spectator* wrote in May 1860 that 'the plan meets many objectives – by its gradual operation, by the premium which it puts upon self education by identifying the more intelligent and therefore more influential portion of the working classes'.[59] Against this, supporters of Holyoake's strategy found hard opposition on their political left from people who resisted the cooperation with radical liberals that the educational strategy implied. Marx expressed the views of such people in the *New York Daily Times* in March 1859 when he wrote of:

> the new fancy franchises that are partly derived from Lord John Russell's abortive schemes of 1852 and 1854 and are partly due to the genius which hatched the convoluted perplexities of Lord Ellenborough's unhappy India bill. There are, first, some so-called educational qualifications which, as Mr Disraeli ironically remarked, independent as they are of scientific acquirements betoken the education of the classes concern 'to have involved some considerable investment' and may, therefore, be considered to belong to the general category of property qualification. The right of vote is consequently to be conferred upon graduates, the clergy of the Church of England, ministers of all other denominations, barristers, pleaders and conveyancers, solicitors and proctors, medical men, certified schoolmasters, in a word on the members of the different liberal professions or as the French used to call it in Mr Guizot's time on the "capacities";…all these new franchises while admitting some new middle-class sections are framed with the express purpose of excluding the working classes and chaining them to their present station of political "pariahs"….[60]

Marx had emphasised how something like the educational strategy included some elements of the disenfranchised but excluded other sections. There was a further issue: whether the people Holyoake's educational strategy was aimed at actually wanted it. One way of looking at this is to focus on them as a potential or actual aristocracy, not of labour, but of ideas. The evidence suggests that while this layer of working-class self-improvers and activists clearly valued knowledge, they supported a much more inclusive view of the suffrage than Holyoake offered. For example, by 1862 George Howell and other trade union leaders such as Odger and Applegarth had already picked up the Chartist mantle and organised to demand manhood suffrage.[61]

Beyond this, although the popular take-up of Holyoake's strategy was quite small it succeeded in influencing some liberal politicians. Although it was the strength of the organised trade unions which underwrote the alliance that was the Reform League, the kind of work done by Holyoake at the level of radical ideas provided some of the framework for this to happen. It is important to grasp that Holyoake and his followers were of no more, and perhaps of less, significance than the 'extreme sections', to his left. These sections, coming often from the same kind of class and occupational structures as the educational aristocracy, reached very different conclusions from Holyoake.

This differentiation within the sections of the working class which the educational strategy was aimed at, and the split ideas and consciousness that existed in the heads of many advanced workers has been rarely picked up on in secondary sources. It was not that the new working-class labour and trade union leaders, whether an aristocracy or not, were against cooperation with the middle class. Rather they were in favour of it, but on specific issues and on a more advanced-platform than that which Holyoake put forward. Grugel, in his biography of Holyoake, is mistaken when he writes that:

> the labour aristocracy had not completely forsaken their Chartist heritage, Their goal was still universal suffrage, but they were by no means as defiant and as conscious that they belonged to a separate class as their Chartist forbears had been. The labour aristocracy was generally composed of reasonable men who believed in the British political tradition and who respected the law. Many moreover, were also willing to accept a bill which granted something less than universal suffrage. Holyoake's counsel for moderation exemplifies that of most working class leaders.[62]

The educational strategy was characteristic of the battles around the suffrage which dominated working-class politics in the ten years after the collapse of Chartism. It was also centrally about which radical ideas and what kind of radical education were now appropriate for radical workers and, as importantly, what they planned to use the ideas and education for. However, the educational strategy was far too closely associated with elitist ideas of the radical middle class for artisans or craft workers to sign on to it. Their perspective was more complex than Holyoake's solution allowed for.

Firstly, the working-class radicals of the 1850s and early 1860s were still very much within the framework of Chartist inclusivism on the vote. The distinction between workers who had stable and secure employment and who could therefore be relied upon to use their vote wisely, and others who could not, was not one that made a great deal of sense to those concerned. George Howell's employment experience in this period, for example, suggests that his hold on a permanent job was as tenuous as that of the most unskilled worker. Indeed the rising, if very small, layer of labour organisers like Howell had a peripatetic existence, whether still working at their trades or trying to make a living out of organising various campaigns. In his biography of Howell, Leventhal notes how, once employed in organising one campaign, he would use this as a springboard for other related campaigns which he might then go on to be employed to organise once the original one had run its course.[63]

Secondly, the labour leaders did not look at the suffrage in the same way as Holyoake. They saw the need for a separate, if connected, approach between the economic position dictated by their class, which was dealt with by trade unionism, and the political questions raised by this organisation, which were dealt with by ad-hoc structures and by pressure on the newly constructed Liberal Party. It was of course the activities of the Government and the 'Master and Servant' Acts still in use in the 1860s, that constantly reminded trade unionists, should they be minded to forget, of the strongly political dimensions to their attempts to organise industrially. As Royden Harrison has noted, '[i]n the 1860s, the politically conscious workman felt closer to the Tolpuddle Martyrs than he did to the Chartists. He was much more likely to meet with imprisonment as a result of a trade dispute than he was as a result of his political activities'.[64]

The labour leaders took a wider perspective on change than Holyoake, whose position had been worked out after twenty years of defeats. They did not see the need to enfranchise themselves to the exclusion of others when, by organising within the framework of Liberalism, general progress on the franchise might be achieved which would obviate the need for complex mechanisms such as the educational strategy.

While commentators may now argue that the educational strategy fitted the narrowed perspectives and horizons of the labour aristocracy, in fact they were not as narrow as all that. It was their one-dimensionality, focused on piecemeal reform as the only option open to radicals, that caused the gulf between their impact and that which Chartism had made as recently as ten years earlier. However, even if Holyoake's policies for progress on the suffrage did not really fit the wider mood on the question, and despite the fact that the ideas of secularism appealed to only a very small number of working-class radicals, it was Holyoake and, more generally, secularist organisation that endured and grew beyond the 1850s, where Ernest Jones and Chartism did not.

Holyoake was able to make the successful transition and become a working-class liberal politician while still maintaining much of his previous support. Miles Taylor has noted that 'Holyoake's range of political friends was considerably more catholic than that of Jones'.[65] It is true that Holyoake was effectively challenged as the leader of secularism by Charles Bradlaugh as the 1850s turned to the 1860s. However, Holyoake understood better than Ernest Jones how radicalism could operate in the new post-Chartist environment. He worked with liberals where he could, but did not hesitate to oppose or go beyond liberal politics and ideas when necessary. By contrast, Ernest Jones resumed his career as a lawyer, moved to Manchester and only when Chartist organisation was firmly behind him did he embrace, and was in turn embraced by, radical liberalism.

**Notes**

1. Perry Anderson, *Arguments within English Marxism*, London, 1981, p. 46.
2. John Foster, *Class Struggle and the Industrial Revolution*, London, 1974.
3. W.E. Adams,. *Memoirs of a Social Atom*, p. 230.
4. Ibid., pp. 161-2.
5. Joseph McCabe, *Life and Letters of G.J. Holyoake*, London, 1908, p. 305.
6. Margot Finn, *After Chartism*, Cambridge, 1993.
7. John Saville, *1848*, op. cit. pp. 204-5.
8. I. Prothero, *Artisans and Politics in early Nineteenth-Century London*, London, 1979.
9. W.E. Adams op. cit., p. 226.
10. Ibid.
11. F. Leventhal, *Respectable Radical, George Howell and Victorian working-class politics*, London, 1971; Owen Ashton, *W.E. Adams*, Tyne & Wear, 1991.
12. *The Reasoner* 14 August 1859
13. Lee Grugel, *George Jacob Holyoake*, Philadelphia, 1976, p. 105.
14. Ibid.
15. John Vincent, *The Formation of the British Liberal Party 1857-1868*, Harmondsworth, 1972
16. Barbara Blaszak, *George J. Holyoake and the Development of the British Co-operative Movement*, Lampeter, 1998, p. 88.; p. 26.
17. Grugel op. cit., p. 106.
18. Grugel, op. cit., p. 106.
19. Blaszak op. cit., p. 22.
20. Grugel, op. cit., p. 107.
21. Grugel, op. cit. , p. 110.
22. W.E. Adams, *An Argument for Complete Suffrage*, Manchester, 1860.
23. W.E Adams, *Memoirs of a Social Atom*, New York 1968 edition. op. cit.
24. W.E Adams, *An Argument for Complete Suffrage*, Manchester, 1860, p. 2.
25. John Saville, *Introduction to Memoirs of A Social Atom*, op. cit.
26. W.E. Adams, *An Argument for Complete Suffrage*, Manchester, 1860, p. 6.
27. Ibid., p. 7.
28. Ibid., p. 7.
29. Ibid., p. 7.
30. Ibid., p. 9.
31. Ibid., p. 12.
32. *The Daily News*, 20 February 1860.
33. *The Westminster Review*, 1 January 1859.
34. G.J. Holyoake, *The Workman and the Suffrage*, London, 1859, p. 6.
35. Ibid., p. 7-8.
36. Ibid., p. 8.
37. Ibid., p. 8.

38 Ibid., p. 8.
39 Ibid., p. 8.
40 Ibid., p. 9.
41 Ibid., p. 12.
42 *The Daily News*, 20 February 1860.
43 *The Reasoner* 7 March 1860.
44 Ibid.
45 *The Reasoner* 6 April 1860.
46 Ibid.
47 Ibid.
48 Ibid.
49 Ibid.
50 *The Reasoner* 6 May 1860.
51 Ibid.
52 Ibid.
53 Ibid.
54 Ibid.
55 Ibid.
56 Ibid.
57 W.E. Adams, op. cit., p. 400.
58 *National Reformer* May 1860.
59 Quoted in *The Reasoner* 27 May 1860.
60 *New York Daily Times* 17 March 1859..
61 Leventhal op. cit. p. 47.
62 Grugel op. cit. p. 106.
63 Leventhal op. cit.
64 Royden Harrison, *Before the Socialists*, Aldershot, 1994 2nd Edition, p. 21.
65 Miles Taylor 2003, op. cit., p. 181.

## Chapter 6
## Beyond Chartism:
## radical education and radical politics in the later 1850s

### Introduction: the landscape of radicalism

By the late 1850s Chartism as an organised national presence was beginning to fade, even from its reduced presence earlier in the decade. More importantly the idea of a revolutionary overthrow of the market capitalist system in favour of, perhaps, a plebeian democracy was also dimming. Not only had continental Europe failed to provide encouraging longer term examples, but the possibilities for some change within the system, without resort to physical force, also appeared open, if not to the rank and file of Chartism, certainly to those who had been or were still leading it.

Edward Thompson has labelled this strategy a process of warrening capitalism from end to end rather than attempting to overthrow it. For Thompson the concept of the 'rabbit warren', as Staughton Lynd has suggestively labelled it,[1] where a society is 'criss-crossed by underground dens and passageways created by an oppositional class',[2] was a way of addressing the debate about how the transition from capitalism to socialism might take place. Traditional marxist thought had seen the earlier transition from feudalism to capitalism as taking place after the bourgeoisie had spent a lengthy period building bourgeois institutions – for example trading houses – in feudal society. However it was not held to be possible for socialists to do this under capitalism. This meant that when capitalism was overthrown, socialism would not appear complete, but would remain to be built. Trotsky refined the theory by arguing that the workers party could fulfil some of the elements that bourgeois institutions had done under feudalism, thereby speeding up the transition.

For Thompson writing in 1960 and then in 1965 the concept of a sharp unprepared break from capitalism, arguably an old style revolution, was not realistic. Rather he saw the transition as being prefigured in existing society, in much the same way as bourgeois society had prefigured itself under feudalism. And he saw this as the preparation for a breakthrough towards socialism. It will be noticed that his model misses out a role for the party and sees socialism appearing in a more complete form than envisaged in some traditional Marxist thought.

In its historical practice the process covered several different concepts. At one end may be seen the 'dull' practice of labourism, where trade unions struggled to reach bargaining positions with employers and sought partnership agreements.[3] Given the relatively unstable state of mid-century capitalism, these were rarely long lived. At the other end may be seen attempts to opt out of the market system, of prefiguration, around some of the co-operative schemes. Somewhere in the middle may be found a huge range of institutions that sought to protect and advance the interests of workers within the system. None of this ruled out revolutionary thoughts and the worker who fought hard for basic negotiating rights, might also be thinking of emigrating out of British capitalism altogether for a new life in America.

It can be seen, with mutual improvement societies and working men's colleges, how the ad hoc mechanisms of radical education and discussion which stretched back to the 1790s, now became entrenched as warrens within the structure of civil society but at the same time became divorced from a direct political agenda. Such an agenda reasserted itself with the socialist Sunday schools from the 1880s. With *Evenings with the People* and Marx and Engels critique of Jones's strategy what can be grasped is a battle for the hegemony of ideas – what would actually be discussed in and inform the warrens as they were being built. Marx and Engels wanted an advanced strategy that would lead to the early formation of a workers' party. Thompson's concept of warrens – of working-class independence – also led to such a party, but over a much longer timescale and in a less directly confrontational way.

The key is to grasp that the warrening of capitalism provided relatively stable oppositional bases for the working class within the system. This was a step forward but also potentially a step back. Once such a base had been established, to challenge its survival with a revolutionary outbreak became much more difficult. Around this forwards/backwards movement debate was a sharp interchange of ideas and strategies, on the one hand from Ernest Jones and on the other from Marx and Engels. By the early 1860s both had had to accept elements of a new political landscape where the new Liberal Party found much working-class support and trade unions had started to become a much more significant and permanent presence.

These included newly developing areas not discussed here such as co-operatives. G.J. Holyoake's *Self Help for the People*[4] was the bible of the new movement. It was above all else, successful, with rising membership and sales, and this is a characteristic feature of the warrening process. It was also a double-edged and contradictory process in terms of political radicalism, such was the landscape against which the ideas and structures detailed below were worked out.

Antony Taylor makes the point that the political landscape in London in the 1850s was different to that in other centres such as Manchester: there was more space for independent labour politics. The same was true, although the precise balance of forces was different, of Newcastle upon Tyne. Taylor has noted that 'In London in particular the increasingly metropolitan orientation of the NCA and the vigorous club and public house culture that had sustained local branches of the movement…enabled the Chartists to continue their activities unchecked into the 1850s'.[5] Indeed, London and Newcastle may have had a certain pecularity in allowing room for working-class politics, with perhaps the only other regional example being in Rochdale.[6]

One useful indicator of how the London landscape had changed is to look at the spread of trade union branches. The Friendly Society of Operative Stonemasons had 14 branches in London from 1859. The Bricklayers had 18 branches, beginning in 1850, of whom around half had over 100 members, The Amalgamated Society of Carpenters and Joiners had 24 branches dating from 1860 the Ironfounders 8 branches from 1859 and the Engineers had 16 branches from 1860, the majority of which were large.

This provided a substantial weight of organised labour and it is perhaps no accident that the new radical leaders who began to emerge in the early 1860s, such as George Howell, came from this trade union background.[7] It would be easy to make the assumption that these people had little in common with or relation to the worlds of Chartism, radical education and really useful knowledge. However the reality was that they had often been formed politically precisely in this milieu, They had, however, developed their ideas in the post-Chartist environment.

The milieu that the new generation of radical leaders faced was one where international and sometimes global developments were making a significant impact in domestic politics as British capitalism began to consolidate its imperial advantage. At the same time, and sometimes because of this they came under the influence of Marx and Engels. Still confined in the late 1850s to a narrow layer of radical activists, often emigres, by 1864 both were in a position to play a leading role which centred around the level of ideas in the International Working Men's Association.

In early 1858, Marx examined the impact of the Orsini affair on British politics. Orsini, an Italian republican, had tried to assassinate Napoleon in Paris but failed and was guillotined for his efforts. Orsini had been living in Kentish Town, North London, and the bombs he used were made in Britain and financed by the middle-class radical Allsopp. Joseph Cowen, later radical

MP for Newcastle, was also involved. The links between radical educational activities and Orsini could have not been stronger. Orsini stayed with Cowen at Stella Hall, Blaydon and the local mechanics' institute conferred honorary membership upon him. Orsini recalled that the working-class radicalism of the north-east was 'a good school for me'.[8] This proved, if nothing else, that there was serious intent behind the developing reformist politics. Palmerston, acting in league with Napoleon III, tried but failed to prosecute several alleged accomplices in the English courts. He also failed in his attempt to push a renewed Aliens Bill through the House of Commons. Marx wrote, 'If Orsini did not kill Louis Napoleon he certainly killed Palmerston...the significance of the late vote is as a proclamation that Britain has ceased to play second to French Imperialism'.[9] Interestingly, despite the developing rift between Marx and Ernest Jones, Jones also carried this Bonapartist analysis of Palmerston in the *People's Paper*.

While Palmerston may have had dictatorial tendencies he could be, and indeed was, removed from office by means of the limited democracy then existing. Moreover, unlike Napoleon Palmerston did not engage in wholesale repression of the working-class movement. There was no doubt, however, that the English party system was in deep crisis. It took a succession of meetings and manoeuvres in 1859 to bring to life the modern Liberal Party and for a way out of the crisis to be found. John Vincent has argued that a view of the world which focuses on 'Parliamentary history, the Parliamentary party and its policies'[10] and therefore sees the formation of the Liberal Party as having taken place at Willis's Rooms in London in 1859 is fundamentally mistaken. He makes the entirely valid point that the crucial change was not at the top of politics but the 'adoption of that Parliamentary Party by a rank and file'.[11] When he does focus on the top of the political process, Vincent again argues that the decisive moment in Liberal formation was the transition from Palmerston to Gladstone in the 1860s. To underline his point that real changes in Liberal and liberal politics took place outside of the Parliamentary process he notes that at the meeting at Willis's Rooms in 1859 the Parliamentary Party 'only ratified by acclamation an arrangement already made between the leaders'.[12] However, there can be no doubt that changes in the working class in the later 1850s underwrote the possibility of the formation of the modern Liberal Party and the roles of key figures such as Palmerston, Bright, Mill and Gladstone were increasingly influenced by a developing working-class constituency.

Marx's and Engels's correspondence for the same period reflected a rather different set of concerns. There was discussion about relations with various emigres, about illnesses which Marx and Engels contracted, and most particuarly about relations with publishers. In his letter of 16 January 1858 Marx made the revealing comment, not covered in his published writings, about the significance of India for British politics: 'In view of the DRAIN OF MEN and BULLION which she will cost the English, India is now our best ally'. Elsewhere there were some pertinent comments on the Chartist movement, and the NCA in particular. Marx wrote in late 1857: 'In last Sunday's issue of Reynolds there is a significant attack upon those APOSTATES who advocate UNION with the MIDDLE CLASS, Meaning Jones, I haven't seen the laddie for a long time, He seems to be avoiding men, for which he must have his raysons, However I shall probably surprise him ONE FINE MORNING'.[13] Several weeks later Marx returned to the question of Jones:

> What do you think of Jones? I still refuse to believe that the chap has sold himself. Perhaps his experience of 1848 lies heavy on his stomach. So great is his faith in himself that he may think himself capable of exploiting the MIDDLE CLASS or imagine that if only, ONE WAY OR THE OTHER, Ernest Jones could be got into Parliament, world history could not fail to take a NEW TURN. The best of it all is that out of SPITE against Jones OF COURSE Reynolds is now posing in his paper as the most rabid opponent the MIDDLE CLASS and of all compromise. Mr B O'Brien has likewise become an IRREPRESSIBLE CHARTIST AT ANY PRICE. Jones only excuse is the enervation now rampant among the working class in England. However that maybe if he goes on as at present he will become either DUPE of the MIDDLE CLASS or RENEGADE The FACT that he should now seek to avoid me as anxiously as he once used to consult me over the merest trifle is evidence of anything but good conscience.[14]

Marx was extremely critical both of Jones' isolation from the small group around himself and Engels, and more particuarly of his continued overtures to the middle class. He also understood that Jones' course allowed others, like G.W.M. Reynolds and O'Brien, who were politically to the right of him and considerably more sectarian, to assume the mantle of Chartist leadership, whilst paradoxically portraying Jones as to the right of them. As Miles Taylor has noted 'Jones was now speaking alongside the very parliamentary radicals and "middle-class" reformers whom he had dismissed as the enemy for most of the 1850s'.[15] Engels, too, criticised not only Jones but also Harney. Of Harney, now editing the *Jersey Independent* and involved with republican refugees from Bonapartist France, he wrote: 'He's a rotten little blighter and Jersey is just the right place for him'.[16] As regards Jones he commented that he too: 'is evidently up to some pretty tricks. The obese Livesay [sic] whom he appointed CHAIRMAN of his conference is a wretched little bourgeois who swears by Miall and who, in company with Sturge and Co engineered the COMPLETE SUFFRAGE SECESSIONS as long ago as 1842 when all the petty bourgeois withdrew'.[17] Following the 1858 Conference organised by Ernest

Jones which attempted a union with some middle-class radicals and had the practical effect of splitting the NCA, causing the collapse of the *People's Paper* and allowing the initative on reform to pass to middle-class radicalism, Marx wrote to Engels:

> Our friend Jones HAS DECIDELY SOLD HIMSELF AT THE LOWEST POSSIBLE PRICE TO THE BRIGHT COTERIE. The idiot has ruined himself politically without rescuing himself commercially how little his apostasy – the laddie is preaching UNION of THE MIDDLE AND WORKING CLASSES – has availed him [he has sold the Peoples Paper to the Morning Star fellows and has retained a mere couple of columns in the sheet for himself].[18]

Engels' political conclusions to this state of affairs were comparatively well known, However, they have considerable bearing on a detailed analysis of radicalism and education for this period. If a key leading section of the working-class radical movement had, in effect, gone over to the middle class this had considerable implications for independent working-class education, Engels wrote:

> one might almost believe that the English proletarian movement in its traditional Chartist form must perish utterly before it can evolve in a new and viable form. And yet it is not possible to foresee what the new form will look like. It seems to me that there is in fact a connection between Jones' NEW MOVE, seen in conjunction with previous more or less successful attempts at such an alliance, and the fact that the English proletariat is actually becoming more and more bourgeois, so that the ultimate aim of this most bourgeois of all nations would appear to be the possession, alongside the bourgeoisie, of a bourgeois aristocracy and a bourgeois proletariat, In the case of a nation which exploits the entire world this is, of course, justified to some extent.[19]

He added: 'Reynolds will become a prominent personage thanks to Jones' manoeuvre.'[20]

Engels drew a link between a labour bureaucratic layer of working-class leaders, developing by the late 1850s, the role of imperialism and the embourgeoisment of the working class. These were radically new ideas for the late 1850s. There is no doubt that the questions to which Engels referred were and remain important trends and influences in the British Labour Movement. Their relative influence in the late 1850s and their use as an explanation for the activity of Jones was much more problematic. It was unclear, for example, how precisely Jones had been bought off by the bourgeoisie. Miles Taylor notes that he did receive some money from middle-class sources but the 'bulk of these contributions were publicly accounted for in the pages of the *Peoples*

*Paper*.[21] Certainly, because he partially collapsed Chartism into middle-class radicalism, Jones despaired of the possibility of independent working-class action or, at the very least, gave the impression of doing so. However, at this stage the working class could hardly be characterised as having been bought off. Indeed major struggles lay ahead, as Marx argued in 1859 when he noted that opportunities would be missed because of Jones's actions. Jones's errors were at root political. By his sectarianism he had allowed the rise back to prominence of middle-class radicalism, and then, due to his lack of understanding of the ebbs and flows of working-class struggle, he had gone into alliance with the radical middle class.

Engels' analysis did not fully explain matters. However, in the more general sense, namely when he was explaining the development of reformism, the split between politics and economics and the failure of independent working-class politics he was undoubtedly correct. What was emerging was a limited space for material reform and a much enlarged role for imperialism in the Crimea, India and China. Engels' assessment that Chartism had to be completely eradicated before a new movement could be built again in the long run was ultimately correct. The parties of the 1880s, the Social Democratic Federation and the Independent Labour Party were formed on a new basis, with a new generation of working-class activists and with only a slight historical memory of Chartism. On the other hand however, the proto-parties of the First International and Reform League were formed very clearly on the basis of Chartist ideas on the ballot. Finally Engels view of the increased importance of Reynolds was also correct. Marx wrote on this point to Engels: 'Reynolds is a far greater rogue than Jones, but he is rich and a good speculator, The mere FACT THAT HE HAS TURNED AN OUT AND OUT CHARTIST shows that this position must still be a profitable one'.[22] Eventually Marx and Engels stopped paying active attention to Chartism which, in any case, had ceased as an effective national organisation by 1859. Marx did however note that Jones's capitulation to the middle-class radicals had effectively set back the proletarian movement, at the very time that circumstances for its progress were becoming more favourable. Marx and Engels' assessment of the complete collapse of an independent political movement among the working class is questionable. Breuilly, for example, points to Chartism being able to act as a vehicle or protest where it retained its organisation.[23] There can be no doubt that their identification of the trend was correct however. Small and invariably sectarian groupings did survive. Their survival was important and a significant matter for the later development of socialist politics, but they could not, and in practice largely did not, seek to provide a substitute for a mass movement.

The implications of all this for radical education were considerable. A reading of the *People's Paper* for 1857 showed this in practice but it could also be looked at theoretically, The direct link between political action and radical education had been broken. No doubt individuals maintained at least the idea of a link. In general, however, those workers looking for educational and political instruction would no longer turn to Chartist activity as the central provider. Nor, it would appear, were the Chartists themselves engaged in politically developing a new layer of activists through educational mechanisms, although Jones had tried with his *Evenings with the People*. The framework had changed. The new activist of the late 1850s now possessed a more limited political horizon and looked for a more 'practical' education through the cooperative or temperance movements. Such a search for knowledge could, although it did not always do so, lead to a political. affiliation to the Liberal Party which sought to harness such interests in a wide, if unstable, electoral coalition, There is truth in Richard Johnson's assessment that '[b]y the 1860s a section of the skilled organised working class had joined the Liberal agitation for a compulsory state system, while insisting on a secular curriculum and some measure of state control'.[24] Nevertheless, his view that 'the provided forms of schooling won out because they were better adapted to the new conditions and its relationships of times space or power or so it seemed in the, short run',[25] must remain debatable.

Really useful knowledge had not entirely disappeared but it had shifted its focus and terrain. There was now more demand for really *practical* knowledge about, for example, how to run a cooperative business within the context of a capitalist economy. The impact of the destruction of an independent working-class political party was therefore to remove directly political education from the agenda for all except a small minority. Paradoxically this was true even when radical education was elevated to the status of a strategy. Political radical education was a means to an end not an end in itself: this was the beginning of educational reformism. Again it was a process which developed throughout the later 1850s and beyond rather than a dramatic turning point at a particular moment. Holyoake noted in *Self Help for the People*, when discussing Co-operative support for Guiseppi Mazzini, that there was belief in Rochdale that 'cooperation was not divorced from citizenship' and went on to underline that 'whenever the Rochdale Society opens a new branch they open a new news-room'.[26]

### Ernest Jones and Evenings With The People, 1856-58

*Evenings With the People* spanned the period from when Chartism was still dominant in working-class radicalism up to 1856 and the period when it began to decline from 1857. A series of lectures at St Martins Hall in central

London were reprinted as tracts, often with critical comment from *The Times* associated with them. The lectures made a considerable impact at the time and survived as tracts into the long hinterland of post-Chartist radicalism up to the 1880s. The purpose of *Evenings With the People* was primarily educational. The aim was to restate a core of Chartist ideas – on emigration reform, foreign affairs, unemployment and the Church, and provide a political programme for late Chartism. There was less sign of the social radicalism of the 'Charter and Something More'. Jones had returned to basic Chartist principles although the subjects addressed were certainly wider than they would have been before 1848. The style of the lectures – long on detail and comparatively weak on analysis – was suited to a popular audience and designed for a large circulation. There was entertaintment as well as education.

There can be no doubt that *Evenings with the People* established Ernest Jones as the pre-eminent leader of late Chartism and the key radical leader of the period in general. No other leader could hope to attract comment in *The Times* on the efficacy or otherwise of their ideas, as Jones did with the lectures.[27] Even Miles Taylor notes of them that 'if there was little novelty, there was plenty of stirring entertainment'.[28] Jones re-established a radical hegemony for late Chartism. While he could no longer achieve organisational dominance over working-class radicalism, the kind of ideas which were central to *Evenings With the People* were those which were accepted by the vast majority of working-class radicals. It was not the ideas but what, if anything, ought to be done about them in practice which caused difficulties. Jones' hegemony stood over a radical movement that was increasingly splintered and disunited. This may be why Jones chose to address a series of single issues in his lectures rather than trying to lay down an overall radical strategy as he had done earlier in the decade. As developments were to show later in 1857 he had increasing doubts as to what such a strategy might be.

The events which led Ernest Jones to seek an alliance with the more advanced section of non-Chartist radicalism including some middle-class radicals have been accurately described by John Saville. Saville has noted the dual nature of Jones' project. On the one hand he has argued that Ernest Jones 'endeavoured to pursue a conciliatory policy towards the middle-class radicals'.[29] On the other hand Saville has noted that Jones's aim to maintain independent Chartist organisation was 'by no means incompatible with his desire for unity with middle-class radicalism'.[30] The impact on Jones of trying to pursue this dual strategy against the background of continued Chartist decline was noted by W.E. Adams, 'Ernest Jones kept the old flag flying till he was almost starved into surrender…A shabby coat buttoned close up round the throat teemed to conceal the poverty to which a too faithful adherence to a lost cause had reduced him'.[31] It is the longer term significance of these events and the analysis of them that remains open to question.

There seems little doubt that a combination of Jones's refusal to look beyond the traditional ranks of Chartism towards the trades and his belief that he, alone, could revive the Chartist movement led him to conclude that progress on the full programme of the Charter was now blocked and that it was necessary to attempt a united radical move on a more limited demand – manhood suffrage – in order to pave the way for further advance. While Jones was able to hold a conference in February 1858 which included numbers of non-Chartist radicals and was able to secure a degree of agreement on a reform campaign to secure manhood suffrage, his proposals for reform still went much further than any significant middle-class radical leader was prepared to go. His problem lay not in making too many concessions to middle-class radicalism but in his inability to grasp that he needed both to work with the radicals and maintain an independent working-class movement. Indeed, Miles Taylor finds Jones guilty of a 'lurch into the centre-ground of British radical politics'.[32]

The conference itself provided the best guide to how the political changes which Jones had sought would change the nature of radical education. This was the first Chartist conference where representatives of organised labour, the trades, attended as a separate and distinct grouping. It was a sign of Jones's isolation that they were grouped with middle-class radicals rather than treated as key partners in the fight for the suffrage, Moreover, they were now in a position to begin to launch their own journals and their own discussion groups and their need for Chartism was, perhaps, less than the need of Chartism for them.

Very few delegates opposed to the new move had been elected. In itself this was clearly not representative of the feelings and ideas held by those who still saw themselves as Chartists and now looked to G.W.M. Reynolds or Bronterre O'Brien rather than Jones. The most outspoken opponent of Jones, Henrette, was subjected to considerable ridicule. The discussion at the conference represented a new temper, which provided a moderate and conciliatory tone in the proceedings. Edward Hooson, a supporter of Ernest Jones from Manchester, was one of a number who drew educational implications from this change of mood. It was suggested that the Chartists would need to work with advanced Liberal politicians like John Bright. Accord with the radical middle class, if it could be reached, would clearly have implications for the form and direction of radical education. Even the emphasis on how far the Chartists were prepared to go to meet middle-class radicalism did not provide a basis for really effective campaigning. Holyoake argued that Chartism came with manhood suffrage in one hand and a stick in the other. Against this policy he argued that 'I would no more lend myself to set up a tyranny of the working classes over gentlemen and scholars, than I would sit quietly under a tyranny of the rich over the poor which under present arrangements certainly occurs'.[33] The key issue concerned both the impression and impact which the conference created. Jones was prepared to go only so far to meet the middle-class radicals. In reality therefore he continued to maintain a position of independent working-class politics. However, the impression which he now created was that he was quite prepared to deal with the radicals at almost at any price.

From a historical perspective his proposals for working-class suffrage reform movement were far removed from the most advanced middle-class proposals put forward by Bright. The overall impact of the whole affair was to demobilise Chartism and to spread confusion over what the issues and ideas now were which divided middle-class from working-class radicalism. Jones had laid the basis for the Reform League and for the ultimate victory of reform. He had also laid the basis for working-class support for the Liberal Party and a clear policy on the suffrage. For him it was something to be won through a fight rather than conceded by reform minded politicians. On the front page of *The Cabinet Newspaper* at the beginning of 1859 he argued: 'People! This is the problem you have to solve for 1859: Shall the franchise be the game of a class or the work of a people? With you rests the issue and with you we will do our utmost in the coming struggle'.[34] Jones argued that 1859 would be 'the Reform Year' if 'the people will it'.[35] He went on to warn against a ratepaying suffrage and suggested that this model of reform which fell a long way short of manhood suffrage, had only made progress because of the failure of the working class to organise actively against it. Certainly Jones's warning 'Beware, fellow countrymen! The old trick is about to be tried again, You will be sold once more if you do not take care'[36] did not sound like the language of someone who himself was supposed to have sold out his political independence to the middle classes.

This argument remained central to working-class political education. The suffrage had now replaced the Charter as the key political demand of the working class. Discussion and advice on how it could be won and what reform exactly would constitute a victory represented the issue of really useful knowledge in the highest order. While Jones had the mechanism in *The Cabinet* to spread this knowledge, circulation remained low. Even so the paper carried key arguments on the suffrage. For example, William Hill reported from Stalybridge on a call for a 'Conference of the Reformers'. By this he meant a unity conference between those still advocating the full Charter and those calling for manhood suffrage only. The background to this was the renewed assertion of the independence of working-class politics from middle-class reformers laid out by Jones.

Something further was needed, and provided, by the continuing rump of Chartist organisation. Reports from Chartist localities indicated a still thriving movement where it continued. For example an open air meeting on Caledonian Fields in early January 1859 was 'well attended'.[37] A veteran Chartist, Savage, read the Editorial from *The Cabinet* while another member of the old guard, James Bligh, highlighted the key political tasks of the moment which he felt to be 'a good Reform Bill' and the need to 'watch the would be leaders'.[38] From Bermondsey it was reported that 'Progress is being made'.[39] From Windy Nook in the North East Mr Watson from Newcastle 'commented strongly on the programme of Mr Bright clearly defining the rating clause, finally showing the same to be of no use to the working class of this country'[40]. The rise in the late 1850s of the Northern Reform Union, which had Tyneside Chartism as a central element, showed that Chartist ideas and activists could still help to inspire wider reform movements.[41] In an editorial several weeks later Jones attacked the Reform Bill which Bright had brought forward on the grounds that it was far too limited as it left four million adult male workers without the vote.[42]

Even as the 1850s turned to the 1860s Jones kept the Chartist message alive, but its educational impact became progressively more limited. Although *The Cabinet* gave increasing space to the activities of trade unions, these organisations now had their own means of both organisation and communication. Set against this were the increasingly bitter disputes amongst Chartists, ex-Chartists and post-Chartists which reached a peak with the libel action which Jones won against G.W.M. Reynolds. The squabbling over the legacy of Chartism left less space for any of the remaining Chartist groupings to address the future and allowed other radicalisms to take their place. The general point was that while *The Cabinet* and Jones still addressed issues, particularly manhood suffrage, which were of central importance to the working-class movement, these issues were increasingly addressed more effectively elsewhere. A key example was the Northern Reform Union, based in Newcastle and led by Joseph Cowen jnr and Richard Reed. This mobilised considerable numbers on the basis of suffrage reform, but on a marginally less radical programme than Chartism.[43]

### From Chartist Institutes to Mutual Improvement Societies, 1856-1860

This had a significant impact on the context, tone and style of radical education. Most of the Chartist educational activity that was reported in the *People's Paper* was, in fact, post-Chartist and often originated amongst those Chartists who chose to pursue an educational strategy for change. Several reports referred directly to activity which related to the still existing Land Company. One example was the Chartist Free Library, which opened at eight every evening at the Alma Coffee House, Edgware Road. This library was, formally, at least, the library of the London and O'Connerville Mutual Improvement Society.[44] Later in the same year a report direct from O'Connorville noted that:

> the attempt of the official manager under the Winding Up Act to sell the school house of O'Connorville having aroused the friends of education, such a misfortune is not likely to befall the Chartist farms. A most useful school is being established there at the lowest charges each scholar being presented with a handsome little bible and prayer book.[45]

While the education on offer may have been cheap, there was little evidence that there was any specifically radical intent, and some, as with the provision of prayer book and bible, that it may have been otherwise.

Stalybridge, on the other hand was, and remained, highly political in its provision of radical education. A report in early 1857 talked of a tea party the proceeds of which were to go to the Chartist Institute: 'The Chartists of this locality have now two rooms each capable of holding nearly 300 persons. They have already spent a considerable sum of money in purchasing furniture for their new room and when it is completed no Institute will have better accommodation for educating youth than our own'.[46] The emphasis on youth and on training up a new generation of radical political activists was unusual in a late Chartist movement often fixated on the 'Old Guard' of pre-1848 Chartists. The report went on to suggest that Stalybridge 'might spur on other localities, who disseminate knowledge while spreading political information. Our institute keeps increasing in numbers and shortly we shall have a school that will be an honour to Chartism....'[47] This report, issued by William Hill, made a highly pertinent distinction between knowledge which was seen as a good thing itself and the dissemination of political information which was here seen as a parallel rather than a fully integrated activity. A further report appeared in the *Peoples Paper* in summer 1858. The occasion was another social party and again the key figure was Hill who was reported as saying, 'He perceived the progress the institution had made since their last party ten weeks ago, £8 worth of books had been placed in the library, while several pounds had been spent in embellishing and adorning the institution; in addition to which arrangements were made for purchasing another library case'.[48] Here progress and knowledge were firmly linked but it was the progress of the Institution itself which took pride of place rather than the impact of the political knowledge which was disseminated. The most significant feature of the Stalybridge Chartist Institute was its continuation long after the collapse of Chartism as a national organisation. However, if the Institute remained within a notional framework of Chartist ideas it survived by accurately reflecting rather than leading the ideas of the workers that patronised it.

Neville Kirk has argued that at Stalybridge 'the onus for working-class advancement was increasingly placed upon the shoulders of workers themselves'.[49] This took place within the context of a retreat from independent working-class politics. Kirk therefore goes on to argue that 'leading figures at the Stalybridge Institute believed that the tasks of educational and personal improvement should provide the primary focus for the Institute'.[50] Given a working-class desire for independence that was turning in upon itself Neville Kirk misses how the Chartist Institute still followed a specific political strategy which was distinctively post-Chartist. Stalybridge in the later 1850s had a large variety of organisations which attracted working-class support. There were several mutual improvement societies, usually under the control of religious groups. There was Mossley Cooperative Society and there were also Turkish baths. While not necessarily mutually exclusive each of these institutions suggested a different path for working-class organisation. The Chartist Institute placed politics at the centre of its strategy, but this did not necessarily mean that it was Chartist politics of the type advanced by Feargus O'Connor or Ernest Jones.

*The Ashton Reporter* carried occasional reports of the activities of the Institute in the late 1850s and early 1860s. In October 1859 the paper noted that a speaker at the Institute had argued that workers must improve their own social and moral position.[51] They must, in other words, reform themselves and then the authorities would grant them the reforms they desired. This was very much a working-class version of the educational strategy for change favoured by G.J. Holyoake. Neville Kirk has followed Tholfsen in noting that education at Institutes such as Stalybridge 'was seen as intrinsically worthwhile'.[52] While this is correct, it is correct only if Stalybridge is seen within the general context of radical politics in the north west. There were alternative strategies available to the working class, In this sense the Stalybridge Institute represented an educational strategy where radical ideas and their transmission to a wider working-class audience came first. In this it was spectacularly successful. Not only did it attract 500 people to a fund raising evening for the Institute in October 1859[53] but it also had the funds and the desire to expand itself in order to take on more scholars. The central point that Neville Kirk has missed is that this was not a success for residual Chartism. It was a success, and a large one, for an important strand of post-Chartist politics.

In September 1860 the *Ashton Reporter* noted that 'The deification of the home was a recurrent theme in the lectures given by the men at the Stalybridge Chartist Institute'.[54] Here it was argued that the working man who spent his time in intellectual self-improvement would not only be better able to instruct his children but would provide for a happier domestic environment all round. While this view may have been more that of the journalist than a precisely accurate description of what had been said, there is little doubt that where women did participate in radical educational endeavours in the north-west in the later 1850s, they did so in an environment defined by male working-class radicalism, as were the ideas discussed.

Stalybridge was not the only Chartist institute which survived the demise of Chartism as a national organisation. Newcastle and some of the clubs controlled by supporters of Bronterre O'Brien in London also continued. However, as Nigel Todd has pointed out, Joseph Cowen Jnr. visited a large number of regional centres in 1858 and found a popular campaign for the suffrage only in Rochdale.[55] But the context of Chartism now meant that though the knowledge gained did not feed directly into political activism, the acquisition of knowledge was nevertheless seen as a broadly political activity. The struggle for knowledge, if not party political, was still firmly identified with a working-class struggle for change. Here then was defined a more limited focus of working-class independence than that represented by Chartism, but it was independence all the same.

There was an immense contradiction which opened up as the 1850s turned into the 1860s. On the one hand, the organisation of working-class interests in terms of trade unions was growing rapidly. Yet, just as rapidly, the independent political representation of these interests was declining. This meant that while the new trade unions and cooperatives often did have a capacity to provide education, the content of the education was often merely useful rather than really useful knowledge. In terms of radical education the matter went further. Key contradictions existed between what could be labelled an almost autodidactic educational culture and the influence of Liberalism which represented, at heart, the interests of capital. The reconciliation of these two, if they were to be reconciled, remained a central area of exploration.

Nottingham NCA No. 2 Branch had set up a People's Improvement Library and the Quarterly Meeting was able to report 70 members and 46 books purchased during that quarter, bringing the total number held to over 90. Opening hours were 11-12.30 on Sundays and 7-8 in the evenings.[56] Again, while there was a political connection, there was no specific evidence of direct political intent, aside from self-improvement by means of knowledge. At Greenwich and Deptford a library had been set up at the Fox, Union St, Greenwich. The subscription was one penny weekly and 'Democrats' were invited to participate.[57] An earlier report indicated that subscribers could take a book home to read, while the library itself was run by the already post-Chartist formulation 'the friends of progress'.[58] Previous trends in radical education did continue. For example, a report in the *The Reasoner* for Spring 1859 from Barrowford noted : 'we are keeping a good night and Sunday school and we have opened a free library'.[59]

The emphasis on libraries and self-knowledge was clearly susceptible to a degree of commercial exploitation. This was not necessarily successful although Abel Heywood in Manchester did provide an example of a leading figure who gained commercial success in this way. One well documented case was that of the General Circulating Library of T. Riley which advertised 'cheap reading'. The library contained a 'choice, rare and select stock of books worthy of the attention of Free inquirers and liberal minded readers, A general stock of Stationery, Book Binding. *The Reasoner, National Reformer* and all the liberal publications of the day in stock or had to order'. The library was in Halifax. This appeared in May 1860[60] but similar references appeared several times in the late 1850s. The converse to private provision were those of the Literary Institutes such as the one at Royton, reported in the first issue of the *National Reformer* as having 'about 94 members, all young men, the most active being freethinkers. They have two comfortable rooms for reading and classes, well lighted'.[61]

The more libraries and institutes such as these developed, the more politics became incidental. Yet, on the other hand radical activists, while they may not have been a part of this were aware of it. Hence, for example, *The Reasoner* set up a Book and Secular Tract Distribution Depot: 'We have made up a fresh lot of packets of Secular Books and Tracts to meet the demand so often made for Secular Tracts for Distribution. Each packet contains a book of not less than 1s in value and tracts of not less than 2s in value. This new batch contains some works given specifically for this purpose, There are also portraits of Cobbett, Mazzini, Strauss, These tracts are well adapted for propagandist purposes.'[62] *The Reasoner* serviced a movement not entirely of its own creation, in which its influence was uncertain, although still potentially significant. Indeed, the dominant feature of radical educational activity and provision in this period can be seen as in and against this dichotomy of secular propaganda and mutual instruction. The most frequently mentioned improvement society was that in Coventry. All reports appeared in *The Reasoner*, indicating at least a notional secular affiliation. The first for this period read:

> Some few years ago you inserted in the *The Reasoner* a paper read by me to the above society and you appended to it some remarks about the desirability of such societies for female education. Within this last twelve months our members have acted upon your suggestion and so far as to give the fair sex a fair opportunity of mental improvement. A reading room has also been started recently to open at six o'clock on Saturday evenings…Now factories are generally closing at an early hour on Saturday this suggestion may be worth something,

We intend to commence a Secular Sunday School...for "adults and young persons...as there is nothing of the kind in Coventry".[63]

The next report, which appeared in November, gave a detailed history of the society, laying claim, it must be suspected, to Coventry as a model society which others should follow:

> The Coventry Mutual Improvement Society, which commenced in 1851, has through the continued perseverance of its founders who are all working men, not only kept its position as a thoroughly free and independent society but has of late made rapid strides in the direction of more extended usefulness. Its members who had declined to ten in that season of trial and difficulty which it had, in common with many working mens societies, to pass through, are now nearly six times that number. It is evident that so large a number of persons have great power in extending the work of education, however humble their position in life maybe. Its members now think they would be doing their duty to that large class of persons who have been totally excluded from weekday schooling, if they did not at least endeavour to reserve some from that degradation which must ever attend ignorance, They therefore, with this object in view, started a Sunday school for adults and young persons above the age of fourteen on Sunday November 7th. The school will be conducted on purely Secular principles, no theology whatever will be allowed to be discussed in the room in school hours. The school opens in the morning at half past nine o'clock and closes at twelve. It has been decided that those persons who attend this school for three months shall have free use of the Society Library which now consists of upwards of 250 readable volumes.[64]

The report was, as usual, from the secretary W. Shuttlebottom. A report in Spring 1859 reproduced a circular which had been printed to publicise the Society:

> It is now more than seven years since a few young men in this city fully sensible of the great usefulness of Mutual Improvement Societies determined upon founding one that should be entirely free from any sectarian test and independent of external control. The only qualification imposed upon candidates for membership being good moral character. During that period they have held weekly meetings for mutual instruction and through donations from friends and by occasional small purchases of books they have accumulated a library of upwards of 200 volumes for the use of the members at their homes; and further, having in view the fearful evil of public house drinking, they have held tea parties and social gatherings thus providing innocent recreation as well as instruction for the members friends. All this has been effected entirely by the voluntary contributions of the members. Desiring to extend the usefulness of their society the members have recently commenced a Sunday School and an

evening school for the instruction of as many children and young persons as they are able to accommodate – preference being given to those whose education has been entirely neglected.[65]

A further report was published in early 1860 and noted 'Our Sunday School which started at a much inferior room is now doing much more good and we feel naturally proud that as an educational society we are endeavouring to do something beyond our own circle to help the rising generation.[66]

The Mutual Improvement Society and its partial successor, the working men's club, were central to the rehabilitation of 'useful' as opposed to 'really useful' knowledge. Of course the resurgence of usefulness had to be on a new basis to that found prior to 1832, which is perhaps why it is mentioned in the context of a great or extended form of usefulness. According to John Foster, the mutual improvement societies were the preserve of the labour aristocracy and a potential bridge into the middle class. In other words they were a way of acquiring knowledge to develop supervisory and specialist skills now beginning to be needed by capital. Evidence from Coventry does indicate that the societies appealed to what has come to be known as the ''respectable' sections of the working classes. Respectable for what purpose however was another question. Neville Kirk has noted that 'self-help and respectability were sometimes seen as a means of both individual and class empowerment, as the means of enabling the membership, as conscious agents of history, to develop sufficient powers of reason, organisation, independence and confidence to fashion their own destinies.'[67]

Firstly, and significantly, Coventry maintained a secularist affiliation. All the above reports appeared in *The Reasoner*. The affiliation may have been largely notional, but it is clear that secularism held an appeal for a minority of articulate working-class men and women. In terms of organisation they would need to have been educated, at least to a fair standard of literacy, to make any sort of sense of what secularism was about. On specific issues a wider audience might be reached. It seems possible in the case of Coventry that the key determinant of its Secularist affiliation was opposition to religious interference.

The Mutual improvement Society at Coventry had been active since 1851 and frequently reported its activities in *The Reasoner*. These reports related how the society had broken away from religious control and set itself up independently. The emphasis on independence and the class status of its activists was a key feature of mutual improvement societies. The social and political outlook of these men may be of interest. To an extent this would have been determined by events. Their Secularist outlook was provoked by religious interference and the period when the membership declined to ten must also have made a considerable impact. No existing study is able to suggest a reason for what Coventry implied was a general crisis in such societies or its date. Obviously it was some time between 1851 and the late 1850s. Informed speculation might suggest that it was in the mid-1850s during the period of the Crimean War, when much radicalism suffered a severe crisis. The emphasis on self and mutual help, which the crisis no doubt fostered, should not be underestimated.

The stress on mutual improvement rather than self-improvement was significant however. The mechanism for improvement was, as with all educational strategists, education. Education was to be provided in a collective manner. The strategy was for the core of activists in the Society themselves to provide education for a wider audience. Here the emphasis on those who had lived in degradation leading to ignorance and those who had been exposed to the 'fearful evil of public house drinking' was important. Formal education was not necessarily the initial key. Rather this was to provide counter-attractions to the public house. Tea parties and social gatherings were held. The emphasis was on formal education, however. Both Sunday and evening schools were set up, in due course (almost ten years after the society was founded). The order of progression was also clear enough. Those who attended one of the schools regularly for three months were allowed use of the library and thence presumably into the society itself, where they too could become educators.

What age of person was to be instructed is not clear from the reports. The trend, in the late 1850s, was towards educational provision for young adults who had failed to receive education as children. Yet this was not usually the function of secularist Sunday Schools which had a tradition of providing an alternative to religiously funded and controlled Sunday provision. It might be expected therefore, that the evening school catered for young adults. However, it is unclear if the children and young adults were exclusively male. Little detail was provided but there was an unusual indication that attention was paid to attracting women through the mechanism of a reading room. Probably the key element behind all this was the extension of early closing on Saturday afternoons. This enabled the shopping and leisure activities of Sunday morning to occur on Saturday afternoons or early evenings, leaving Sunday free, potentially, for educational purposes. Of course, other, sometimes commercial, attractions were available or beginning to become so but there was still a potentially significant new opening to be exploited here for the radical educationists.

Reports of the activity of other mutual improvement societies were sporadic, as many were quite consciously outside the sphere of overt radical politics. These echoed a similar pattern. For example, Dudley Mutual Improvement

Society reported that 'a Working Man's News Room has been opened where, for a penny a week, the members enjoy the privilege of reading the weekly and other papers. It promises to succeed'.[68] The question about the effectiveness of mutual improvement was under discussion in radical circles. For example in late 1857 at Caledonian Fields, North London (a Chartist locality) a discussion was opened where it was argued that mutual instruction had been tried and failed. To this Bligh replied: 'Perseverance alone would gain us the Charter and perseverance in obtaining knowledge would alone fit us to make a proper use of our rights when we get the power'.[69]

Conversely in the late fifties, Secularism was still able, here and there, to give an organised radical expression to education. For example, Thomas Whittaker, the secretary of the New Howland St Institution, which was to replace John Street when it closed on June 8th 1858, wrote to the Vestry of St Pancras: 'It is true we advocate Secular Education and we are not at all singular in that, as is evidenced by the many Secular Schools now established throughout England. The Secular Schools have been and are being established to prevent the massed from being longer left without any education at all'.[70] Whether Whittaker was accurate in claiming such a large network of secular schools is dubious. It is likely that such schools did exist, from time to time, in many of the major centres of population. Certainly, there is evidence that teachers were offering services to secular education. For example, Hugh Fulton, who in the 1860s became teacher at Howland Street, advertised in *The Reasoner*, 'Mr Hugh Fulton public lecturer begs, most respectfully to intimate to his Secular friends and the public generally that he is, wishful to enter into engagements. Formerly a schoolmaster he has no objection to conduct a day, school in conjunction with his platform duties. His course comprises Politics, Theology, Literature, History and Biography'.[71] At least some Chartists followed what may be called the educational strategy for change, a trend that particularly identified with secularist politics. One example was from a lecture given at Manchester Secular Society in summer 1858 where the speaker Mr Child from Brighton said '...Education to become general and useful...must be compulsory and Secular, only when we have established a national system of Secular Education can we expect men to win their social and political rights'.[72]

### Working Men's Colleges and other alternatives

The years 1857-60 were difficult times for radicals, and radical education was no exception. The collapse, in the main, of the political framework which had inspired and supported such education, while it did not destroy it, prevented much in the way of significant advance. Where an overt political connection remained it was sometimes in the hands of educational strategists, who saw education, above all, as the key to transforming society.

The period thus saw the continued development and increased significance of radical education which had no, or only notional, links to radical politics. Such education, frequently undertaken by mutual improvement societies, may perhaps not be regarded as radical at all. Against this must be considered three factors, Firstly, it was almost exclusively patronised by working men, and occasionally women. It was set up either because of lack of alternative provision or in opposition to it. Secondly, it was almost invariably secular. Thirdly, unlike others it discussed politics and had a view of knowledge as political, although in a much diminished form.

An alternative trend, also concentrating on these points and looking towards a more formal basis for adult working-class education, were the Working Men's Colleges. The original College had been set up in 1854 by middle-class radicals, most of whom were Christian Socialists, as one of the earlier fruits of the beginnings of the break-up of Chartism. The real success of the Working Men's College lay in the fact that radicals such as Maurice and Ludlow were able to attract a small but significant layer of working-class Chartists and secularists who were not only able to provide legitimacy for the College but also run its day-to-day operation.

The later 1850s saw the London College consolidate its initial success and several other Colleges began to function in Salford, Manchester and Wolverhampton. In each case those attending were considerably more working class than those who had been attracted to Mechanic's Institutes, although there was still a preponderance of clerks and other semi-skilled non-manual workers. The key point was that the Colleges were not hostile to operatives or factory workers and did in fact attract them in considerable numbers.

The subjects taught, which were dictated by their popularity amongst students, were neither what the Christian Socialist founders had expected or in conformity with a model of 'really useful knowledge'. Rather they represented what might he called really *practical* knowledge. A significant number of students came to the Colleges to learn basic education which they had earlier missed. They were not turned away in the hope that they might eventually progress to more advanced subjects. History, literature and political economy found but sparse following compared to French and Latin, and, as J.F.C. Harrison has noted, there was a pattern of development during the early years which was not what the founders had anticipated.[73] The number of students who attended showed that the College was meeting a real need, but it was not quite the need which the founders had originally thought it was their mission to meet. However, it might be considered that many of the students already knew a considerable amount about history, books, politics and economics. Perhaps they did not trust the Colleges to teach them in a liberal manner in such areas, a mistrust almost certainly ill conceived, or perhaps they now sought the kind of education which previously had only been available to their 'betters'.

By 1860 the Working Men's Colleges had begun to be a major player in formal working-class education. Unlike many Mechanics' Institutes they did not bar working-class radicals. This represented a victory for the struggles of the Chartists and others in the previous twenty years. Whether they agreed with them or not the, middle-class radical backers of the colleges now had to take working-class students on their own terms. Indeed, there was a considerable dispute when a report in the *People's Paper* suggested that Maurice had been the founder rather than the facilitator of the London College. The colleges reflected a situation where a working class had begun to develop which was more stable, and was able to see a future within the existing system and sought the knowledge to be able to progress in that context. This schema applied equally whether the student had in mind to become a skilled worker or foreman or an activist in the now developing labour movement.

Some of the seeds of radical education in the 1860s were laid in the late 1850s. Co-operative education had its roots in this period. The maintenance of secular education provided a heritage for a rejuvenated Secularist movement under Bradlaugh. The continuing activity of small pockets of Chartist radicals was to be a feature of working-class life for the next 30 years and more. The most notable change however was that such education was now focused more on the young adult than the child. The dominant Chartist trend in radical education was moving toward a role as an adjunct to that provided elsewhere. The direct political links were broken in places but the political context and the milieu of radical activism remained. However, this activism often saw radical education as part of a wider agenda of political activity, ranging from co-operation to trade unionism and republicanism rather than the centre of a strategy for change which it had been for a significant group of radicals, led by Holyoake and others in the years after 1848.

The late 1850s was a time of organisational transition for radical leaders and radical ideas. Ernest Jones's *Evenings With the People* can be seen, in retrospect, as a last attempt to provide a Chartist framework of ideas for radical activists and radical education. *The Times* praised one of Jones's early lectures in the following terms: 'With an eulogy of Chartism and an exhortation to abide by it, concluded a discourse that was certainly a masterpiece'.[74] However, such was the impact of the series of lectures that by early 1857 the same paper slammed a speech by Jones at Smithfield in London with the cry that 'there it no good reason why the monopoly of the trade of Demagogues should be left to Ernest Jones and his partners in discord'.[75]

However, in order to understand the evolution of radical education in this period it is important to grasp that the series of lectures that comprised *Evenings With the People* were not simply political rallies. Jones styled them as 'political soirees' and sought to combine 'elevating Recreation' with 'Political Instruction'. In practice this meant that Jones's political speech was combined with vocal and instrumental music. Jones himself argued that the aim was to take politics out of the Tavern. In other words, Jones's project was to place the whole basis of working-class political and recreational culture on a more sober and critical basis. Jones had ten more years as a radical leader before his untimely death in 1869, but already he was involved with the transition from Chartism to radical Liberal politics.

In the early 1860s new radical leaders started to come forward who had little or no connection with Chartism, or were associated only with its final period after 1848. People like Joseph Cowen Jnr and Charles Bradlaugh, while certainly not disowning Chartism, had other, post-Chartist, strategies and ideas to pursue. Moreover, they did so in a climate where organised labour and co-operation were now major features of life for any radical activist.

Joseph Cowen Jnr who had been a youthful Chartist activist in 1848 and was now a successful Tyneside businessman. In January 1858 he set up the Northern Reform Union (NRU), which was launched at a meeting at the Newcastle Chartist Institute. As Cowen's modern biographer Nigel Todd has noted, 'these meetings were planned carefully to position the NRU as the heir to the Chartist crown yet distanced from Chartism in order to cultivate the middle classes'.[76] Cowen focused the NRU on the ideas of manhood suffrage which were similar to but rather narrower than the old Six Points of the People's Charter. He was concerned above all, however, to give the politics of reform a new image. As Todd has noted, 'The Union was located in Newcastle's imposing Grainger Street at smart offices "beautifully lighted by pane and gas, and as handsomely and completely fitted up as a merchant's office in Manchester"'.[77]

The composition of the NRU gives a significant clue as to the constituency that a progressive radical education could look to in the late 1850s. NRU branches revolved around Radicals, Chartists, Secularists and those active in co-operative, benefit and teetotal societies, trade unions and mechanics institutes.[78] The instrument which Cowen used to forge this alliance towards new forms of radical ideas and activity was the *Newcastle Daily Chronicle* which he had gradually taken control of between 1857 and late 1859. Todd notes of the impact that the *Chronicle* made that 'the old world of Chartism gave way to new landmarks'.[79] While, as Ashton and Pickering argue,[80] the NRU was not immediately successful at the ballot box, it laid down the parameters within which radical Liberalism on Tyneside had to work, and saw Joseph Cowen Jnr returned as a Liberal MP.

## Conclusion

Recent studies by movement theorists such as Sidney Tarrow help to explain the general processes at work here in terms of an incorporation of radical activism and ideas within the existing system. Protest became institutionalized, while political activism began to become professionalised. This is an important process to understand in terms of radical activism in the later 1850s. There had developed a tendency for radical activists, black-listed from or unavailable for employment, to take a job within the broad radical movement, perhaps as a teacher or lecturer, as a journalist or someone involved in a radical business such as the Land Plan or insurance and benefit societies. The numbers of professional activists were small then, and have remained so, but their position was significant. By 1860 a few had taken paid positions with trade unions and Co-operative societies, while others began to pick up occasional sponsorship from radical Liberals. Yet others such as W.E. Adams began to find influential positions in the new wave of regional papers launched after the final repeal of the Stamp Duty in 1855.

They did not, of course, give up radical politics, but nevertheless they had been brought within the existing political framework, at least for most purposes and for most of the time. Changes in the structure and framework of radical activism also meant changes for radical education in this period. One area already noted was the development of a limited radical middle-class patronage with Joseph Cowen as the leading example. A second was the development of a series of institutions such as Co-operatives and trade union branches which had some grasp of really useful knowledge but increasingly within the framework of the developing liberal capitalist state structure. A third area was the development of institutions of mutual improvement. Nowhere better could be seen the complexity of changes in radical education at this period.

The focus here has been on examples of politically radical mutual improvement societies, but there was a wide range of other societies. Neville Kirk has demonstrated for north-west England that any suggestion that such societies were the exclusive presence of workers seeking individual betterment and advancement is wrong. The occupations of those attending mutual improvement societies went far beyond the layer of skilled workers who may have comprised a labour aristocracy.

In fact, it is possible to track societies which were entirely radical and independent in comparison to those which avoided politics altogether. The key point that is missing from existing studies is that many of the societies became important sites of class struggle and the battle of ideas between working- and middle-class radicalism. Workers had different reasons for attending the societies and took different things from them. A study of the reading rooms in Carlisle underlines this point.[81] Their importance and development can be seen as part of a specific moment of radical education which arose from the decline of Chartism before a new radical landscape had been formed. As the 1850s drew to a close the range of providers of radical education had extended considerably. So, however, had the meaning of what radical education was, Workers could find discussion, books, lectures and conviviality at surviving Chartist and Secularist institutes, mutual improvement societies, temperance societies and Co-operative reading rooms.

This education was often rather less overtly politicised than it had been ten years previously. The decline in sales of working-class and left-wing papers underlined that the specific radical milieu had shrunk. However, as the rapidly expanding sales of *Reynolds's Newspaper* also indicated, there was still a huge market for general radical ideas to the left of the Liberal Party. It was certainly not the case that radical education had now simply become education for individual self-improvement only. Matters were more complex.

Individual self-improvement in itself was now sharply political and it begged the question, often answered in the negative, as to whether 'the system' was open even to educated working men and women. Where educational provision was made under the auspices of radical middle-class sponsors, as was the case with Working Men's Colleges and temperance groups, the audience attracted was often anything but the respectable labour aristocratic worker of labour history mythology. In reality the audience was more working class and not at all amenable to studying subjects which the sponsors thought were good for them.

These contradictory organisational developments and political ideas, present as Chartism broke up as a national presence, were something that radicals were well aware of at the time.

Thomas Wright, a far from typical journeyman engineer, who wrote 'The Great Unwashed', also produced a short story, 'Bill Banks' Day Out'.[82] In it he relates the story of Bill Banks, a stoker and his wife Bessie Banks' trip, with others, to Hampton Court one Saint Monday. In the story Banks is at times rough and at times respectable, both drinking and thinking. The story was written in 1868 but it captures well the temper and mood of a developing working class that was conscious of its status, well aware of old traditions like Saint Monday but also looking for self improvement.

Colin Barker,[83] writing about the European left and labour movement in the same period, has argued that it needs to be understood not as one thing or another but as a 'field of argument' where competing and sometimes contradictory trends were at work.

**Notes**

1   Staughton Lynd, Labour/Le Travallieur, 50, p. 178.
2   Ibid., p. 182.
3   Patrick Joyce, *Work, Society, Politics*, Brighton, 1980.
4   G.J. Holyoake, *Self Help For The People*, London, 1858.
5   J. Breuilly et al, (Eds) *The Era of the Reform League*, Mannheim, 1995, p. 15.
6   John Vincent, *History of the British Liberal Party, 1857-1868* Harmondsworth, 1972, p. 131.
7   See also for Thomas Burt, Lowell J. Satre, *Thomas Burt, Miners' MP, 1837-1922: the Great Conciliator*, London, 1999.
8   Nigel Todd, *The Militant Democracy*, Tyne and Wear, 1991, p. 9.
9   Karl Marx, 26 February 1858, In Marx and Engels, *Collected Works*, Volume 40, London, 1983.
10  John Vincent, op. cit.
11  Vincent op. cit.
12  Vincent op. cit.
13  Karl Marx 25 December 1857, op. cit.
14  Karl Marx 16 January 1858, op. cit.
15  Miles Taylor, op. cit., p. 183.
16  Friedrich Engels, 19 February 1858, op. cit.
17  Ibid.
18  Karl Marx 21 September 1858, op. cit.
19  Friedrich Engels, 7 October 1858, op. cit.
20  Ibid.
21  Miles Taylor, op. cit. p. 184.
22  Karl Marx, 8 October 1858, op. cit.
23  John Breuilly et al, *The Era of the Reform League*, op cit, p. 15.
24  Richard Johnson, *Really Useful Knowledge* in Tom Lovett (Ed) *Radical Approaches to Adult Education*, London, 1988, p. 25.
25  Ibid.
26  G.J. Holyoake, *Self Help for the People*, London, 1857, p. 152.
27  *The Times*, 1857.
28  Miles Taylor op. cit. p. 180.
29  John Saville, *Ernest Jones*, London, 1952, p. 63.
30  John Saville, Ibid.
31  W.E. Adams, *Memoirs of A Social Atom*, p. 230.
32  Miles Taylor op. cit. p. 183.
33  G.J. Holyoake, *The Workman and the Suffrage*, London, 1858.
34  *The Cabinet Newspaper*, 1 January 1859.
35  Ibid.
36  Ibid.
37  Ibid., 15 January 1859.

38  Ibid.
39  Ibid.
40  Ibid.
41  See Owen R. Ashton and Paul A. Pickering, *Friends of the People*, London, 2002, Chapter 5 'A Newspaper genuis, Richard Bagnall Reed'.
42  Ibid., 5 February 1859.
43  Ashton and Pickering, op. cit.
44  *People's Paper* 3 January 1857.
45  Ibid., 13 June 1857.
46  Ibid., 10 January 1857.
47  Ibid.
48  Ibid., 3 July 1858.
49  Neville Kirk p. 223.
50  Ibid.
51  *The Ashton Reporter*, 29 September 1860
52  Neville Kirk, *The Growth of Working Class Reformism in Mid-Victorian*, London, 1985, p. 213.
53  Ibid., 8 October 1859.
54  Ibid., 29 September 1860.
55  Nigel Todd, op. cit., p. 45.
56  *People's Paper* 21 March 1857.
57  Ibid., 18 April 1857.
58  Ibid., 21 March 1857.
59  *The Reasoner*, 10 April 1859.
60  *National Reformer*, 12 May 1860.
61  Ibid., 14 April 1860.
62  *The Reasoner*, 11 August 1858.
63  Ibid.
64  Ibid., 14 November 1858.
65  Ibid., 3 April 1859.
66  Ibid., 5 February 1860.
67  Neville Kirk, 1999, p. 31.
68  *The Reasoner*, 6 March 1859.
69  Ibid., 14 November 1857.
70  Ibid., 10 February 1858.
71  Ibid., 30 June 1858.
72  Ibid., 4 August 1858.
73  J.F.C. Harrison, *History of the Working Mens College 1854-1954*, London, 1954.
74  *The Times*, 9 October 1856.
75  Ibid., 19 February 1857.
76  Nigel Todd op. cit., p. 48.
77  Ibid., p. 44.
78  Ibid., p. 47.
79  Ibid., p. 50.
80  Ashton and Pickering, 2002, op. cit.
81  Brian Graham, *The Carlisle Working Men's Reading Rooms*, Nottingham, 1983.

82 Thomas Wright, *Bill Banks Day Out*, London, 1868.
83 Colin Barker, *In the Middle Way*, International Socialism, 101, 2003 p. 74.

## Chapter 7
## The Politics of Radical Education in the 1860s: 'Really Useful Knowledge' and the 1870 Education Act

If we take the view that a battle of ideas between the working classes and the middle classes is always present in one form or another in society, then it becomes impossible to sustain interpretations of post-1848 British history which contemplate only the collapse of Chartism and a total capitulation to the Liberal Party by former working-class radicals by the early 1860s. Rather, what can be seen is a process of struggle for influence, for ideas and for political change, which led almost in a contrary fashion not only to the 1870 Education Act but also to the election of Benjamin Lucraft, a supporter not of the Liberal Party but of the First International, to the London School Board.

The radical politics and ideas of the 1850s shaped those of the 1860s particularly because the 1850s was a period of dissolution of forms and concepts of radical politics and organisation that had existed for 20 years or more and also as a result of the emergence of new landmarks on the radical map such as organised labour and co-operative societies. However, if the emphasis in the 1860s switched to respectable working men and reform, that decade also saw an echo of the violent confrontations of earlier decades with the Sheffield trade union 'outrages'. The most recent history to address the period has noted that 'where some have stressed the equipoise of the 1850 to 1880 period [there are] examples of continuing struggle and resistance...both conflict and conciliation governed the activities of the organised working-class'.[1]

There were some particularly significant markers. *Reynolds's Newspaper*, which had been a minor radical paper in the late 1840s and early 1850s, was able, brilliantly, to exploit the repeal of the newspaper stamp in 1855. By the early 1860s it had a weekly readership in excess of 300,000 copies. It was popular in format, and popular in politics. This latter meant, by and large, an emphasis on Chartist ideas yet with a radical focus provided by single issue campaigns; for example, on conditions for ordinary soldiers in the army. By the 1880s *Reynolds's Newspaper* was supporting the Social Democratic Federation and always saw itself as radical in politics. The fact that it sold many times the number of copies of the liberal broadsheet papers is highly significant and almost entirely uncommented on. Rohan McWilliam has noted that, 'Integral to the creation of a working-class public sphere was the radical press, for example... *Reynolds's Newspaper* which commenced publication in 1850 and lasted 'till 1967, blending sensational stories with political polemic. The press helped generate a movement culture, the awareness of belonging to a movement'.[2]

The repeal of the stamp also saw a rapid growth of liberal and radical provincial papers highlighting the trend towards the growth of radicalisms on a regional basis rather than with a national focus.

John Vincent has noted that 'Before 1855 the press was dominated by and took its tone from the traditional holders of power who dominated Parliament. After 1861 the press was a chiefly popular institution, representative of classes with little weight in Parliament'.[3] However, while Vincent has argued that the new papers were 'democratic but not Radical, cheap but respectable'[4] and that they killed the old type of Chartist tract, the reality was that the main beneficiary of the change was precisely *Reynolds's Newspaper*, the key post-Chartist working-class newspaper.

The 1850s also raised the question of working-class engagement with Liberal politics and this became the dominant theme of the following decade. What has often been missed from historical accounts particularly, for example, the recent work of E. Biagini,[5] is that the engagement was far from total. In fact what came with this engagement was also the construction of an independent working-class politics that specifically did not engage fully with the Liberal Party. This often took the form of what appear to be quite eccentric movements, such as Foreign Affairs Committees and the Turkish Bath movement, but in a period of retreat for radical politics and reformulation of radical political ideas these provided the basis for independent activity.

Another key issue is what Martin Hewitt refers to, in the context of post-1848 Manchester, as the cash nexus.[6] If the working class was to take the road of pragmatic labourism, it was not an easy option by any means. It required funding and time to provide the infrastructure of the new radicalism, whether it was the trade union hall or the co-operative store. Some of this money could be collected from the working-class, but not enough of it. It required hard choices about how to deal with the patronage of the radical middle class and, ultimately, which of their ideas could be lived with or accepted and which could not. As Nigel Todd has demonstrated, this process was probably pioneered most effectively in Newcastle where the configuration of radical liberalism in the 1860s was different to that of Manchester.[7]

A new form of independent working-class politics and independent working-class radical ideas began to develop as a result of this battle to co-exist within the system of market capitalism and constitutional democracy. It meant, as Marx noted when he came to write the address of the First International, a softening in the tone of language since the days of Chartist ascendancy. It also meant, however, a deeper base of organisation within society as the working class, in Gramscian terms, began to erect the trenches and battlements with which it could fight within the system.

While it is important to focus on the 'extreme sections', namely those working-class radicals who were to maintain a clear independent working-class political organisation and ideology in the 1860s, it is also important not to ignore the more mainstream leadership of post-Chartist politics. George Howell was clearly part of this, as were some people clearly identified with the extreme sections like Jones's ally James Finlen. Others, such as the veteran radical Benjamin Lucraft were neither part of the new wave of trade unionists nor the extreme sections. Lucraft became the leader of the North London Political Union (NLPU), an off-shoot of the Chartist and middle-class reform conference in February 1858, which Lucraft had chaired jointly.

Lucraft was over fifty in 1860 and an experienced radical and trade unionist, but he had only come to national prominence in the later 1850s. The NLPU was able to attract new layers of activists interested in manhood suffrage but these were not middle-class radicals but trade unionists like George Howell. The NLPU may be seen, then, as the meeting of a post-Chartist and trade unionist outlook on reform, which was given a more concrete political focus with the birth of the International Working Men's Association on which Lucraft sat, until he resigned over the Paris Commune in 1871.

### The changing landscape of radical politics and ideas in the 1860s

According to Edward Royle in a recent article which compares the similarities between Chartism and Owenism, 'This joint Chartist-Owenite legacy proved to be more widespread and enduring than that other "Charter and Something More" of the Marxist-socialist tradition'.[8] It is an interesting point, not only because it takes as a given that there was a legacy from Chartism in the 1860s and beyond, but also because it recognises that the legacy was a disputed one.

Engels summed up one view of the working class in the 1860s when, writing to Marx on the results of the 1868 General Election, he noted that

> everywhere the working class is the rag, tag and bobtail of the official parties, and if any party has gained strength from the new voters it is the Tories…it all shows up the disastrous political ineptitude of the English working class. The parson has shown unexpected power and so has the cringing to respectability. Not a single working-class candidate had the ghost of a chance but my Lord

Tom Noddy or any parvenu snob could have the workers' votes with pleasure....[9]

Engels' view has coloured many historical commentaries on the post-Chartist working class but it is far from the whole picture. On one key point Engels was absolutely right. There was no significant independent working-class political force at the 1868 Election. But this fact suggests other perspectives.

Newly enfranchised working-class voters were faced with a choice between two bourgeois parties, the Liberals and Tories. While it has traditionally been thought that the Liberals were more favourable to working-class politics, and allowed a handful of working-class politicians such as Ernest Jones to stand on their ticket, the Tories also made a bid for working-class support, based on working-class hostility to Liberal employers and their belief in a Gradgrindian political economy.

There is no doubt that where backward elements of the working class had been enfranchised by the 1867 Reform Act the Tories would have been a considerably more appealing party than the Liberals. However at the same time Marx was involved with the Land and Labour League – formed out of some of the working-class elements of the Reform League – which he hoped would form a new independent working-class party. In the event this did not happen, which suggests that Engels' analysis was broadly correct. However, it was not possible simply to write off the working class, not grasping that there were significant elements that did not support either the Liberals or Tories but were grappling towards new forms of independent labour representation.

Both Marx and Engels were active in trying to organise independent working-class political activity; Engels in Manchester, Marx in London. Marx was central to the formation of the First International and exercised real influence over the trade union and working-class elements of the Reform League. For both there was a political balance to strike. Many of those with whom they worked were prepared to deal with radical Liberals, a position to which they were firmly opposed. They concentrated, therefore, on ensuring that the demands that were put forward were distinctively working-class. The call for manhood suffrage, for example, was beyond anything that Gladstone wanted or would be able to get through in the 1867 Reform Act. In these activities the role of Ernest Jones, the best known working-class leader in the 1860s, was of vital importance, and Marx and Engels recognised this.

Until the recent biography by Miles Taylor the trajectory of Ernest Jones in the 1860s has been little discussed. In his introduction to a recent volume of Chartist studies, *The Chartist Legacy*, Asa Briggs points out that a narrative history of Chartism remains to be written and that a particular point of dispute has been the date when it should start and end.[10] At the moment, however, while it is commonly understood that events following on from Peterloo in 1819 led directly to the formation of the Chartist movement in 1837, the decade of the 1860s has been little studied in respect of Chartism. It is still argued that Chartist organisation ceased by 1860 at the latest and that after that Chartism disappeared from the political scene. Antony Taylor, in an essay in *The Chartist Legacy*, discusses the use that Liberals and socialists made of the legacy of Ernest Jones. However, he focuses on the 1880s and 1890s and does not draw out precisely what aspects of Jones's political trajectory in the last decade of his life led to the dispute over his legacy.[11] The work of Margot Finn follows a similar pattern, focusing on the dispute between liberals and social-democrats over Jones' heritage in the 1880s, rather than the events of the 1860s that provided the basic materials for the dispute. However Finn does make it clear that Jones was not willing to reach a compromise with the Liberal Party which would involve him becoming a party functionary.[12] He was prepared to speak on Liberal platforms to put across a post or neo-Chartist viewpoint on manhood suffrage, and speak for the Reform League. However, unlike Holyoake he did not become an ornament of the League, nor did he take up a formal leadership role within it. There was always, in Finn's analysis, a distance maintained between Jones and the Liberal Party. It is in this gap that the disputes over the heritage of Jones thrived.

However, what is known of Jones's political career in the 1860s can provide a useful way of understanding some of the currents of political organisation and ideas in the period. The first account is in John Saville's 1952 biography where he devotes a handful of pages to an account of Jones's activities in the 1860s.[13] While still very much seen as a Chartist figurehead, and consciously harking back to Chartist days in speeches, Jones went some way to reaching an accommodation with the Liberal Party before he died in 1869. The nature of the accommodation and the changing ideas that it may have represented are issues of some importance. For Miles Taylor the same process is regarded as evidence of Jones's ability to reinvent his political leadership to suit circumstances.

For Saville, over time Jones softened his tone and began to concentrate on key planks of the Liberal political platform such as land reform while praising the role of Cobden and Bright as political leaders. There is no question this did occur, but the issue is whether it was a necessary hypocrisy in the absence of a working-class party, as Marx and Engels appear to have thought, or a capitulation on the part of Jones, whose time might more profitably have been spent organising such a party. These are matters of interpretation of Jones's political trajectory, but they are important ones if the nature of working-class politics and ideas in the 1860s is to be grasped.

From 1859 when he moved from London to Manchester until his death at the age of fifty ten years later he practised as a lawyer. It is apparent that initially he had some trouble attracting briefs but before too long he began the transition to becoming a successful barrister. It would be unusual for this not to have had some impact on his political views, even if this concerned only the networks of people to which he now related. However, it is also clear that he took on a considerable number of political briefs, relating to Fenians and trade unionists, and that he sometimes turned down profitable briefs particularly to meet public speaking engagements.

John Saville has argued that in the 1860s Jones was an influential supporter of existing movements rather than a leader of them. Since he was fully occupied as a lawyer this is an undeniable reality. However, whether it was also a deliberate political choice is less clear. There is some evidence that Jones felt that his basic political position was well enough known, and that deviations from this might be permissible if they could be shown to advance reform in some way. After all he had tried a similar gamble in 1858 with the Political Reform Union, and while this had not been an immediate success it did much to influence the Manhood Suffrage Associations that underwrote the passage of the 1867 Reform Act.

Despite Miles Taylor's work there is still not a direct, biographical account of what Jones thought his strategy was in the 1860s. This can only be pieced together from his activities and writings. In this sense the interpretation on offer here is more optimistic than that offered by Saville. Before Jones died he had stood as a Liberal Parliamentary candidate and was set to contest a further seat with some possibility of success. This allowed the radical wing of the Liberal Party to claim him as part of its political heritage. The key to this claim, however, surely lay with his untimely death. Had he lived, as a radical Liberal MP in the mould of Joseph Cowen he might well have ended up being marginalised from official Liberal politics and been one of those who were active around the formation of the Social Democratic Federation. A clue to Jones's thinking and his relationship to the Liberal Party may be gleaned from his last speech to a working-class meeting at Chorlton Town Hall in January 1869, a few days before he died. He argued that 'there was a personal reason why he desired soon to get into the House of Commons, and that was that he could not afford to wait very long. What little work there was in him must be taken out speedily, or it would be lost altogether...when a man got to be fifty he desired to make the best use of his time'.[14]

Thus the evidence suggests that Jones's political strategy changed during the second half of the 1860s. The most recent study of Jones by Miles Taylor underlines this point.[15] Taylor uses very much the same evidence and reference points as John Saville and concurs with his assessment that by the late 1860s Jones had made an accommodation with radical Liberalism. Taylor is less good than Saville at charting the changes in Jones's ideas and strategy that this implied, since in his view Jones's entire career was based on opportunistic accommodations to various stances and causes.

The argument here, however, is that Jones was quite consistent in pursuing his underlying political principles. He had been reluctant to remain as a leading member of the Reform League, demanding of Gladstone that real progress on suffrage reform must be in the Liberal Party programme before support could be forthcoming. He made it clear that he was opposed to the rump of Whig Liberalism, and his allies in the Liberal Party, such as they were, represented a small group on the far-left of middle-class radical politics. In early 1867 his response to Professor Blackie in Edinburgh, on the issue of democracy, was very clearly framed in a 'which side are you on?' progress or reaction context.[16] Yet, and perhaps crucially, after the passage of the Second Reform Bill Jones, in going forward as a Liberal candidate for Hulme in Manchester, had to determine which side he was on.

The best public marker to Jones's thought in this period was his speech on Labour and Capital, made in Glasgow, Manchester, London and Birmingham in October and November 1867, just under a year before he stood unsuccessfully as a Liberal candidate.[17] There was, or appears to have been, a marked change from the views he expressed at the beginning of 1867. It is true that he raised the argument that labour is the source of all wealth, and defended the role of both trade unions and strikes in forthright terms. This, at the very least, underlined his position on the far left of official Liberalism. Yet he also called for Labour to be 'at least a partner, an equal partner' in society, which, while still radical and certainly in tune with the ideas of trade union leaders, was not the language of the First International. Despite Miles Taylor's biography it his focus on the land question that continues to provide the biggest puzzle. John Saville has noted that 'his emphasis upon the evil of the land monopoly, in itself unexceptional, was typically middle class in its failure to consider the problem in the wider context of property relationships in general'.[18] What Saville means by this is that while nationalisation of the land was by the late 1860s, an argument current in radical working-class circles, Jones specifically does not call for this. Rather he called for the repeal of the laws of settlement and entail and of primogeniture which he argued would, along with tenant-right, be sufficient to settle many on the land. Perhaps this is so, but there was a clear dividing line between working-class radicals and Liberals on the land issue at this period and it was precisely on the question of nationalisation. Jones had signalled which side he was on. However he had heavily qualified it by prefacing his remarks by suggesting that his comments followed if the argument of supply and demand was accepted. His earlier remarks suggested that he did not, except for reasons of debate, accept this. There was ambiguity here, which had a political purpose which was well recognised by those active at the time, including Marx and Engels who grasped what Jones's 'bourgeois hypocrisy' was all about.

It is not just Ernest Jones personal trajectory, however, that helps to achieve a clearer direction on changes in radical ideas and politics in the 1860s. It is also the wider context in which he operated. Broadly speaking this was one where many second rank Chartist leaders had decided to give some support to a reconstituted Liberal Party. As Neville Kirk has underlined, the precise profile of the Liberal Party and whether or not it would accommodate working men and former Chartists varied from area to area and from town to town.[19] In the north-west the accommodation was made in many places. In London it was not, while in Joseph Cowen's Newcastle it was, if anything the Liberal Party that had to accommodate itself to organised labour and radicals. Cowen had set up the Northern Reform Union on a professional basis in January 1858, with offices in central Newcastle and republican activist Richard Reed as the full-time paid secretary.[20] But an accommodation on the basis of political organisation was not the same as an agreement on ideas or underlying philosophy. At the same time there were always minorities of radicals who refused to have anything to do with the Liberal Party, and these could have a significant impact. It is against this changed landscape of radical ideas and politics that Jones's trajectory must be judged. Indeed, it was this background against which Jones himself had to work, and it can be seen, from letters that he wrote to Marx from 1865 onwards, uncovered in Moscow Archives by Dorothy Thompson, that twenty years in the leadership of Chartism had not prepared Jones for the problems that he met at this period.[21]

Jones was determined to keep the demand for manhood suffrage, and nothing less, as the key working-class demand in the suffrage agitation. In a letter to Marx from Manchester written on 7 February 1865 Jones outlined some of the problems with this strategy. Firstly, while meetings of workers were taking place around the country, they were nearly all supporting demands which amounted to less than manhood suffrage. In effect they were supporting a demand that would probably not lead to many of them securing the vote. Jones noted that while there were others who supported a manhood suffrage campaign, many who might be supposed to be in favour, such as the trade unionist Potter and the radical Manchester publisher Abel Heywood, in his view would stifle rather than promote such a campaign.

Jones also pointed out that there was neither the organisation, the people or the money to finance a demonstration for manhood suffrage in Manchester and he pleaded with Marx to organise one in London which might show a lead elsewhere. In a second letter of 10 February 1865, in response to a reply from Marx, Jones emphasised the importance of London radicals leading a campaign for manhood suffrage. He also underlined his commitment to independent working-class organisation and opposition to what he called 'sham liberals'. However Marx had other ideas. While he was happy to see the link between the working-class elements of the Reform League and the First International, Marx wanted to build up the International rather than the agitation for manhood suffrage. Marx wrote to Engels on 13 February 1865 and mentioned the letter he had received from Jones, but noted that he had received no indication that Jones was prepared to help build the forces of the International in Manchester. For Jones the priority was manhood suffrage; for Marx and Engels it was the International.

Jones continued to correspond with Marx throughout 1865, and through the correspondence some idea of the tensions in the radical working-class movement at this time can be gathered. Jones was determined to pursue a policy of manhood suffrage, and although short of money for the campaign, drew a sharp distinction between those who supported this demand and what he referred to as 'sham reformers'. He mentioned to Marx that he had turned down money to include the idea of an educational suffrage in the campaign. However, it is clear that the manhood suffrage movement in Manchester gathered far greater support than Jones had imagined possible. At the same time Jones saw the key battle as between working-class and middle-class reformers and the different conceptions of reform that each possessed. In particular he was concerned to draw working-class activists away from middle-class formulations of reform which fell short of manhood suffrage. To his annoyance he was not always successful. Indeed a Manchester reform conference had voted down manhood suffrage by around 95 to 40 votes. Where Jones differed with Marx, was that he was not minded to focus those 40 votes into the organisation around the International, which was Marx's prime concern. Jones did not see the key importance of this new development.

Hence after 1865, at least as shown by the surviving correspondence, Jones and Marx exchanged letters rather less frequently. Marx was annoyed that Jones failed to build support for the International in Manchester. However as Jones noted in a letter to Marx of 12 May 1866, several key people who might have become supporters, such as Hooson and Greening, had gone over to the middle-class reform movement. By contrast, Jones disagreed with the decision of the Reform League to regard the Liberal Reform Bill as at least a step towards manhood suffrage and resigned from the League. By November

1868, Jones was asking if Marx could help to secure his nomination as an independent working-class candidate for Greenwich. This was after his failure to get elected at Manchester, but Marx, according to Dorothy Thompson, did not agree to help Jones out.[22]

Wider political changes and developments in the 1860s had their impact on radical education. In the period of intense debate about the franchise before the 1867 Reform Act, arguments about the educational franchise were focused by a Bill introduced into the Commons by Clay. *The Working Man,* a paper edited anonymously by Holyoake and designed to appeal to the working-class forces around the Reform League, carried much material and correspondence about the educational franchise. *The Working Man* also provided an interesting guide to what might have been considered really useful knowledge in the mid-1860s when it launched a prize essay competition for working men. Subjects included the franchise, trade unions, strikes, education, co-operation, working-class housing, Sunday recreations and domestic economy. Not all of the correspondents to *The Working Man* were in favour of a form of educational suffrage. W. Glazier of 2 Mildmay Street, Islington wrote in the paper in March 1866 that 'the old leaven of Chartism is not yet dead. The mass of those working men who are interested in political matters go in for manhood suffrage'.[23]

Ernest Jones's views on education in the 1860s underlined clearly how he saw the fight for manhood suffrage as an educational issue, rather than education being the key to the vote. In his 'Democracy Vindicated. A Lecture delivered to the Edinburgh Working Men's Institute' which he gave on, 4 January 1867 he noted that

> Instead of wanting education to fit them for the franchise, they need the franchise to enable them to obtain education. Look at America, where manhood suffrage has created the best educated people in the world. Look at the co-operative societies where from their profits, the working men unanimously vote large sums to establish schools and libraries for working men. Education! Give them manhood suffrage and in six months education would be made compulsory throughout the country...The laws favour education, in some states make it compulsory; but in fact it is mainly promoted by the spirit of the people.[24]

His comments on education provided a useful snapshot of where advanced working-class thought on this issue was by the late 1860s. He harked back, first of all, to the argument used by Feargus O'Connor against William Lovett almost thirty years earlier, that the franchise was the means to education, and not the other way around. This was not simply an acknowledgement of old Chartist arguments, however. It was also a signal that proposals for what were termed 'fancy franchises' were still very much in the public domain.

Elsewhere in the speech he queried whether if the qualification for the vote was to be a financial one based on rates, such people were in fact more educated than those working-class people who did not own property and did not pay rates.

The examples that Jones went on to use were also of interest. The 'North' in the US Civil War had won with the support of most working-class people in Britain and it made sense, therefore, to hold that country up as a model of the kind of democratic practice that could be achieved. Since it had both manhood suffrage and a good education system it was an excellent debating point. Closer to home the value of the co-operative societies educational efforts was also demonstrated. They proved in practice that working-class people were interested in education and were prepared to make sacrifices to open institutions that could provide it. Jones emphasised that education should be compulsory, a point first raised in the 1851 Chartist programme but not achieved by the 1870 Act. He did not, however, call for education to be secular. Such calls were now the province of Bradlaugh and the National Secular Society and Jones was keen in the lecture to emphasise that he remained a Christian.

### Independent Working-Class politics and ideas ten years after the demise of Chartism

The Liberal candidature of Ernest Jones at the post Reform Act General Election of 1868 and his subsequent victory in a test ballot in an ensuing by-election provide a useful benchmark by which to test change and continuity in radical politics and ideas in the ten years since the demise of organised Chartism. A number of commentaries on the 1860s have noted that Jones stood as a Liberal in Manchester and lost, and have taken this as a sign that either working-class voters would not support the Liberals, perhaps preferring the Tories, or that the Liberal Party of the late 1860s was not able to successfully assimilate working-class candidates.

In fact, as recent studies by Antony Taylor and Miles Taylor of what exactly took place in the 1868 Manchester election underline, matters were a good deal more complex than this.[25] The contradiction of Jones's candidature at Manchester was expressed by two opposites. On the one hand the Tory Reform Bill had enfranchised a far wider layer of the working-class than Gladstone's Liberal measure had envisaged. This meant that the Liberal Party had little choice but to adopt some working-class candidates in areas where this vote was significant. At the same time, as Taylor notes, 'In the 1860s memories of the 1840s in the city were too strong to allow Liberalism to adopt Chartism as part of its historical baggage as it did after 1880'[26]. In reality the Manchester Liberals were prepared to adopt Jones as a candidate for a very genuine reason, namely electoral success. However they were not prepared to adopt Chartist ideas, except in areas where there was already a general agreement, for example on the establishment of secular state education.

This left Jones in a very awkward position since although officially adopted as a Liberal candidate he was not part of the official culture or milieu of Manchester Liberalism. If, of course, Jones had been a trade unionist then it could be seen at once why the party of Manchester commerce could not welcome him. But Jones was a barrister, albeit a radical one, and therefore very much on the same class terms as his new colleagues. Even so the tensions were too great for a rapprochement, and this position quite clearly reflected a wider contradiction in the independent working-class movement. If working-class radicals could be members but not really part of the Liberal Party then a number of positions were possible. These could range from those who preferred to remain entirely independent, for example the ex-Chartists in Carlisle who were particularly critical of Jones in this period, to those who abandoned their radical past and assimilated into the Liberal Party.[27] This process, it should be noted, was a good deal easier in areas where the Liberal Party had not the history that it had in Manchester. As Antony Taylor has noted, Jones 'hovered uneasily on [the] margins'[28] of the Liberal Party. However, if this was the entire story of the Manchester election of 1868 it is likely that Jones would still have been returned as a candidate. In reality matters were clouded because an independent, ex-Liberal candidate, Mitchell Henry, split the vote. As Antony Taylor has noted, 'It was therefore Henry who denied Ernest Jones a seat in Parliament';[29] a point confirmed by Miles Taylor.[30]

Henry had been adopted as the Liberal candidate in Manchester to represent the working-class constituency before the passage of the 1867 Reform Act. With the wider franchise pushed through by Disraeli the Manchester Liberals determined to find a candidate who could appeal to the newly enfranchised working-class constituency. As a result they dropped Henry and nominated Jones. Henry, however, refused to accept the change and stood as an independent. The main subject of his campaign was Jones's Chartist past and in particular his status as a 'lawyer';[31] these became the central issues in the 1868 Manchester election.

Taylor has noted that 'The hostility with which Henry opposed Jones and the issues that he raised with regard to his Chartist past meant that the legacies of Chartism dominated the 1868 election, more so even than during Abel Heywood's two previous candidatures for the city in 1859 and 1865. The persistence of the Chartist tradition was therefore remarkable and proved sufficiently durable amongst working-class electors to make mainstream Liberal politicians reluctant to condemn the movement outright'.[32] This assessment places in a new light familiar arguments that Chartism was simply assimilated into Liberal politics during the 1860s. In fact, as can be seen, there was tension rather than assimilation. The resilience of Chartist ideas amongst workers may have been far greater than has been supposed.

When Jones lost the election the usually accepted story had been that the Liberals challenged the successful Tory candidate and that Jones was selected to stand for the Liberals in a by-election, which he was likely to win, but died before it could take place. Again, this story was the product of a liberal mythology that was built up around Jones. As Taylor has underlined, while the Liberal Party went to the lengths of organising a test ballot of Liberal voters between Jones and Milner Gibson, which Jones won, the reality was that their legal attempt to unseat the successful Tory candidate failed; a point not covered by Miles Taylor.

Jones had already decided that the Liberal Party did not offer a way forward and that 'by 1869 he was...thinking of contesting Greenwich as an independent candidate against the Liberal Party'.[33] However by the end of January 1869 Jones was dead. But there can be little question that while the Liberal Party tried to use Jones' affiliation with it, which had lasted perhaps two years, to attract working-class support in the 1870s and even into the 1880s, the lesson learnt by working-class activists was that they required independent organisation. This did not preclude relations and even deals with the Liberals, but the idea of working within the Party's structure was not a major feature of post-Chartist radical politics.

In fact another model altogether from the 'working from within' strategy that Jones had pursued proved to be much more successful. This involved working with middle-class Liberals and radicals while remaining independent of them. Both the *Beehive* and *Reynolds's Newspaper* supported secular, free and compulsory education. While the 1867 Reform Act was seen as, at best, a step towards universal suffrage by working-class radical activists, the extension of the suffrage raised educational reform to a high priority on the political agenda. J.S. Hurt has pointed out that those newly enfranchised by the 1867 Act and dissenters who had voted heavily for Gladstone in 1868 provided a powerful grassroots force to help a campaign to open up and democratise education.[34] The campaigning force in education was the National Education League (NEL). At the core of the NEL were middle-class dissenting Liberals, including the Birmingham Liberal MP George Dawson, who chaired the first meeting of the NEL in Birmingham in October 1869. He wanted to wrest control of education entirely out of Church and voluntary hands. Yet the 1870 Forster Act did not propose to go this far. Board schools were to fill in rather than replace voluntary provision. Most of the working-class radicals associated with the Reform League and then with the Land and Labour League and some who sat on the executive of the IWMA were involved with the NEL. However, on occasion they also acted independently of it and sent their own delegations to Gladstone.

The more middle-class supporters of the NEL, who were by far the majority, were concerned that school boards should be limited in extent to avoid what Hurt accurately suggests they saw as 'the risk of setting up popularly elected boards on any large scale'.[35] This risked taking education out of the control of the middle-class altogether, whether for or against reform. The Trades Union Congress in 1868 called for 'free, national, unsectarian and compulsory education' and urged affiliates to join the NEL. Around twenty trade union organisations did, but they were kept in a separate section, rather than in the mainstream branches run by the middle class. There are two ways to look at this reality. One is to suggest, as Hurt does, that the level of trade union support was small. The other more realistic way is to grasp that for any form of affiliation to occur and to be accepted was itself a significant new development.

The organised trades were led by those who placed a premium on education, often having struggled themselves to get it, and who represented, in general, skilled workers who already saw to it that their children were educated. They had a concern shared with middle-class supporters of the NEL that it was important to educate the children of the unorganised, as they saw them, or the 'dangerous classes' as the NEL majority without doubt classified them. Yet the trade unionists also had a wider perspective which saw a universal value in everyone having access to education at all levels up to university. This marked them out as far more advanced than the NEL leadership. Even so there were limits. At a meeting of working-class supporters of free and rate aided working-class education held independently of the NEL in London on 16 June 1870, a motion moved by Daniel Chatterton, a well-known supporter of Holyoake's 'extreme sections' for fully secular education, found only twenty supporters. Chatterton was not amongst the delegation of working men, led by Cremer, who went on 25 June to see W.E. Forster.

### 1870-71: Benjamin Lucraft, the Land and Labour League, the London School Board and the Paris Commune – Puzzling it out

Without question the passage of the 1870 Act ushered in a new era for radical working-class education, although it took some years for the government to root out dame schools and other informal mechanisms of working-class education. For the first time in many working-class areas there was the prospect of widespread state provision of elementary education. As the work of Phil Gardner has demonstrated there was significant working-class resistance to state education.[36] Some of this may have been of a backward nature – an opposition to formal education. Others may simply have sprung from the practical reality that family life could not hang together without the income from children's work. Some opposition was certainly political since, as with vaccination laws, there were sections of the working-class that opposed state interference in their affairs. Statism has since become such a dominant trend in working-class politics that it is easy to forget that there have been strands which opposed the involvement of the state in working-class affairs – those of employment and trade unions as much as education – on the grounds that it compromised independent working-class politics.

The dominant position was that which supported the 1870 Act and sought to influence the school boards that were set up to administer it. Elections for the boards remained on a relatively restricted franchise, and took place during working hours. Further as can be seen with the attempts of Ernest Jones to enter parliament, there was no independent working-class political organisation beyond a local level which could have put forward a coherent national programme for school board elections.

However, Joseph Cowen was elected to the Newcastle School Board in January 1871[37] and Benjamin Lucraft to the Finsbury School Board in London. Lucraft was a well-known figure in London working-class Chartist political circles and had been one of the Chairs of the 1858 Chartist conference. He was on the extreme left of the Reform League, a key figure responsible for organising the large central London working-class demonstrations that became a feature of the pre-1867 Reform agitation. He was also associated with the First International and still supported these politics and had this political base when he was elected to the school board.

Indeed, it is this area of Lucraft's political activity that provides a puzzle. He was a member of the International Working Men's Association from 1864 to 1871 and, as John Saville's biography of him notes, 'he played an active and committed role in its political work'.[38] Indeed, Lucraft was at the inaugural meeting of the IWMA on 28th September 1864 and at that meeting joined its provisional committee which went on to become the General Council. None of these facts are mentioned in the only contemporary biography of Lucraft, by Dyer, who commends him as the model of Gladstonian liberalism.[39] When Lucraft was elected to the London School Board in 1870 he was a member of the Land and Labour League, the most advanced working-class organisation of the period.

However, in the following year he broke with the International over its support for the Paris Commune. He became a radical Liberal and, in practice, an early Lib-Lab politician, and was re-elected to the school board on a number of occasions. That these experiences provoked his break with the International is a possibility. Lucraft is particularly interesting in the context of a study of post-1848 radicalism and radical education. For a number of reasons he had a particularly long and active political career, stretching at least from the 1858 conference to 1890. His significance and political position remains disputed both by his contemporaries and his biographers. Finally, he became the first ultra-radical to be elected to the London School Board in 1870, a position he held for twenty years.

There is no question that Lucraft did make a significant political break when he resigned from the First International over the Paris Commune in June 1871. However, he had been elected to the London School Board before he made this break. Further, because of his ultra-radicalism during the 1860s he was deselected from the executive of the Reform League for being too extreme. This was not entirely in character with his political trajectory during the 1850s or the 1870s, which might explain why both F.M. Leventhal in his biography of George Howell and Royden Harrison in *Before the Socialists* see Lucraft as an ultra-radical figure while John Saville, in the *Dictionary of Labour Biography*, points out that he was never a first-rank leader and after 1871 was very much in conformity with the Lib-Lab politics of labour activists of the period.[40]

Lucraft was not the only radical with an educational profile. A spoof in the *Penny Beehive* which named an alternative cabinet of leading radicals had James Finlen as minister for education, reflecting, no doubt, the popular impression that radicals such as Finlen still placed emphasis on ideas and education. Finlen, too, had been an active Chartist in the 1850s, and although he had disagreed with Jones, had in time become one of his leading lieutenants. He remained active in London working-class radicalism in the 1860s, particularly in defence of Fenianism, before apparently retiring to obscurity in Liverpool. Royden Harrison has noted of this period that 'it would be difficult to over-stress the analogy between the early seventies and the late eighties. It extended even to the language of protests'.[41] It is possible to go even further than this and see in the development of the labour movement and radicalism at this period and its interaction with government the basis for the model which has operated until the present day.

This is clear when the trajectories of Lucraft and Finlen are examined. Lucraft was certainly on the extreme left of the Reform League, although he had complained at a Land and Labour League meeting in 1869 of the sentiments of the League's president Hennessey that the occasional shooting of an Irish landlord did no harm. Lucraft had sat on the General Council of the IWMA, as had Odger, and resigned with him over the publication of *The Civil War in France*. However, unlike Lucraft Odger did not distance himself from the role that he had played in the International prior to 1871. A clue to the reason for the different reaction may lie in a *Spectator* article which specifically called into question how Lucraft could be an elected member of the

London School Board and a defender of the Commune. It may be suspected that it was this pressure that made Lucraft resign from the International.

The same may well have been true for James Finlen, who had represented Finsbury at the 1851 Chartist Convention. Following his defence of Fenian prisoners Finlen was attacked in the press and in Parliament and his name became associated with the expression of extreme views on Ireland and Republicanism. Phrases such as a 'social Finlen' and 'polished Finlenism' were used to describe not only those with similar views but also the likely fate that lay before them. Finlen was witchhunted out of public life and was discovered by George Howell on a visit to Warrington in 1888-89 living under an assumed name. In both cases the successful attacks on radicals were only possible because the age of mass circulation papers had started to develop, as had basic literacy, which meant that the words and deeds of Finlen and Lucraft now reached a much wider audience than they might have twenty years previously.

The situation in respect of radical political organisation around 1870-71 was one of great fluidity. At one level there was the revolutionary example of the Commune and sympathy for the plight of the Communards that reached even to the middle classes as it had not done in 1848. At another level was the concrete advance of the 1870 Act and elections to local school boards. At a third level was the question of what kind of working-class political organisation and what kind of ideas could meet these new challenges.

### The geography of radicalism, 1870

What is certain is that the work of radical education and spreading radical ideas continued after 1870. Developments in terms of railway travel, communications and newspaper publishing meant that a national network of radical meetings and venues was now possible as never before. During the years of *The Reasoner*, while Holyoake had made regular lecturing tours to various parts of Britain, secularist organisation and regular meetings remained very much a London focused affair. The advent of the National Secular Society in 1866 saw this change dramatically. Secularism now acted as a proto working-class party. This meant that it now had a national organisation which focused very largely on building support for its ideas and strategies in working-class areas. The Guide to the Lecture Room published in the *National Reformer* during 1870 still had extensive coverage of London meetings. These were now far outnumbered by what the paper termed, in its London-centric manner, 'provincial' venues.

In addition the paper listed the London branches of the Land and Labour League, providing a link to radical politics that had never existed so overtly during the period when Holyoake had hegemony over the movement. Indeed, the paper also listed meetings of the International Democratic Association in Hatton Garden, which described its aim as being for 'the advancement of Republican and Socialistic principles'. Like a number of other developments in the late 1860s and early 1870s this marked a sharp leap forward in terms of the language and ideas that were becoming acceptable within the radical mainstream, even if the supporters of this particular current were probably not usually particularly numerous.

A number of the venues advertised that they ran Sunday schools. The focus here was specifically on secular education for young people rather than the Sunday childcare operation which later came to be associated with some elements even of the socialist Sunday school movement. The City Road Hall of Science did so from 2.30 to 4 p.m. on a Sunday, as did the Huddersfield Secular and Eclectic Institute, which also opened on a Sunday morning at 10 a.m. The Newcastle on Tyne Secular Society at 33 Clayton St also ran a Sunday school, morning and afternoon. Of course, radical Sunday schools were not a new phenomenon but they held a new importance after the passage of the 1870 Education Act had started to address issues of weekday provision. It is reasonable to see the radical Sunday Schools of the 1860s as the forerunners of what became the typical form of radical education by the turn of the century. Radical educational initiatives were now focused firmly on schools as a top-up rather than an alternative to provided education.

Interplay between practical attempts at radical education, educational suffrages and the fight for manhood suffrage had been central to understanding working-class radical politics in the 1860s. More than this, while the 1860s is often seen a period of defeat for working-class politics, this was far from the experience of those active at the time. Neville Kirk has noted that 'increased satisfaction with their past and present achievements and boundless optimism in the prospects for future progress were the products not only of considerable advance made by sections of organised workers after the mid-1840s, but also of the greatly enhanced readiness on the part of the state and influential social groups to accommodate some of organised labour's claims to recognition, protection and advancement'.[42] There were indeed significant advances. For example, by 1875 there were over half a million trade unionists and with the Trade Union Act of 1871, the Criminal Law Amendment Act of 1871, the Conspiracy and Protection of Property Act of 1875 and Employers and Workmen Act of 1875, trade unions acquired a legal status. This had an impact on ideas. Chartist ideas which had argued that little progress was possible without total political reform, no longer fitted so exactly the circumstances in which workers found themselves. There had been limited political reform and there was some progress. This fitted rather better the ideas of those who argued that change was possible on a piecemeal basis. However, the harsh realities of mid and late Victorian society, particularly during economic downturn, still provided a considerable basis for those who wanted wholesale not piecemeal change. For example, the passage of the 1867 Reform Act, while ultimately achieved peacefully, provoked a sufficient struggle to promote a new layer of ultra-radical working-class activists. It was these people who filled the ranks of the First International and the Land and Labour League and carried the battle for radical ideas to a new generation.

## Notes

1. Donald M MacRaild and David E Martin, *Labour in British Society 1830-1914*, London, 2001.
2. Rohan McWilliam, *Popular Politics in Nineteenth-Century England*, London 1998, p. 72.
3. John Vincent, *The Formation of the British Liberal Party 1857-1868*, Harmondsworth, 1972.
4. Vincent op. cit.
5. See for example: Eugenio Biagini, *Liberty Retrenchment and Reform: Popular Politics in the Age of Gladstone, 1860-1880*, Cambridge, 1992;
   Eugenio Biagini (ed), *Citizenship and Community: Liberals, Radicals and Collective Identities in the British Isles, 1865-1931*, Cambridge 1996;
   Eugenio Biagini and Alistair Reid, Eds, *Currents of Radicalism: Popular Radicalism, Organised Labour and Party Politics in Britain, 1850-1914*, Cambridge, 1991.
6. Martin Hewitt, *The emergence of stability in the industrial city, Manchester 1832-1867*, Aldershot, 1996.
7. Nigel Todd, *The Militant Democracy*, Whitley Bay, 1991 Ch. 5.
8. Edward Royle, *Labour History Review*, Spring 2000.
9. Engels to Marx, 18 November 1868.
10. O. Ashton, S. Roberts and R. Fyson, Eds, *The Chartist Legacy*, Woodbridge, 1999.
11. Antony Taylor in *The Chartist Legacy*, op. Cit.
12. Margot Finn, *After Chartism*, Cambridge, 1993.
13. John Saville, *Ernest Jones, Chartist*, London, 1952.
14. Frederick Leary, *The Life of Ernest Jones*, London, 1887, p. 81.
15. See Miles Taylor, op. cit., Chapter 7 *The People's Advocate*.
16. Ernest Jones, *Democracy Vindicated*, London, 1867.
17. Ernest Jones, *Labour and Capital*, London, 1867.
18. John Saville, op. cit. P. 80.
19. Neville Kirk, *Change, Continuity, Class*. Manchester, 1998, p. 93.
20. Nigel Todd op. cit., p. 44.

21  Dorothy Thompson, *Bulletin of the Society for the Study of Labour History*, No.4, Spring 1962.
22  Ibid.
23  *Working Man*, 24 March 1866
24  Ernest Jones, *Democracy Vindicated*, op. cit.
25  Antony Taylor, '"The Best Way to Get What He Wanted". Ernest Jones and the Boundaries of Liberalism in the Manchester Election of 1868'. *Parliamentary History*, Volume 16/2, September 1997, pp. 185-204.
26  Ibid.
27  See Miles Taylor, op. cit., p. 242. for Carlisle.
28  Ibid.
29  Ibid.
30  Miles Taylor op. cit. p. 248.
31  Miles Taylor op. cit. p. 246.
32  Ibid.
33  Ibid.
34  J. S. Hurt, *Education in Evolution: Church, State and society in popular education, 1800-1870*, London, 1972.
35  Ibid., p. 61.
36  Phil Gardner, *The Lost Elementary Schools of Victorian England*, London, 1984.
37  Nigel Todd, op. cit., p. 85.
38  John Saville, *Dictionary of Labour Biography, Volume V11*, London, 1984.
39  George Dyer, *Benjamin Lucraft, A Biography*, London, 1879.
40  John Saville, op. cit.
41  Royden Harrison, *Before the Socialists*, 1965, p. 245.
42  Neville Kirk, *The Growth of Working-Class Reformism in Mid-Victorian England*, London, 1985, p. 152.

## Chapter 8
## Conclusion

A spirited and most interesting conversation arose between different members on most questions of the day effecting the working classes, the general opinion being that the time had now come when an association like this was required to discuss the questions effecting their well being, to express their opinions and assert their rights in a determined, calm and perfectly open and fearless manner. This conversation was most especially useful to the young members in consequence of the older speakers being known as old and tried workers in the Chartist movement.
*Report in The Beehive of the decision of Greenwich and Deptford Manhood Suffrage Association to affiliate to the First International, February 1865.*[1]

In concluding this study in 1870-71 a number of questions have been raised. How far had the working class moved since 1848 from looking for change from below to hoping that it would come, by means of reform, from above? How far were at least sections of the working class now inside the system of Parliamentary pressure and politics? While constitutionalism and plebeian democracy had been important strands in working-class politics, had the electoralism so familiar from later years, taken root by 1870? How different was the working class of 1870 to that of 1848 or 1832? These questions provide a key framework for gauging where radical ideas and education had travelled to by 1870.

A key element is the sexual composition of the workforce. It may be thought that factors of gender, following the work of Sonya O. Rose and Anna Clark,[2] those of race and ethnicity raised by Neville Kirk,[3] and the links between them in an imperial context highlighted by Catherine Hall,[4] have little to do with radical education and ideas held by workers. In fact, they go to the centre of an understanding of what the working class was and which model is used to understand it for the period from 1848 to 1870.

A model which sees the working class as an undifferentiated and static mass is no longer tenable. This owed much to implicit postmodernist caricatures by historians such as Patrick Joyce[5] of positions that were never held by Marxist historians. In reality, as Edward Thompson noted, the working class was unmade and made in each new generation.[6] It was made up of conflicting interests which sometimes united, but also frequently erupted into disagreement. It can be of little surprise to find workers divided against each other, for example in the Murphy riots in the north-west of England from the mid-1850s,[7] in a social and economic system that was designed to facilitate just this. More significantly, what brought workers together to challenge capital must be examined. The model of 'labourism' put forward by Perry Anderson and Tom Nairn,[8] which saw the working class in 1870 as grey, timid and conservative, is not one which fits the complex reality.

The geography and maps of radicalism and radical ideas, the contours and horizons of working-class politics in 1870 were different from those of 1848. When maps and contours are fleshed out it becomes apparent how limiting the categories of labourism and the labour aristocracy are. The world in 1870 was still recognisable to the Chartist but it was also one that was characterised by modest working-class organisational advance within a political system that itself had changed in a number of ways, including the 1867 Reform Act. There remained a fluidity to organisation in the 1860s which hardened in later years. Radical activity most often focused on single-issue movements which were tightly organised but loosely defined in terms of membership. The inclusive/exclusive characteristics of party organisation were not the central feature that they had been with the National Charter Association twenty years earlier, or were to be later with the Social Democratic Federation and Independent Labour Party. Secularism, Republicanism and trade unionism did have, however, more strictly patrolled boundaries and these often formed the organisational core of the wider movements for change and reform.

Royden Harrison, along with John Breuilly one of the few historians to study the labour history of the 1850s and 1860s in depth, has noted that, 'by and large historians with an interest in politics have been drawn away from the mid-Victorian period by the seemingly greater excitements of Chartism and the birth of the Labour Party'.[9] The 1860s are known for landmark features such as the founding of the First International in 1864, the Second Reform Act in 1867 and the foundation of the TUC in 1868. They are even better known for two events that occurred at the end of the period of this study: the 1870 Education Act and the Paris Commune of 1871. However, the struggles of ordinary working people, particularly during the 1860s, remain obscure. Royden Harrison has argued for a contrast with the pre-1848 period that was 'above all one of spirit – as anyone who compares the *Northern Star* with the *Beehive* [even the early *Beehive*] must quickly recognise'.[10] Chartist ideas were still current but they were expressed less strongly as workers grew weary of defeats and looked for some way to make progress. E.P. Thompson has described this process as one of warrening capitalism from end to end, where defensive positions and structures from trade unions to co-operatives were carefully constructed. Many of the changes that took place after 1848 can be explained, at a general level, by reference to changes in the nature and relations of production. Some employers did begin to recognise trade unions, while wages and employment prospects showed moderate advances for much of the twenty year period after 1848. Yet if Harrison is correct that the main change in the working class was more of spirit, then issues of ideas and radical education remain central.

By 1870 the kind of balance sheet of ideas that had to be drawn and understood by radical workers was considerably more complex than it had been in 1830. The existing political system, although still not in any sense a modern democracy, had shown itself, when under pressure from below, to be capable of reform. At the same time the battles around the legal status of trade unions underlined the hard fight that serious reforms still required. The status of British workers in 1870, with some influence inside the political system, was very different to their German counterparts, who found their political organisations banned, and to those in France, who with the Commune in 1871 suggested an altogether different way of going about things. Yet the nature of working-class organisation and ideas was actually very similar. The idea that progress could occur within the system, albeit through the often difficult work of building up, organising and sustaining pressure from below, appealed to many involved in trade unions and co-operatives and was the model of political development held across Europe. Against this the reversals and failures of such a strategy, which were many, combined with the lack of employment and social safety nets for most workers, was sufficient to allow for a continued revolutionary edge, both to working-class organisation and to the ideas held by a minority, such as the followers of Bronterre O'Brien examined by Stan Shipley in his study of *Club Life and Socialism in mid-Victorian London*.[11]

Royden Harrison's view that the labour movement of the late 1860s and early 1870s had much in common with its counterpart of fifteen or twenty years later can be sustained by reference to individual activists such as the London shoemaker and trade unionist Charles Murray, who had been a Chartist and was still active in the Social Democratic Federation thirty years later. Some organisations such as the O'Brienite-influenced Manhood Suffrage League also sustained themselves over this period. However, the idea of a broadly united radical labour movement, as there had been in the 1830s and 1840s, is more difficult to demonstrate. Antony Taylor and John Breuilly argue that in the late 1860s 'the alliance between the trades and radicalism…collapsed'.[12] Miles Taylor, by contrast, sees the death of Ernest Jones in the 1860s as the end of an era of 'gentleman leaders' in the Henry Hunt, Feargus O'Connor mould.[13]

It is true that some policies of Gladstonian Liberalism such as land reform and Irish Home Rule, when given a radical edge, could provide temporary unity for most working-class and middle-class radicals. Indeed Joseph Cowen became a radical Liberal MP for Newcastle precisely on this basis. Nigel Todd has shown how, while Cowen's public statements were often conventionally 'radical' Liberal, what he actually did and supported in practice was rather further to the left.[14] However, in general, the interests of the two classes were simply too far apart in most cases to make this a permanent unity. Further to the left the populist radicalism of *Reynolds's Newspaper* provided a uniting factor. However this unity was mainly around what was seen as the 'enemy'– the aristocracy and corrupt figures in Government – rather than an agreement about what might be done to change things. It was here that the left and Marx and Engels in particular hoped to see a new independent working-class force arise, rooted in the trade unions, that would have the weight and influence to force change. But matters were not so simple. The attempt to make the link between the basic concepts of trade unionism, independent organisation, solidarity and a fight for decent wages and conditions and a broader political programme proved to be more complex than was thought. Agreement over what kind of political programme was required, in essence a set of ideas about what was wrong with society and series of demands and strategies to address them, was not easy to achieve.

Even as early as 1870 the issue of the relation of working-class politics to Parliamentary representation was important. The Reform League had splintered after the passage of the 1867 Act. Those who wanted to go further – primarily working-class radicals – founded the Land and Labour League. Others were involved with the National Secular Society led by Charles Bradlaugh. In some areas, particularly London, this was a far more serious and working class organisation than the League. On the other hand some of the leading working-class radicals in the Reform League founded the Labour Representation League (LRL), which focused on getting working men elected to Parliament, implicitly with Liberal Party support. The LRL did attract trade union support where the NSS and LLL did not.

While the presence or absence of radical political working-class organisation helped to focus, or otherwise, the radical ideas and strategies, these existed independently. Just as much as in 1848 workers in 1870 struggled to make sense of the political and economic system in which they found themselves and it was in the questions that this process raised that the milieu of radical education continued to exist. Arguments about continuity and discontinuity of radical education and ideas in the period after 1848 are too mechanistic to explain the realities of what took place. It is more useful to see radical education as a series of waves which ebbed and flowed depending on specific contexts and conjunctures.

There was always the continuing presence of radical education and ideas in the 1850s and 1860s. Indeed because of developments in rail travel, newspaper production and the beginnings of the creation of a national political culture, radical ideas and education, in general, had a stronger presence in 1870 than in 1848. Radical political organisation was not as strong and 1870 saw no challenge to the British state as in 1848. On the other hand, in 1867 the government had been forced to give way on the Second Reform Act and left-wing ideas were considerably more advanced in 1870. Nationalisation, for example, had become a familiar concept, and working-class organisation measured in terms of trade union membership was much stronger.

The key to grasping the significance of radical education and ideas, both before and after 1870, is to understand the factors that allowed the thoughts and strategies worked out in small meetings and low circulation papers to break out and influence mass political movements. Despite the defeats of 1848 the process of really useful knowledge continued up to the 1870s. While changes from 'above' such as the repeal of the Newspaper Stamp in 1855, the 1867 Reform Act and the 1870 Education Act had their impact, the process of exploitation implicit in a system of market capitalism continued to provoke an interest in ideas which could explain what was happening and how it might be changed by pressure from 'below'.

The 1870 Education Act was a watershed for radical education. History is often seen in terms of 'victory' and 'defeat' and it is important to understand who thought they had gained and who thought they had lost from the Act. However, historians also need to understand the longer term impact of such a significant change in the state's attitude towards education. For Phil Gardner the Act represented an attack by the government on the private working-class schools that he has studied and an attempt to control the education of working-class children through official channels. He has pointed out that the 1870 Act 'has commonly been seen as a step..in bringing effective elementary schooling within the reach of all'.[15] In fact, while it did not outlaw private working-class schools it began a period of attrition on behalf of the state against them, which led to a further measure in 1876 which legally defined 'certified efficient schools' and which, in general, was specifically designed to exclude the kind of schools that Gardner has uncovered. In reality, while the government could not outlaw such schools without also causing problems for middle-class private schools, they could undercut support for them. Gardner argues that the government targeted working-class parents. However they also coopted much working-class radical organisation behind the 1870 Act.

Hence, as Gardner notes, there was 'no organised support'[16] for parents who wanted to resist the government.

At the other end of the spectrum can be seen a proto-Fabian position, later echoed by the Webbs, which believed that the more the state involved itself in civil society, the more a kind of socialism was gaining power. As has been argued consistently in this study, while there was truth in both positions, the reality on the ground was a process of struggle. The government did hope to control working-class education, but it did not have the means to simply impose this control. It had to be done with a degree of consent and this meant that some concessions had to be made to working-class radical political demands in respect of education. In particular a strong element of local democratic control over schools – the local school boards – had to be conceded. The ability of working-class radicals to get elected on to such boards was very limited, and the arrangements for elections were deliberately designed to make as sure as possible that this was the case. However, working-class radicals were elected to school boards around the country and had some influence. Brian Simon has noted how, after the election of George Potter to the London School Board in 1873 a committee was appointed to 'enquire into the endowments available in the London School Board area which might [or should] be applied to education'.[17] The school board arrangement, although a very limited experiment in democracy was still felt by government to allow too much working-class influence into the system. The 1902 Act abolished the school boards.

While Miles Taylor sees Chartism 'dwindling' after 1848,[18] Royden Harrison has noted that Chartism did not 'vanish without trace' after 1848 but 'played various and surprising roles'.[19] One of these was to sustain a militant really useful knowledge amongst a minority of working-class activists such as Charles Murray and James Finlen. These activists never made their peace with Liberalism and their presence exerted a pressure for change upon it. Taylor and Breuilly argue that those active in manhood suffrage campaigns in the late 1850s 'also enlisted in the Reform League and remained active in all the major metropolitan reform causes in the intervening years'.[20] At the same time, new generations of working-class activists began to develop who, if they did not have the heritage of the struggles of the Chartist period, did not also have the experience of the defeats. A new confidence in ideas and language began to develop which could harness a wider working-class movement on occasion. The case of the Tichborne Claimant underlines the sometimes peculiar ways in which these currents worked themselves out in the absence, until the early 1880s, of a national working-class political organisation. Historical models have their uses in avoiding attempts to explain history in terms of local peculiarities and exceptionalisms. However, the reality of class relations and class struggles as an historical process where victories and defeats happen, and where radical ideas and education ebb and flow through various forms from radical papers to radical schools, suggests a reality more complex than any model.

**Notes**

1. *Beehive*, 12 February 1865.
2. Sonya O Rose, *Limited Livelihoods, gender and class in nineteenth century England*, London, 1984; Anna Clarke, *The Struggle for the Breeches*, London, 1995.
3. Neville Kirk, op. cit. 1985.
4. Catherine Hall and Leonore Davidoff, 'Gender and the Middle Class' in Patrick Joyce (Ed) *Class*, Oxford, 1995, p. 309.
5. Patrick Joyce op. cit. pp. 322-31.
6. E.P. Thompson, *Making of the English Working Class*, Harmondsworth, 1968.
7. Neville Kirk, *The Growth of Working Class Reformism in Mid-Victorian England*, London, 1985. See Chapter 7, *Class, Ethnicity and Popular Toryism*
8. Perry Anderson, 'Origins of the Present Crisis', *New Left Review* 23 and Tom Nairn, 'The English Working Class', *New Left Review*, 24.
9. Royden Harrison, *Before the Socialists*, London, 1965 edition, p. 2.
10. Ibid., p. 7.
11. Stan Shipley, *Club Life and Socialism in Mid-Victorian London*, London, 1971
12. Breuilly and Taylor (Eds.) op. cit. p. 267.
13. Miles Taylor, 2003 op. cit. see 'Introduction'.
14. Nigel Todd, op. cit., pp. 96-7.
15. Phil Gardner, op. cit., p. 189.
16. Ibid., p. 192.
17. Brian Simon, *Education and the Labour Movement*, London, 1965, p. 129.
18. Miles Taylor, 2003, op cit, p. 138.
19. Royden Harrison op. cit.
20. A. Taylor and J. Breuilly [Eds] op. cit., p. 22.

# Appendix 1
# Glossary

*Beehive*
A trade union focused paper that started in 1861. It was run by ex-Chartists sympathetic to Bronterre O'Brien

**Charter and Something More**
The left-wing programme adopted by the Chartists in 1851. 'Something More' referred to economic as well as political democracy, primarily nationalisation of the land and some parts of the economy.

**Democracy**
A term borrowed from the French it meant the popular will, or, in the British case, those who were actually excluded from the formal democratic process by lack of a vote.

**Dem-Soc**
From the French term suggesting someone who supported an early view of social democracy rather than socialism which was often connected with 'utopians' such as Fourier at this time. Similar in meaning to The Charter and Something More.

**Educational Strategy**
A plan, primarily put forward by G.J. Holyoake but also supported by the extreme wing of the Liberal Party such as J.S. Mill, which proposed some form of educational test and qualification whereby workers could gain access to the suffrage.

**Extreme Sections**
Those on the far left of working-class politics, often influenced by Marx and Engels, but sometimes also anarchists. They certainly numbered amongst their ranks Late Chartists such as Charles Murray and most were to come together in the Land and Labour League in the late 1860s. They were those opposed to any form of co-operation or agreement with the Liberal Party.

### Fraternal Democrats
The far left Chartist grouping led by G.J. Harney. Founded in 1846, it had given way to other organisations by the early 1850s. Did not have its own paper but its activities were widely reported in the Northern Star and the Red Republican. Worked closely with Marx and Engels and with refugees from continental liberation struggles.

### Labourism
A term used in particular to describe the limited and reformist perspective of British labour in the period after 1848. There is an implied criticism of attempts to win gains and improvements in the here and now rather than the pursuit of a longer term, hegemonic and hence revolutionary strategy. An alternative perspective put forward by E.P. Thompson was that having seen revolution fail in 1848 the working class determined to 'warren' capitalism from end to end, suggesting that labourism may have been more dynamic and less conservative than is sometimes imagined.

### Land and Labour League
The Land and Labour League was formed in 1868 from amongst those working-class sections of the Reform League that wanted the fight for an extension to the suffrage to continue after the passage of the 1867 Reform Act. The League was a broad organisation stretching from secularists like Bradlaugh to land nationalisers and trade unionists. It contained many of those who offered solidarity to the Paris Commune in 1871. Marx hoped that the League would form the basis of a new working-class political party and it did begin to publish a monthly, then weekly, paper, *The Republican*. However by the early 1870s it had collapsed as a national organisation, although the precise reasons for the collapse still await an historian.

### Late Chartist
Broadly a supporter of Chartism from 1851 to the final demise of Chartism on a national scale in 1860. Most Late Chartists subscribed to the politics of the Charter and Something More, a left-wing version of Chartism that focused on nationalisation.

### Mass Platform
The term given by historians, although also used at the time, to the radical strategy of extra-Parliamentary outdoor meetings to agitate for the suffrage. Judged by some to have run its course with the defeats of 1848, it proved a successful tactic in the passage of the Second Reform Bill in 1867.

### National Charter Association
The world's first working-class political party, formed in 1841 it finally collapsed in 1860. The date of the final end of the NCA is itself subject to his-

torical dispute, highly relevant to this study. For Neville Kirk, the NCA effectively ended with the 1858 conference, when a split called the National Political Union, opposed to co-operation with middle-class radicals took place. For John Saville it was the demise of the Chartist press, with the closure of the Cabinet Newspaper in 1860, that signalled the final end of the NCA. Meanwhile, Taylor and Breuilly make the point that far from marking the end of the NCA, the 1858 conference in fact provoked new activity and organisation.

*National Reformer*
One of the great radical papers of the third quarter of the nineteenth century, the paper was secularist in opinion and radical working class in its politics. It was associated with Holyoake, W.E. Adams and Charles Bradlaugh.

*Northern Star*
*The* national Chartist paper which ran from 1838 until 1852. Owned by Feargus O'Connor it was based first in Leeds but later moved to London. By far the bestselling newspaper of the period, sales easily outstripped those of *The Times*.

*Northern Tribune*
Newcastle journal published in the mid-1850s by Joseph Cowen, later owner of the *Newcastle Weekly Chronicle* and Liberal MP for Newcastle. The *Northern Tribune* is probably the earliest and perhaps the purest expression of the body of ideas known as Late Chartism.

*People's Paper*
The paper of Late Chartism it was edited by Ernest Jones and ran from 1852-1858. Marx was a frequent contributor.

**Post Chartist**
A working-class activist in the 1860s who had been a Chartist but was now focused on a campaign to extend the suffrage. Post-Chartism was also a set of ideas which held on the principles of Chartism while campaigning on a narrower basis.

**Radical**
As Raymond Williams noted in *Keywords* the description 'radical' can apply to the political right as well as the political left. Its precise meaning therefore depends on its usage in an historical and chronological context. In this work it is specifically used in conjunction with the term working class to mean the politically active section of that class. It does not imply support for socialist or communist ideas but a desire for change and reform of a general nature.

More specific currents are defined by the group or set of ideas to which they were affiliated, for example, the Fraternal Democrats.

**Radical Education** – *see 'Radical'; 'Really Useful Knowledge'.*
Radical education is a broad term covering both formal and informal educational mechanisms. 'Radical' could take the form of independent working-class or artisan run and attended schools, particularly in major cities like London. Here the actual content of the education provided might not have been particularly radical – as was the case with the Chartist Land Schools. Radical education could, however, take the form of discussion and dissemination of radical ideas, strategies and tactics. These would more often be focused at an adult rather than a child or juvenile age range and would also be more likely to be found in radical papers, meetings and discussion groups than in a formal school environment. In the wider context of the political impact of radical education, Prothero has noted 'educational activities had different implications in the presence or absence of a strong radical movement; extensive repression led to radical strategies concentrating on…forms such as educational activities, front organisations, benefit and co-operative societies, as well as conspiracies'.

**Really Useful Knowledge**
A term used by Richard Johnson to describe the body of political knowledge that working-class radicals developed in the Chartist era. Johnson first wrote about the subject in *Radical Education* Nos. 7 & 8 and developed his ideas in a number of subsequent articles. The term was actually used by radicals in the 1830s and 1840s, but Johnson was able to show how it combined elements of political and economic democracy.

*Reasoner*
The journal of working-class secularist thought. Edited by G.J.Holyoake, it ran from 1846 until 1861.

*Red Republican*
Journal started by G.J. Harney in 1850 after his final break with Feargus O'Connor and the *Northern Star*. The most advanced of the late Chartist publications, it carried the first English translation of the Comm*unist Manifesto*. It changed its name to the *Friend of the People*, after finding problems with distribution of the title *Red Republican*.

**Ruling Class**
The term 'ruling class' was hardly used during the period of this study, except by the small group around Marx and Engels. There was however a clear sense of controlling group in society. The structures of the state were very limited in 1848, but began to grow after this, arguably as a reaction to it. Those

in authority ranged from senior police officers, government ministers, army commanders and *The Times* newspaper. They represented a narrow range of propertied and, increasingly, industrial interests. Secondary sources vary in how they describe the ruling class. David Goodway focuses on the 'authorities' and in particular the police and army. John Saville distinguishes between those who maintained the rule of capital and those whose interests were being defended by their activities.

## Suffrage

Broadly speaking anything, in working-class politics, used to refer to any extension to the 1832 Reform Act. It was often qualified by terms such as 'manhood', 'universal', or, in more limited meanings, 'ratepayers'.

## Working Class

The category 'working class' should not be taken unproblematically for the period of the study: 1848-1870. As David Goodway underlined in his study of the London trades in 1848, and Raphael Samuel also demonstrated in his study 'The Workshop of the World', the working class in the mid-Victorian period was not dominated by the factory proletariat or the white collar clerk of the late Victorian period. Small production with artisanal labour remained a central feature of the working class in 1870, as in 1848. The writings of Thomas Wright make the point. The working class was also gendered. Women were not absent from the workplace, but often followed different occupations, as suggested by the studies of Henry Mayhew. The artisanal working class, often skilled, may be seen as the bedrock of independent working-class education in the third quarter of the nineteenth century. By contrast, radicals and Chartists made some effort to organise the new factory proletariat. Here, however, the emphasis had to be on the provision of mass schooling, of a secular and gratuitous kind.

# Appendix 2
# Biographies

John Saville, in a brief introduction to the tenth volume of the Dictionary of Labour Biography – the last he edited – reflects on the reasons for the choice of entries in the series over the best part of forty years. In summary he notes that they were lives that were not already in the Dictionary of National Biography, were of interest and where material was available.

Christopher Godfrey, in his earlier work on Chartist biography, argues a case for looking at Chartists as people whose political activities may well have started before and continued after they were Chartists.

In the case of the lives detailed here the criterion is more specific: a small group of radical figures who had a particular impact on radical education in the third quarter of the nineteenth century.

The key sources for these biographies are:
Christopher Godfrey, *Chartist Lives*, London, 1987.
John Breuilly et al, Eds, *The Era of the Reform League*, Mannheim, 1995.

*W.E. Adams, (1832-1906)*. A central radical figure from the 1860s onwards when he was employed as an editor by Joseph Cowen Jnr, proprietor of the *Newcastle Chronicle*. He was a youthful Chartist before 1848 and played a central role in setting the terms and tone of the debate amongst radicals in the post-Chartist period of the 1860s and after.

*Charles Bradlaugh, (1833-1891)*. He spoke at Kennington Common in 1848 and was active in the later stages of Chartism. Edited the *National Investigator* (1852-54) and the *National Reformer* (1862-1891). Youngest member of Reform League executive; Elected MP for Northampton 1880, but did not take oath or seat.

*Joseph Cowen Jnr. (1829-1900)*. Financed *English Republic* (1851-55); *Northern Tribune* (1854-55); *Newcastle Daily Chronicle* (1860); *Weekly Chronicle* (1863); Liberal MP for Newcastle (1873-1886). A leading figure in post-Chartist radicalism, he was also briefly a member of Newcastle School Board from 1871.

*Sir Charles Dilke, (1843-1911)*. A Liberal MP and minister in the final quarter of the nineteenth century. He had an orientation to radical working-class circles in the later 1860s and opposed Forster's 1870 Education Bill, moving an amendment for directly elected school boards rather than committees of boards of guardians.

*James Finlen, (Dates unknown)*. A French polisher, newsagent and insurance agent. Delegate to 1851 Chartist Conference; 1854 Labour Parliament; ally of Jones to 1858; Reform League lecturer in 1866; pro-Fenian in 1867, he was hounded out of public life because of his far-left views and died in obscurity.

*G.J. Harney, (1817-1897)*. Editor of the *Northern Star*, the *Democratic Review* and the *Red Republican*. Central leader of left-Chartism and advocate of revolutionary ideas. Did not play a leading role in late Chartism, living first in Jersey and then America from the mid-1850s.

*G.J. Holyoake, (1817-1906)*. Editor of *The Reasoner* (1846-61); Self Help for the People 1858. A key influence in the post-1848 period.

*Ernest Jones, (1819-1869)*. Came to prominence as an ally of Feargus O'Connor in the mid-1840s, but later became the leading Chartist supporter of Marx and Engels, at least in terms of their political projects if not their theories. An advocate of national, secular and compulsory education, and editor of the central paper of late Chartism, *The People's Paper* (1852-58).

*Benjamin Lucraft, (1809-1897)*. Present at Kennington Common in 1848; Co-Chair of 1858 Chartist conference; Reform League 1866; International Working Men's Association and Land and Labour League, but split over the Paris Commune; elected to the London School Board for Finsbury in 1870, and stood unsuccessfully as a Liberal MP.

*Charles Murray, (died 1889)*. Boot closer. NCA 1852; O'Brienite, anti-Jones; Prominent in the Association for Promoting the Repeal of the Taxes on Knowledge. One of those responsible for carrying radical ideas and strategies from the Chartist period to the birth of the Social Democratic Federation in the 1880s.

*G.W.M. Reynolds, (1814-1876)*. He spoke at Kennington Common in 1848; founded and edited the mass circulation radical newspaper, *Reynolds's News*.

*W.P. Roberts, (1806-1871)*. Chartist lawyer; an active lecturer; supported Ernest Jones's attempt to win a Manchester seat in 1868; retired to Heronsgate House on the O'Connorville estate after 1869.

*T.M. Wheeler, (1811-1862)*. General Secretary, NCA 1842; spoke at the Chartist Convention in 1848; Secretary of the Shareholders of the People's Paper from 1852; In 1858 he became anti-Ernest Jones and helped to form the rival National Political Union.

# Bibliography

**Archives (Major Sources)**

Howell Collection, Bishopsgate Institute
including:
G.J. Holyoake diaries, papers and correspondence.
Reform League papers.
Ernest Jones papers.

J. MacDougall (ed.) The Minutes of Edinburgh Trades Council, Scottish History Society, 4th Series, Volume 5, 1968.

British Library
W.J. Linton papers, diaries and scrapbooks. Prose and verse written and published in the course of fifty years, 1836-1886.

Tyne and Wear Archives Department, Newcastle upon Tyne:
Joseph Cowen Papers, including Newcastle Foreign Affairs Committee 1855-6; Northern Reform Union 1858-62.

Lancashire County Record Office

Preston Archives: Scrapbooks on the Preston Lock-Out 1853-4.

**Parliamentary Reports:**
Hansard 13 May 1848, 3rd Series, Volume XCVIII
Select Committee on the National Land Company, Parliamentary Papers, Reports from Committees, 1847-8, Volume XIX.
Select Committee on Public Libraries, May 1849.
National Association For the Promotion of Social Science. Trades Societies and Strikes, London, 1860.
Stalybridge Mechanics Institution, Catalogue, 1878 (BL Pressmark 2725 d 200).

**Newspapers and Periodicals:**
*Christian Socialist*, 1850-52.
*Cooper's Journal*, 1850.
*Eliza Cooks Journal*, 1849-54 (Volume X111)
*English Republic*, 1851-55.
*Evenings with the the People*, 1856-57.
*Household Words*, 1854
*London Investigator*, 1857-59.
*Louis Blanc's Monthly Review*, 1849.
*National Sunday League Record*, 1856-59.
*Northern Tribune*, 1854-55.
*Notes to the People*, 1851-1852.
*The Beehive*, 1860-1870.
*The Cabinet Newspaper*, 1858-60.
*The Co-operator Issues*, 1860-70.
*The Democratic Review*, 1849-50.
*The Democrat and Labour Advocate*, 1855.
*The Free Press*, 1855-56.
*The Friend of the People*, 1850-52.
*The Friend-in-Need Journal*, 1858.
*The Irish Felon*, 1848.
*The London News*, 1858.
*The Manchester Guardian*, 1852-3.
*The National Reformer*, 1861-
*The National Union*, 1858.
*The Northern Star*, 1838-152.
*The People's Paper*, 1852-58.
*The Reasoner*, 1846-61.
*The Red Republican*, 1849-51.
*The Republican Record*, 1855.
*The Spirit of the Age*, 1848-9.
*The Star of Freedom.*
*The Times*, 1848.
*The Vanguard*, 1853.
*Vegetarian Advocate*, 1848-1851.
*Working Men's College Magazine*, 1859-1862.
*Yorkshire Tribune*, 1855-1856.

**Books (Primary)**
Adams, W.E., *An Argument for Complete Suffrage*, Manchester, 1860.
Adams, W.E., *Memoirs of a Social Atom*, edited John Saville, New York, 1968.

Ashworth, J., *The Preston Strike*, Manchester, 1854.
Combe, G., *What should secular education embrace*, Edinburgh, 1848.
Considerant Victor, *The Last War*, London, 1850.
Crossley, J., *Ernest Jones, What is he, What has he done*. Manchester, 1868.
Devyr, Tom, *The Odd Book of the Nineteenth Century*, New York, 1882.
Dyer, George, *Benjamin Lucraft, A Biography*, London, 1879.
Ellis, Ethel, *Memoir of William Ellis*, London, 1888.
Ellis, W., *A few questions on secular education*, London, 1848.
Ellis, W., *The conditions of well-being as taught in the Birkbeck Schools as they ought to be taught everywhere*, London, 1851.
Finlen, J., *Defence of Himself*, London, 1868.
Frost, Thomas, *Forty Years Recollections*, London, 1880, Reprinted, New York, 1986.
Gammage, R, *History of the Chartist Movement*, [Merlin edition, 1968, New York, edited John Saville]
Heavisides, E.M., *Poetical and Prose Remains*, Stockton on Tees, 1850.
Hill, S., *Bygone Stalybridge*, Stalybridge, 1907.
Holyoake, G.J., (as Francis Pears) *The skin, baths, bathing and soap*, London, 1859.
Holyoake, G.J., (as Landor Praed) *History of the rise and progress of Middlesbrough*, Newcastle, 1863.
Holyoake, G.J., *A logic of facts*, London, 1848.
Holyoake, G.J., *A secular catechism for children*, London, 1854.
Holyoake, G.J., *Bygones Worth Remembering*, London, 1906.
Holyoake, G.J., *History of the Fleet Street House*, London, 1856.
Holyoake, G.J., *Literary Institutions: their relations to public opinion*, London, 1849.
Holyoake, G.J., *Organisation not of arms but of ideas*, London, 1853.
Holyoake, G.J., *Self Help for the People*, London, 1858.
Holyoake, G.J., *Sixty Years of An Agitator's Life*, London, 1892.
Holyoake, G.J., *The child's first letter book*, London, 1852.
Holyoake, G.J., *The child's first reading book*, London, 1853.
Holyoake, G.J., *The child's first work book*, London, 1854.
Holyoake, G.J., *The child's second letter book*, London, 1852.
Holyoake, G.J., *The Government and the Working Man's Press*, London, 1853.
Holyoake, G.J., *The Liberal Situation*, London, 1865.
Holyoake, G.J., *The richman's six and the poor man's one day*, London, 1856.
Holyoake, G.J., *Self Help by the People. The History of the Rochdale Pioneers*, London, 1893.
Holyoake, G.J., *The social means of promoting temperance*, London, 1859.
Holyoake, G.J., *The workman and the suffrage*, London, 1859.

Holyoake, G.J., *Practical Grammar*, 1844.
Jones, Ernest, *Democracy Vindicated*, London, 1867.
Jones, Ernest, *Labour and Capital*, London, 1867.
Jones, Ernest, *Womans Wrongs*, London, 1856.
Leary, Frederick, *The Life of Ernest Jones*, London, 1887.
Leno, J.B., *The Aftermath*, reprinted, New York, 1986.
Lloyd, Jones, *Progress of the Working Class 1832-1867*, London, 1867.
Lovett, W., *Justice Safer than Expediency*, London, 1848.
Mayhew, Henry, *Mayhew's London*, edited by Peter Quennell, London, 1984.
Mitchell, W., *The Philosophy of Teetotalism*, Stanningley, 1854.
Watts, J., *The Facts of the Cotton Famine*, London, 1968.
Watts, J., *The Workman's Bane*, Manchester, 1864.
Wise, E, *The Law relating to Riots*, London, 1848.

**Books (Secondary)**
Anderson, Olive, *A Liberal State at War*, New York, 1967.
Anderson, Perry, *Arguments within English Marxism*, London, 1981.
Ashton, O., Fyson, R. and Roberts, S., *The Duty of Discontent: Essays for Dorothy Thompson*, London, 1995.
Ashton, O.,Fyson, R. and Roberts, S., eds. *The Chartist Movement: A New Annotated Bibliography*, London, 1995.
Ashton, Owen, *W.E. Adams: Chartist, Radical and Journalist, 1832-1906*, Tyne and Wear, 1991.
Auerbach, J.A., *The Great Exhibition of 1851*, London, 1999.
Barker, Colin, ed., *Revolutionary Rehearsals*, London, 1986.
Belchem, John, *Popular Radicalism in Nineteenth-Century Britain*, London, 1996.
Bellamy, Joyce M. and Saville, J., eds. *Dictionary of Labour Biography*, London, 1976 (continuing)
Biagini, Eugenio F., *Liberty, Retrenchment and Reform*, Cambridge, 1992.
Biagini, Eugenio F. and Reid Alistair J., *Currents of Radicalism*, 1850-1914, Cambridge, 1991.
Breuilly, John, et al, *The era of the Reform League*, Mannheim, 1995.
Breuilly, John, *Labour and Liberalism in Nineteenth Century Europe, essays in comparative history*, Manchester, 1992.
Briggs, Asa, ed., *Chartist Studies*, London, 1959.
Burnett, J,; Vincent, D,; Mayall, D., eds. *The Autobiography of the Working Class, An Annotated Bibliography 1790-1945*, Brighton, 1984.
Callinicos, A., *Against Postmodernism, a Marxist critique*, Cambridge, 1989.
Callinicos, A., *Theories and Narratives, reflections on the philosophy of history*, Cambridge, 1995.

Challinor, Ray, *A radical lawyer in Victorian England, W.P. Roberts and the struggle for workers rights*, London, 1990.
Charlton, John, *The Chartists*, London, 1996.
Chase, Malcolm, *The People's Farm*, Oxford, 1995.
Claeys, G., *Citizens and Saints. Politics and Anti-Politics in Early British Socialism*, Cambridge, 1989.
Claeys, Gregory, *Machinery, Money and the Millennium. From Moral Economy to Socialism*, Cambridge, 1987.
Clarke, Anna, *The Struggle for the Breeches, gender and the making of the English working class*, London, 1995.
Clarke, John; Critcher, Chas and Johnson, Richard, eds. *Working Class Culture. Studies in history and theory*, London, 1974.
Colls, Robert, *The Pitmen of the Northern Coalfield. Work, Culture and Protest 1790-1850*, Manchester, 1987.
Crossick, Geoffrey, *An Artisan Elite in Victorian Society: Kentish London 1840-1880*, London, 1978.
Davin, Anna, *Growing up poor, home, school and street in London 1870-1914*, London, 1996.
Dyos, H.J., *Exploring the urban past, essays in urban history*, edited by David Cannadine and David Reeder, Cambridge, 1982.
Eagleton, Terry, *Ideology*, London, 1991.
Geoff, Eley, *Forging Democracy: The History of the Left in Europe, 1850-2000*, Oxford, 2002.
Epstein, James and Thompson, D. eds. *The Chartist Experience*, London, 1982.
Epstein, James, *Radical Expression, political language, ritual and symbol in England, 1790-1850*, Oxford, 1994.
Epstein, James, *The Lion of Freedom. Feargus O'Connor and the Chartist Movement 1832-1842*, London, 1982.
Evans, Richard, *In Defence of History*, London, 1997.
Finn, Margot, *After Chartism*, Cambridge, 1993.
Foster, John, *Class Struggle and the Industrial Revolution*, London, 1974.
Fraser, Derek, *Urban Politics in Victorian England*, London, 1976.
Gardner, Phil, *The lost elementary schools of Victorian England*, London, 1984.
Godfrey, Christopher, *Chartist Lives. The Anatomy of a Working-Class Movement*, London, 1987.
Goodway, D., *London Chartism 1838-1848*, Cambridge, 1982.
Goss, C., *A Descriptive Bibliography of the Writings of G.J. Holyoake*, London, 1908.

Gray, R.Q., *The Aristocracy of Labour in Nineteenth-Century Britain 1850-1914*, London, 1981.

Groves, Reg, *We Shall Rise Again, A Narrative History of Chartism*, London, 1938.

Grugel, Lee, *G.J. Holyoake. A study in the Evolution of a Victorian Radical*, Philadelphia, 1976.

Gurney, P., *Co-operative Culture and the Politics of Consumption in England 1870-1930*, Manchester, 1996.

Gutman, Herbert, *Power and Culture. Essays on the American Working Class*, edited by Ira Berlin, New York, 1987.

Hambrick, Margaret, *A Chartist's Library*, London, 1986

Harman Chris, *The Fire Last Time*, London, 1998.

Harrison, J.F.C., *History of the Working Men's College 1854-1954*, London, 1954.

Harrison, Royden, *Before the Socialists*, Second Edition, Aldershot, 1994.

Harrison, Royden, *Independent Collier*, Hassocks, 1978.

Harrison, Royden; Woolven, Gillian; Duncan, Robert, *The Warwick Guide to British Labour Periodicals*, Brighton, 1977.

Haywood, Ian, *The Literature of Struggle: An Anthology of Chartist Fiction*, Aldershot, 1995.

Hewitt, M., *The Emergence of Stability in the Industrial City: Manchester 1832-67*, Aldershot, 1996.

Hobsbawm, Eric, *Labouring Men*, London, 1954.

Hobsbawm, Eric, *The Making of the English Working Class 1890-1914*, Worlds of Labour, London, 1984.

Hollis, Patricia, *The pauper press: a study in working class radicalism of the 1830s*, London, 1970.

Hurt, J.S., *Education in Evolution*, London, 1972.

Johnson, Richard, 'Really Useful Knowledge' in Lovett, Tom, ed., *Radical approaches to adult education*, London, 1988.

Johnson, Richard, *The State and the politics of education*, Open University, Course Unit, E353 Part 1, Milton Keynes, 1981.

Johnson, Richard, ed., Making Histories, *Studies in history writing and politics*, London, 1982.

Johnson, Richard, Clarke, John, Critcher, Chas, eds., *Working Class Culture. Studies in History and Theory*, London, 1979.

Jones, D.J.V., *Chartism and the Chartists*, London, 1975.

Joyce, Patrick, ed., *Class*, Oxford, 1995.

Joyce, Patrick, *Democratic Subjects*, Cambridge, 1994.

Joyce, Patrick, *Visions of the People: Industrial England and the Question of Class, 1848-1914*, Cambridge, 1994.

Joyce, Patrick, *Work, Society and Politics: The Culture of the Factory in Later Victorian England*, Brighton, 1990.
Kidd, Alan J., & Roberts, K.W., eds., *City, class and culture. Studies of social policy and cultural production in Victorian Manchester*, Manchester, 1985.
King, J.E. & Dutton, H.I., *10% and No Surrender*, Cambridge, 1981.
Kirk, N., *Change, Continuity, Class*, Manchester, 1998.
Kirk, N., *Labour & Society in Britain and the United States. Volume 1. Capitalism, Custom and Protest 1780-1850*, Aldershot, 1994.
Kirk, N., *The Growth of Working Class Reformism in Mid-Victorian England*, London, 1985.
Koditschek, T., *Class Formation and Urban Industrial Society: Bradford 1750-1850*, Cambridge, 1990.
Lee, A.J., *The origins of the Popular Press in England 1855-1914*, London, 1976.
Leventhal, F., *Respectable Radical, George Howell and Victorian working-class politics*, London, 1971.
Lummis, Trevor, *The Labour Aristocracy 1851-1914*, Aldershot, 1994.
MacRaid, Donald M. and Martin, David. E., *Labour in British Society 1830-1914*, London, 1998.
Marcus, Steven, *Engels, Manchester and the working class*, London, 1974.
Marx, K. and Engels, F., *The Communist Manifesto*, London, Part 1, Socialist Register, Suffolk, 1998.
McWilliam, Rohan, *Popular Politics in Nineteenth Century England*, London, 1998.
Pickering, P.A., *Chartism and the Chartists in Manchester and Salford*, Manchester, 1995.
Prothero, Iowerth, *Radical Artisans in England and France 1830-1870*, Cambridge, 1997.
Rees, John, *The Algebra of Revolution*, London, 1998.
Reid, A.J., *Social Classes and Social Relations in Britain, 1850-1914*, London, 1992.
Roberts, S., *Radical Politics and Poets in early Victorian Britain: The voices of six Chartist leaders*, New York, 1993.
Rose,, Sonya, *Limited Livelihoods*, London, 1992.
Rothstein, Theodore, *From Chartism to Labourism*, London, 1983.
Royle, E., *Radicals, secularists and republicans, popular freethought in Britain 1866-1915*, Manchester, 1980.
Royle, Edward, 'Owenism and the Secularist Tradition: the Huddersfield Secular Society and Sunday School in Living and Learning' in Chase, Malcolm & Dyck, Ian, eds., *Essays in Honour of J.F.C. Harrison*, Aldershot, 1996.

Royle, Edward, *Revolutionary Britannia*, Manchester, 2000.
Rude, G., *History from Below*, Montreal, 1985.
Savage, C., *The dynamics of working class politics*, Cambridge, 1987.
Saville, John, *1848, The British State and the Chartist Movement*, Cambridge, 1987.
Saville, John, *Democracy and the Labour Movement*, London, 1954.
Saville, John, *Ernest Jones*, London, 1952.
Schwarzkopf, Jutta, *Women in the Chartist Movement*, London, 1991.
Sewell, William H. Jnr., 'Towards a Post-Materialist Rhetoric for Labour History', in Barlanstein, L.R., ed., *Rethinking Labor History: Essays on Class and Discourse Analysis*, US, 1993.
Shipley, Stan, *Club Life and Socialism in Mid-Victorian London*, Oxford, 1971.
Simon, Brian, *Studies in the History of Education*, London, 1960.
Slosson, W., *The Decline of the Chartist Movement*, London, 1967.
Stedman Jones, Gareth, *The Languages of Class*, Cambridge, 1983.
Steinberg, Mark, *Fighting Words*, London, 1999.
Stevenson, John, *London in the Age of Reform*, Oxford, 1977.
Tarrow, Sidney, *Power in Movement*, Cambridge, 1994.
Taylor, Antony, ed., *The Era of the Reform League*, Mannheim, 1995.
Taylor, Antony, *Modes of Political Expression and Working-Class Radicalism 1848-1874*, Manchester, 1992.
Taylor, Miles, *The decline of British radicalism 1847-1860*, Oxford, 1995.
Taylor, Miles, *Ernest Jones, Chartism and the romance of politics, 1819-1869*, Cambridge, 2003.
Thompson, D. and Harrison, J.F.C., *Bibliography of the Chartist Movement*, Hassocks, 1978.
Thompson, D., *Outsiders. Class, Gender and Nation*, London, 1993.
Thompson, D., *The Chartists*, London, 1984.
Thompson, D., *The Chartists, Popular Politics in the Industrial Revolution*, London, 1984.
Thompson, E.P., 'The Peculiarities of the English', *The Poverty of Theory*, London, 1978.
Thompson, E.P., *The Making of the English Working Class*, Harmondsworth, 1968.
Tiller, Kate, 'Halifax 1847-1858' in Epstein, James & Thompson, Dorothy, eds., *The Chartist Experience*, London, 1982.
Todd, Nigel, *The Militant Democracy. Joseph Cowen and Victorian Radicalism*. Tyne and Wear, 1991.
Vernon, James, *Politics and the People: A Study in English Political Culture 1815-1867*, Cambridge, 1993

Vincent, David, *Bread, Knowledge and Freedom*, London, 1983.
Vincent, John, *The Formation of the British Liberal Party 1857-1868*, London, 1972.
Voloshinov, V., *Marxism and the Philosophy of Language*, New York, 1973.
Walton, J.K., *Lancashire: a social history*, Manchester, 1987.
Weisser, H., *April 10$^{th}$, Challenge and Response in England in 1848*, New York, 1983.
Wiener, Joel H., *William Lovett*, Manchester, 1989.
Wiener, Joel, *The war of the unstamped: the movement to repeal the British newspaper tax 1830-1836*, London, 1969.

**Journals**

Anderson, Perry, 'The Antinomies of Antonio Gramsci', *New Left Review* 100, 1977.
Ashton, Owen R., 'Chartism in Gloucestershire and the Contribution of the Chartist Land Plan', *Transactions of the Bristol and Gloucestershire Archaeological Society*, Volume 104, 1986.
Bailey, P., 'Will the real Bill Banks please stand up? A role analysis of mid-Victorian working class respectability', *Journal of Social History*, 12, 1979, pp. 336-53.
Belchem, John and Epstein, James, 'The Nineteenth Century Gentlemen Leader Revisited', *Social History* Vol 22/2 May 1997.
Chase, M., 'Out of Radicalism. The Mid-Victorian Freehold Land Movement', *English Historical Review*, Vol CVI, April 1991.
Claeys, G, 'Mazzini, Kossuth and British Radicalism, 1848-1854', *Journal of British Studies*, Volume 28/3, July 1989.
Faherty, Ray, 'The Memoir of T.M Wheeler, Owenite and Chartist'. *Bulletin of the Society for the Study of Labour History*, No.30 Spring 1975.
Flett, Keith, 'But the Chartist Principles did not die', *North-East Labour History Bulletin*, No. 21, 1988.
Flett, Keith, 'Coercion and Consent', *Bulletin of the Society for the Study of Labour History*, Volume 53/3 Winter 1988.
Flett, Keith, 'Progress and Light: Secularism and Radicalism on Teesside after 1848'. *Bulletin of the Cleveland and Teesside Local History Society* No.56 1989
Flett, Keith, 'Sex or Class: The Education of Working-Class Women 1800-1870', *History of Education*, Volume 18/2 1989.
Flett Keith, 'To Make That Future Now: The Land Question in Nineteenth Century Radical Politics', *The Raven*, Volume 5, 1992.
Foster, John, 'Review of the Languages of Class', *New Left Review*, 150.

Gaymer, Regenia, 'Social Atoms: Working-Class Autobiography, Subjectivity and Gender', *Victorian Studies* Volume 30 Spring 1987.
Harris, Keith, 'Joseph Cowen – The Northern Tribune', *North-East Labour History Bulletin* No. 5 1971.
Johnson, Richard, 'Really Useful Knowledge', *Radical Education*, Nos. 7 & 8, 1976.
Kirk, N., 'In Defence of Class', *International Review of Social History*, No 32/1 1987.
Kirk, N., 'The Continuing Relevance and Engagements of Class', *Labour History Review* 60/3, 1995.
McClelland, K., 'Some Thoughts on Masculinity and the "Representative Artisan" in Britain 1850-1880', *Gender and History* Volume 2/1, 1989.
Nicholls, D., 'The New Liberalism – after Chartism?' *Social History* 21/3 1996.
Pickering, Paul, 'Class Without Words', *Past and Present* No112, August 1986.
Sager, E.W., 'The Working-Class Peace Movement in Victorian England', *Histoire Social/Social History* Volume XX11 May 1979.
Samuel, R. 'Reading the Signs', *History Workshop Journal* 32, Autumn, 1991.
Scott, Susan, 'The Northern Tribune: A North-East Radical Magazine', *North-East Labour History Bulletin*, No. 19 1985.
Taylor, A.D., '"The Best Way to Get What He Wanted". Ernest Jones and the Boundaries of Liberalism in the Manchester Election of 1868'. *Parliamentary History* Vol 16/2 September 1997.

# Index

Adams, W.E. 81
  on Ernest Jones 154
  *Memoirs of a Social Atom* 125-6
  *An Argument For Complete Suffrage* 133
  Owen Ashton on 129
Anderson, Perry [& Tom Nairn] 29, 124
*Ashton Reporter* 15

Bailey, Peter *Will the Real Bill Banks Please Stand Up* 14
Bill Banks's Day Out 170
Barker, Colin 36, 65, 85, 170
Belchem, John 76
  politics of space 68-9, 86
Biagini, Eugenio 8, 175
Birkbeck Schools 107
Blanc, Louis 112
Blazak, Barbara 132
Bradford 40
Bradlaugh, Charles 81

Cabinet Newspaper 125, 156-7
Charter and Something More 76, 94, 113
Chartist Conference 1858, 155
Chartist Programme 1851 114
Chatterton, Daniel 187
Chronological Approaches 3
City of London Mechanics Institute School 108
Cliff, Tony 71
coffee houses and pubs 60
Cowen, Joseph 81
  Nigel Todd on 168, 175

Coventry Mutual Improvement Society 161-3

'The democracy' 59

Eagleton, Terry, 44, 75
Education Act 1870 174, 187, 198
educational franchise 129
Ellis, William 107
Evans, Richard *In Defence of History* 4

Female Chartists and meeting places 60
Finlen, James 190
Finn, Margot 34, 127, 178
Foster, John 115
Foucault, Michel 2
Fraternal Democrats 98

Gardner, Philip 21, 187, 198
Gawler, Col. George 35
Goodway, David 100
Great Exhibition 1851 98
Gramsci, Antonio 70
Grugel, Lee 131-2

Harman, Chris 71
Harney, G.J. 111, 116
  *Red Republican*
  *Friend of the People*
  *Democratic Review*
Harrison, Royden
  *Before The Socialists* 143 195-196
Helps, Sir. Arthur 35
Henry, Mitchell 285
Hewitt, Martin 99
Heywood, Abel 181

Hill, Christopher
 Experience of Defeat 90-1
Holyoake, G.J.
 *Self Help For The People* 89, 147
 *The Workman and the Suffrage* 136
 On 1848 80
 On O'Connor 67
Howell, George 81, 176
Hurt, J.S. 186-187

Irish Repealers 54

Jersey Independent 150
John St Institution 106
Jones, Ernest 179
 Evenings With The People 147, 153-4
 Labour and Capital 180
 Professor Blackie 180
 Democracy Vindicated 183
 Manchester Liberal Party 184-186

Kirk, Neville 115
Koditschek, Theodore
 on Bradford 64-5, 106

Labourism 124
Land and Labour League 177
Liberal Party
 John Vincent on 149
London School Board 174, 188, 199
London Trades Council 127
Lovett, William
 The National Hall School 103-5
Lucraft, Benjamin 174, 188-9
Luxemburg, Rosa
 Mass Strike 36

Manhood Suffrage Campaign 182
Marx, Karl on
 Ernest Jones 150-1
 Class Struggles in France 83
 Educational Strategy 141
Mass Platform, The 56, 83
Meeting Times 62
Mayhew, Henry 62

National Charter Association
 Strategy 84-5
National Education League 186-7
*National Reformer* 190
National Secular Society 184, 190
North London Political Union 176
Northern Reform Union 157
*Northern Star* 57

O'Connor, Feargus 38
Orsini Affair 148

Pickering, Paul 56
Prothero, Iowerth 57, 118

Really Useful Knowledge [Richard
 Johnson] 1, 7, 10, 22-24, 117, 127, 153
*Reasoner, The* 48, 59, 102, 125, 133-140, 161

Respectability 163
*Reynolds's Newspaper* 174-5
Royle, Edward 50, 67, 74, 87, 176

Saint Monday
 Meetings on 62
Saville, John 33, 178-9
 on 1848 34
Secular Education 164-5
Secular Schools 99
Select Committee on Public Libraries 104
Tarrow, Sidney 169
Stalybridge 158
 Neville Kirk on 159
Stedman Jones, Gareth
 Rethinking Chartism 2, 31, 95
Sunday recreations 62

Taylor, Antony 178
Taylor, Miles 33, 177, 179-180
Thompson, Dorothy 33-4
Thompson, E.P.
 on class 11
 on experience 73

Tiller, Kate 110
*The Times* 40, 41, 42, 44, 45
Trades Union Congress 187
Trotsky, Leon, permanent revolution 91

Vincent, John 175

warrening capitalism 146
*Working Man, The* 183
Working Men's Colleges 166-7